First World War
and Army of Occupation
War Diary
France, Belgium and Germany

39 DIVISION
Divisional Troops
Royal Army Medical Corps
132 Field Ambulance
3 March 1916 - 11 December 1918

WO95/2578/1

The Naval & Military Press Ltd
www.nmarchive.com
Published in association with The National Archives

Published by

The Naval & Military Press Ltd

Unit 10 Ridgewood Industrial Park,

Uckfield, East Sussex,

TN22 5QE England

Tel: +44 (0) 1825 749494

www.naval-military-press.com

www.nmarchive.com

Contents

Document type	Place/Title	Date From	Date To
Heading	WO95/2578/1 132 Fl Ambulance Nov 16-Dec 18		
Miscellaneous			
Heading	39th Div. No. 132 F. Amb. March April 1916		
Heading	132 F Amb Vol 1		
War Diary	Farnborough	03/03/1916	03/03/1916
War Diary	Le Havre	04/03/1916	05/03/1916
War Diary	Thiennes	06/03/1916	06/03/1916
War Diary	Morbecque	07/03/1916	27/03/1916
War Diary	Gonnehem	28/03/1916	31/03/1916
Miscellaneous	A.G Office At The Base	03/04/1916	03/04/1916
War Diary	Robecq	01/04/1916	18/04/1916
War Diary	Bois De Pacaut	20/04/1916	22/04/1916
War Diary	Robecq	29/04/1916	29/04/1916
Heading	39th Div. 132nd F. Amb. May 1916		
War Diary	Robecq	01/05/1916	31/05/1916
Heading	No. 132 F.A June 1916		
Miscellaneous	G.H.Q 3rd Echelon	04/07/1916	04/07/1916
War Diary	Bois De Pacaut Q.33.b.6.5	02/06/1916	17/06/1916
War Diary	Vieille Chapelle	24/06/1916	24/06/1916
War Diary	R.34.a.9.9 Vieille Chapelle	25/06/1916	30/06/1916
Heading	39th Division. 132nd Field Ambulance. July 1916		
War Diary	Vieille Chapelle R.34.a.9.9	03/07/1916	06/07/1916
War Diary	Bethune	07/07/1916	15/07/1916
War Diary	Mesplaux	17/07/1916	31/07/1916
Miscellaneous	A.D.M.S 39 Div	27/07/1916	27/07/1916
Miscellaneous	Medical Arrangements. 39th Div. (amended 24.7.16)	24/07/1916	24/07/1916
Operation(al) Order(s)	R.A.M.C. Order No. 4 By Colonel G.W. Brazier Creagh C.M.G. A.D.M.S 37th Division.	23/07/1916	23/07/1916
Miscellaneous	39th Division Medical Arrangement (amended 15.7.16)	15/07/1916	15/07/1916
Operation(al) Order(s)	R.A.M.C. Order No. 3 By Colonel G.W. Brazier-Creagh C.M.G. A.D.M.S. 39th Division.	14/07/1916	14/07/1916
Miscellaneous	A.D.M.S 39 Div.	11/07/1916	11/07/1916
Miscellaneous	O.C. 132 Fd. Amb.	06/07/1916	06/07/1916
Miscellaneous	O.C. 132 Fd. Ambulance	06/07/1916	06/07/1916
Miscellaneous	A.D.M.S. 39 Divn.	03/07/1916	03/07/1916
Miscellaneous	O.C. 132 Fd. Amb.	14/07/1916	14/07/1916
War Diary	Mesplaux	01/08/1916	01/08/1916
War Diary	X.14.a.9.6	01/08/1916	10/08/1916
War Diary	Allouagne	10/08/1916	11/08/1916
War Diary	Magnicourt-En-Comte.	12/08/1916	12/08/1916
War Diary	Tincquette	13/08/1916	22/08/1916
War Diary	Honval	23/08/1916	23/08/1916
War Diary	Sus St Leger	24/08/1916	25/08/1916
War Diary	Bois Du Warnimont	25/08/1916	25/08/1916
War Diary	Acheux	27/08/1916	31/08/1916
Heading	39th Div. 132nd Field Ambulance Sept 1916		
War Diary	Acheux	01/09/1916	02/09/1916
War Diary	Divisional Collecting Station	03/09/1916	04/09/1916
War Diary	Acheux	04/09/1916	06/09/1916
War Diary	Bertrancourt	07/09/1916	14/09/1916

War Diary	Bus-Les-Artois	18/09/1916	30/09/1916
Miscellaneous	O.C. 132 Fd. Amb. App. 47.d.	01/09/1916	01/09/1916
Miscellaneous	O.C. 132 Fd. Ambulance App. 47	02/09/1916	02/09/1916
Miscellaneous	O.C. 132 Field Ambulance		
Miscellaneous	A.D.M.S. 39 Div.	01/10/1916	01/10/1916
Miscellaneous	A.D.M.S. 39 Div. App. 56.a	25/09/1916	25/09/1916
Miscellaneous	A.D.M.S. 39 Div. App. 56	21/09/1916	21/09/1916
Miscellaneous	A.D.M.S. 39 Div. App. 52a	09/09/1916	09/09/1916
Miscellaneous	A.D.M.S. 39 Div. App. 53	09/09/1916	09/09/1916
Miscellaneous	O.C. 132 Fd. Amb. App. 55	18/09/1916	18/09/1916
Miscellaneous	O.C. 132 Fd. Ambulance. App 54	14/09/1916	14/09/1916
Miscellaneous	A.D.M.S. 39 Div. App. 52	08/09/1916	08/09/1916
Miscellaneous	O.C. 132 Fd Amb. App 51	06/09/1916	06/09/1916
Miscellaneous	A.D.M.S. 39 Div. App 50	06/09/1916	06/09/1916
Miscellaneous	A.D.M.S. 39 Div. App. 47.f.	04/09/1916	04/09/1916
Miscellaneous	O.C. 132 Fd. Amb. App. 48	04/09/1916	04/09/1916
Miscellaneous	A.D.M.S. 39 Div.	04/10/1916	04/10/1916
Heading	132nd F.A Aug 1916 140/1949		
War Diary	Bus-Les-Artois	01/10/1916	03/10/1916
War Diary	Forceville	05/10/1916	05/10/1916
War Diary	Q.31.a.0.2	05/10/1916	10/10/1916
War Diary	Lancashire Dump	11/10/1916	31/10/1916
Heading	War Diary of 132 Field Ambulance From Nov 1st 1916 to Nov. 30th 1916 (Volume I)		
War Diary	Lancashire Dump	01/11/1916	15/11/1916
War Diary	Warloy	15/11/1916	16/11/1916
War Diary	Bretel	18/11/1916	18/11/1916
War Diary	Watou	21/11/1916	30/11/1916
Operation(al) Order(s)	R.A.M.C. Operation Order No. 17 by Colonel G.W. Brazier-Creagh, C.M.G., A.D.M.S. 39th. Div.	27/11/1916	27/11/1916
Miscellaneous	A.D.M.S. 39 Div. App. 6.a	20/11/1916	20/11/1916
Miscellaneous	A.D.M.S. 39 Div. App. 6		
Miscellaneous	133 Fld. Amb.		
Miscellaneous	134 Fld. Ambulance.	20/11/1916	20/11/1916
Operation(al) Order(s)	R.A.M.C. Operation Order No. 16 by Colonel Brazier Creagh, C.M.G., A.D.M.S. 39th Division. App. 5	17/11/1916	17/11/1916
Operation(al) Order(s)	118th Infantry Brigade Order No. 66 App. 4	15/11/1916	15/11/1916
Miscellaneous	Table A		
Miscellaneous	Report on Medical Arrangements in connection with Operations on November 13th. 1916 App. 3a	13/11/1916	13/11/1916
Miscellaneous	A.D.M.S. 39 Div. App. 1	13/11/1916	13/11/1916
Miscellaneous	A.D.M.S. 39 Division.		
Miscellaneous	A.D.M.S. 39 Div. App. 1.b.	14/11/1916	14/11/1916
Miscellaneous	A.D.M.S. 39 Div. App. 1.a.	14/11/1916	14/11/1916
Miscellaneous	A.D.M.S. 39th Division.	05/12/1916	05/12/1916
Operation(al) Order(s)	R.A.M.C. Operation Order No. 15 by Colonel G.W. Brazier-Creagh, C.M.G., A.D.M.S. 39th. Div. App 3	14/11/1916	14/11/1916
Operation(al) Order(s)	Additional Medical Arrangements in connection with 39th. Divisional Order No. 63 dated 25-10-16 App. 2	25/10/1916	25/10/1916
Miscellaneous	O.C. 132 Field Ambulance	12/11/1916	12/11/1916
Miscellaneous	No. 6/223	12/11/1916	12/11/1916
Miscellaneous	No. 6/223	28/10/1916	28/10/1916
Miscellaneous	O.C. 132 Fld Amb.	25/10/1916	25/10/1916
Operation(al) Order(s)	Medical Arrangements In Connection With 39th. Divisional Order No. 63	22/10/1916	22/10/1916

Heading	War Diary 132nd Field Ambulance December 1916 Vol 10 39th Div		
War Diary	Watou	01/12/1916	13/12/1916
War Diary	Proven	14/12/1916	31/12/1916
Operation(al) Order(s)	Extract from Divisional Routine Order No. 482 App. I	04/12/1916	04/12/1916
War Diary	Watou	01/12/1916	13/12/1916
War Diary	Proven	14/12/1916	31/12/1916
Operation(al) Order(s)	Extract from Divisional Routine Order No. 482 App. I	04/12/1916	04/12/1916
Heading	War Diary of 132nd Field Ambulance From 1/1/17 to 31/1/17 (Volume II) 39th Div		
War Diary	Proven	01/01/1917	14/01/1917
War Diary	Hillhoek	15/01/1917	31/01/1917
Heading	War Diary Of 132nd Field Ambulance From Feb 1st 1917 To Feb. 28th 1917 (Volume II) 39th Div.		
War Diary	Hillhoek	01/02/1917	17/02/1917
War Diary	Wormhoudt	18/02/1917	27/02/1917
War Diary	Steenvoorde	28/02/1917	28/02/1917
Heading	War Diary Of 132nd Field. Ambulance March 1st 1917 To March 31st 1917. (Volume II) 39th Div.		
War Diary	Steen Voorde	01/03/1917	04/03/1917
War Diary	Mont Des Cats	05/03/1917	31/03/1917
Heading	War Diary Of 132nd Field Ambulance R.A.M.C. From April 1st 1917 To April 30th 1917 (Volume II.)		
War Diary	Mont Des Cats	01/04/1917	16/04/1917
War Diary	Proven.	17/04/1917	30/04/1917
Heading	War Diary Of 132nd Field Ambulance From May 1st 1917 To May 31st 1917 (Volume 2)		
War Diary	Proven	01/05/1917	31/05/1917
Heading	War Diary Of 132nd Field Ambulance From June 1st 1917 To June 30th 1917 (Volume II.)		
Miscellaneous	B.E.F. Summary Of Medical War Diaries Of 132nd F.A. 39th Div. 18th Corps. 5th Army.		
Miscellaneous	B.E.F. 132nd F.A. 39th Div. 18th Corps. 5th Army. O.C.-Lt. Col. A. Little Johns.		
Miscellaneous	B.E.F. Summary Of Medical War Diaries Of 132nd F.A. 39th Div. 18th Corps. 5th Army.		
Miscellaneous	B.E.F. 132nd F.A. 39th Div. 18th Corps. 5th Army. O.C.-Lt. Col. A. Little Johns.		
War Diary	Proven.	01/06/1917	20/06/1917
War Diary	Herzeele	21/06/1917	30/06/1917
Heading	War Diary Of 132nd Field Ambulance From July 1st 1917 To July 31st 1917 (Volume 2)		
Miscellaneous	B.E.F. Summary Of Medical War Diaries Of 132nd F.A. 39th Div. 18th Corps. 5th Army.	08/08/1917	08/08/1917
Miscellaneous	B.E.F. 132nd F.A. 39th Div. 18th Corps. 5th Army. O.C.-Lt. Col. A. Little Johns.		
War Diary	Herzeele	01/07/1917	21/07/1917
War Diary	A23.C.2.9	22/07/1917	31/07/1917
Heading	War Diary of 132nd Field Ambulance From August 1st 1917 to August 31st 1917 (Volume 2)		
Miscellaneous	B.E.F. Summary of Medical War Diaries of 132nd F.A. 39th Div. 18th Corps. 5th Army.	08/08/1917	08/08/1917
Miscellaneous			
War Diary	A23.C.2.9	01/08/1917	08/08/1917
War Diary	Meteren.	09/08/1917	31/08/1917

Heading	War Diary Of 132nd Field Ambulance From September 1st 1917 To September 30th 1917 (Volume 2)		
War Diary	Meteren	01/09/1917	30/09/1917
Heading	War Diary Of 132nd Field Ambulance From October 1st 1917 To October 31st 1917 (Volume 2)		
War Diary	Keersebrom. Camp. S.10.D. Sheet 28	01/10/1917	05/10/1917
War Diary	Keersebrom. Camp.	06/10/1917	16/10/1917
War Diary	Voormezeele.	17/10/1917	24/10/1917
War Diary	H.27.C.3.7	25/10/1917	28/10/1917
War Diary	Voormezeele	29/10/1917	31/10/1917
Heading	War Diary (Original) 132 Field Ambulance From-November 1st 1917 To-November 30th 1917 Volume II		
War Diary	Voormezeele	01/11/1917	10/11/1917
War Diary	Woodcote Ho.	11/11/1917	25/11/1917
War Diary	Steenvoorde.	26/11/1917	28/11/1917
War Diary	Watou E.4.b.6.4	28/11/1917	30/11/1917
Heading	War Diary of 132 Field Ambulance From December 1st 1917 to December 31st 1917 Volume II		
War Diary	Watou. E.4.b.6.4	01/12/1917	05/12/1917
War Diary	Watou	05/12/1917	08/12/1917
War Diary	Vieil Moulier.	09/12/1917	09/12/1917
War Diary	Brunembert	10/12/1917	31/12/1917
Heading	War Diary of 132nd Field Ambulance From January 1st 1918 to January 31st 1918 (Volume II)		
War Diary	Affringues	01/01/1918	01/01/1918
War Diary	L'Ebbe Farm	02/01/1918	05/01/1918
War Diary	L'Ebbe Farm. F 29.d.5.8	06/01/1918	22/01/1918
War Diary	Herzeele.	23/01/1918	24/01/1918
War Diary	Bray-Sur-Somme	26/01/1918	27/01/1918
War Diary	Haut Allaines	29/01/1918	29/01/1918
War Diary	Fins	30/01/1918	31/01/1918
Heading	War Diary. Of 132nd. Field Ambulance From:- 1st. February 1918. To:- 28th. February 1918. (Volume 2)		
War Diary	Fins-Nurlu Road. (V.1.8.C)	01/02/1918	28/02/1918
War Diary	Fins-Nurlu Road. (V.1.8.C)	01/03/1918	10/03/1918
War Diary	V.18.C.	11/03/1918	12/03/1918
War Diary	Haut Allaines	13/03/1918	21/03/1918
War Diary	Nurlu.	22/03/1918	22/03/1918
War Diary	Doignt	23/03/1918	23/03/1918
War Diary	H 29. Central	23/03/1918	23/03/1918
War Diary	H.25.d.4.0	24/03/1918	24/03/1918
War Diary	C 27.b.6.2	25/03/1918	25/03/1918
War Diary	Cappy.	26/03/1918	26/03/1918
War Diary	Mericourt-Sur-Somme.	26/03/1918	26/03/1918
War Diary	Warfusee-Abancourt.	27/03/1918	27/03/1918
War Diary	Gentelles.	28/03/1918	28/03/1918
War Diary	Sains-En-Amienois	29/03/1918	30/03/1918
War Diary	Saleux	31/03/1918	31/03/1918
Heading	War Diary of 132nd. Field Ambulance. From:- 1st. March 1918. To:- 31st. March 1918. (Volume 3)		
Heading	132nd Field Ambulance March 1918		
Heading	War Diary of 132nd. Field Ambulance From:- 1st. April 1918. To:- 30th. April 1918. (Volume 3)		
War Diary	Bovelles	01/04/1918	02/04/1918
War Diary	Araines.	03/04/1918	03/04/1918
War Diary	Foucaucourt.	04/04/1918	07/04/1918

War Diary	Frettemeule.	08/04/1918	08/04/1918
War Diary	Oust-Marest.	09/04/1918	09/04/1918
War Diary	Arques	10/04/1918	11/04/1918
War Diary	Watten.	12/04/1918	30/04/1918
Heading	War Diary of 132nd. Field Ambulance From 1st. May 1918. to 31st. May 1918. (Volume 27)		
War Diary	Watten.	01/05/1918	31/05/1918
Heading	War Diary of 132nd. Field Ambulance From 1st. June 1918. to 30th. June 1918. (Volume 28)		
War Diary	Watten	01/06/1918	19/06/1918
War Diary	Bournonville	20/06/1918	26/06/1918
War Diary	Abbeville	27/06/1918	30/06/1918
Heading	War Diary of 132nd Field Ambulance. From July 1st to July 31st 1918. (Volume 29)		
War Diary	Etaples.	01/07/1918	01/07/1918
War Diary	Autingues	02/07/1918	06/07/1918
War Diary	Volkerinckhove	07/07/1918	07/07/1918
War Diary	Lister Camp Rousebrugge	08/08/1917	09/08/1917
War Diary	Lister Camp Rousebrugge	10/07/1918	15/07/1918
War Diary	Tubby Camp	16/07/1918	29/07/1918
War Diary	Tubby Camp Rouse Brugge	30/07/1918	31/07/1918
Heading	War Diary Of 132nd Field Ambulance. From 1st August To 31st August 1918		
War Diary	Tubby Camp Rouse Brugge	02/08/1918	31/08/1918
Heading	War Diary Of 132nd Field Ambulance From 1st September 1918 To 30th September 1918. (Volume 31.)		
War Diary	Tubby Camp Rouse Brugge	01/09/1918	03/09/1918
War Diary	Ballance Camp	04/09/1918	07/09/1918
War Diary	Hernicourt Lens 11.2.D.61.83	07/09/1918	16/09/1918
War Diary	Hernicourt	16/09/1918	18/09/1918
War Diary	Louvencourt F5.9.2 (Lens. 11)	19/09/1918	21/09/1918
War Diary	Buire 62.C.J.28 A.4.4	23/09/1918	26/09/1918
War Diary	Buire	26/09/1918	26/09/1918
War Diary	Marquaix 62.C.L.1d.52	27/09/1918	29/09/1918
War Diary	Marquaix	29/09/1918	30/09/1918
Heading	War Diary of 132nd Field Ambulance From 1st October 1918 to 31st October 1918. (Volume 32)		
Miscellaneous	Schedule of training for Personnel of 105 Sanitary train, 30th American Divn.	03/08/1918	03/08/1918
War Diary	Marquaix	01/10/1918	02/10/1918
War Diary	Biaches	03/10/1918	04/10/1918
War Diary	Templeux LI.d.7.2 Sheet 62 C	05/10/1918	05/10/1918
War Diary	A.D.S.G. 16.d.8.2. Sheet 62b	06/10/1918	06/10/1918
War Diary	Quarries	06/10/1918	08/10/1918
War Diary	Montbrehain I.1.d.2.5. Sheet 62c	09/10/1918	09/10/1918
War Diary	Busigny V.10.d.0.2 Sheet 57 B	10/10/1918	10/10/1918
War Diary	Busigny	11/10/1918	11/10/1918
War Diary	Montbrehain	12/10/1918	16/10/1918
War Diary	Bohain	17/10/1918	20/10/1918
War Diary	Quarry Near Bellicourt	21/10/1918	21/10/1918
War Diary	Marquaix	22/10/1918	22/10/1918
War Diary	Bonnay	22/10/1918	22/10/1918
War Diary	Baizieux	23/10/1918	23/10/1918
War Diary	Vadencourt	23/10/1918	31/10/1918
Heading	War Diary of 132nd Field Ambulance. (Volume 33)		
War Diary	Vadencourt	01/11/1918	05/11/1918

War Diary	Vadencourt U.28.A.1.9	06/11/1918	16/11/1918
War Diary	Picquigny	17/11/1918	17/11/1918
War Diary	Abbeville	18/11/1918	30/11/1918
Heading	War Diary Of The 132nd Field Ambulance. For The Month Of December. 1918. Vol 34		
War Diary	Abbeville	01/12/1918	11/12/1918

WO 95/2578

(1)

132 Fd Ambulance

Mar '16 – Dec '18

39th Div

March } 1916.
April }

No. 132 F. Amb.

Mar 16
Dec 18

132 Jane

Vol 1

Instructions regarding War Diaries and Intelligence Summaries are contained in F. S. Regs., Part II. and the Staff Manual respectively. Title pages will be prepared in manuscript.

Ref. Map France $\frac{1}{40000}$ Sheet or 36A.

WAR DIARY

~~INTELLIGENCE SUMMARY.~~

(Erase heading not required.)

Army Form C. 2118. (1)

132nd Field Ambulance –

Place	Date	Hour	Summary of Events and Information	Remarks and references to Appendices
FARNBOROUGH	3.3.16		Unit entrained for service overseas in the 39th Division in two train loads, 1st Party consisting of 5 Officers, 110 other ranks, 2nd Party 5 Officers + 111 other ranks. Total strength 10 Officers, 221 other ranks. Captain A.S. LITTLEJOHNS. RAMC in Command.	App A. List of Officers.
			First party entrained at 7.20 AM + arrived at Southampton at 9.10 A.M, Second party entrained at 9.15 AM + arrived at Southampton at 11 A.M. Unit embarked on H.M.T City of Benares at 4pm, sailed at 5pm, + after a rough crossing arrived at LE HAVRE about 2.30 A.M. on 4.3.16.	
LE HAVRE	4.3.16		H.M.T. City of Benares arrived alongside quay at 10AM: disembarkation of unit complete at 5pm: unit marched to No 2 Rest Camp LE HAVRE, reaching camp at 7.30pm: en route Entrainment Orders were received. Weather very cold + snowing at intervals. Night spent under canvas.	App 1. Entrainment Orders.
LE HAVRE	5.3.16		Unit marched out of camp at 7.45 AM + entrained at Point No: 3, Gare des Marchandises, entrainment completed at 11.30 A.M. + train moved off at 12 noon.	App 2. Train Orders.
THIENNES	6.3.16		Unit arrived at THIENNES at 7.45 AM + detrained: orders (App 3) were	App 3. ADMS. orders.

T2134. Wt. W708–776. 500090. 4/15. Sir J. C. & S.

Instructions regarding War Diaries and Intelligence Summaries are contained in F. S. Regs., Part II. and the Staff Manual respectively. Title pages will be prepared in manuscript.

WAR DIARY
or
INTELLIGENCE SUMMARY.
(*Erase heading not required.*)

Army Form C. 2118.

(2)

Ref. Map. France $\frac{1}{40000}$. Sheet 36A.

Place	Date	Hour	132nd Field Ambulance. Summary of Events and Information	Remarks and references to Appendices
THIENNES	6.3.16		received from A.D.M.S. 39th Division to proceed to MORBECQUE + open a main dressing station at the Chateau at point D 14. c8 (Ref. Map France $\frac{1}{40000}$ Sheet 36A) with A + C sections. Unit billeted partly in Chateau outbuildings + a farm near by, horses at the latter.	
MORBECQUE	7.3.16		B Section proceeded to STEENBECQUE + formed a dressing station at I 5 c 8 8, sending on two detachments to form small dressing stations at LA BELLE HOTESSE (C 21 d 8.4) + BLARINGHEM (B 23 b 5.4).	
MORBECQUE	11.3.16		"C" Section proceeded to the 25th Field Ambulance situated S.E. of the A in LA LYS R on the ESTAIRES SAILLY road (Ref. HAZEBROUCK map	App (4). orders ADMS.
MORBECQUE	18.3.16		"C" Section returned to Headquarters at MORBECQUE.	
"	19.3.16		"B" Section proceeded to 25th Field Ambulance for instruction, being replaced by "C" Section at the dressing station which they had formed.	App. (5) ADMS. orders
"	20.3.16		"B" Section rejoined Headquarters at MORBECQUE, less a detachment of 1 NCO + 4 men left at STEENBECQUE, the Brigade from whom the section was collecting having left the area. Detachments remained at LA BELLE HOTESSE + BLARINGHEM as before.	

T2134. Wt. W708-776. 500000. 4/15. Sir J. C. & S.

Instructions regarding War Diaries and Intelligence Summaries are contained in F. S. Regs., Part II. and the Staff Manual respectively. Title pages will be prepared in manuscript.

WAR DIARY
or
~~INTELLIGENCE SUMMARY.~~ Ref Map France 1/40000 Sheet 36A. (3)
(Erase heading not required.)

Army Form C. 2118.

Place	Date	Hour	Summary of Events and Information	Remarks and references to Appendices
MORBECQUE	24.3.16		Orders (App 6) to be ready to move on 26.3.16 & withdraw "C" Section (App 6a) from 25th Field Ambulance.	App 6 & 6a. ADMS orders
"	25.3.16		Unit ordered (App 7) to move to MANQUEVILLE (U3) on 27.3.16. Advance party unable to find a suitable site at this place, on 26.3.16 orders were received to march out on 27.3.16 (as in Orders App 7), instructions to be received as to ultimate destination whilst en route to ST. VENANT (P4).	App 7. ADMS orders
"	27.3.16		Unit marched out at 8.45 AM: orders were received at 10.30 AM, whilst en route, to proceed to GONNEHEM (V 18). On arrival there a dressing station was established at V18.C.2.8	App 8. ADMS orders
GONNEHEM	28.3.16		Daily collection of sick from districts by motor ambulances according to orders (App 9) & evacuation by 16 M.A.C. as in orders (App 10).	App 9 & 10. ADMS orders
"	30.3.16		Orders (App 11) for unit to proceed to ROBECQ (P.29) on 31/3/16.	App 11. ADMS orders
"	31.3.16		Unit left GONNEHEM at 2 pm. & marched to ROBECQ & established a dressing station at P29b.64. Very good accommodation available in a brewery.	
			Total cases of sickness admitted to 31.3.16 = 346	
			" " " wounded " " " = 1 (accidental).	

A Whittington – Capt. RAMC
O.C. 132 Field Ambulance.

T2134. Wt. W708–776. 500000. 4/15. Sir J. C. & S.

A 129

O i/c
A G's Office at the Base

Herewith original War
Diary of 132nd Field Ambulance

[signature]
Capt R.A.M.C.
O.C. 132nd Field Ambulance

3-4-16

HW

132 F Amb

Army Form C. 2118.

Vol 2

Instructions regarding War Diaries and Intelligence Summaries are contained in F. S. Regs., Part II. and the Staff Manual respectively. Title pages will be prepared in manuscript.

April 1916 –

WAR DIARY
or
~~INTELLIGENCE SUMMARY~~.
(Erase heading not required.)

Map Reference BETHUNE (Combined Sheet) –

Place	Date	Hour	Summary of Events and Information	Remarks and references to Appendices
ROBECQ	1·4·16		Dressing Station in the mill at ROBECQ: collection of patients from same area, together with 9th Machine Gun Squadron at L'ECLEME (V3c) (App 12): Corps Rest Station at MERVILLE (App. 13) – Beautiful sunshiny weather –	App 12 + 13. ADMS orders re collection + Corps Rest Station
"	4·4·16		"A" section proceeded to MESPLAUX X14.a.8.6 + was attached to 130 Fld. Ambulance for instruction (App. 14)	App. 14. ADMS. Order to MESPLAUX –
	11·4·16		"A" section rejoined Field Ambulance headquarters –	
	14/15·4·16		Orders (App 15 + 16) for unit to move to BOIS DE PACAUT (Q33 b 6.5) + take over from a section of the 129th Fld Ambulance –	App. 15 + 16 – ADMS orders to move – ~~App 17 ADMS order~~
"	16·4·16		Unit moved to BOIS DE PACAUT (Q33.b.6.5) – Dressing Station opened in Chateau for reception + treatment of Divisional Scabies Cases, + evacuation of Divisional Reserve Area – Bearer subdivision held in readiness to move if required (App 17) –	App 17 ADMS orders –
BOIS DE PACAUT	20·4·16		Orders (App 18) for two sections to return to ROBECQ (Q33.b.6.5) to establish site for treatment of Divisional Scabies cases –	App 18. ADMS orders –
"	22·4·16		"A + B" sections moved to ROBECQ + opened dressing station at Q33.b.6.5. for treatment of Divisional Scabies Cases. "C" section remained at BOIS DE PACAUT to collect + treat sick etc of Divisional Rest Area –	
ROBECQ	29·4·16		Arrangements satisfactory + working well at both sites –	

Total Patients admitted during the month including Transfers } 420. (Transfers 58).

A.F. Phillips [?] Major RAMC
O.C. 132 Field Ambulance –

39th Div.

May 1916

132nd F. Amb.

Instructions regarding War Diaries and Intelligence Summaries are contained in F. S. Regs., Part II. and the Staff Manual respectively. Title pages will be prepared in manuscript.

WAR DIARY or ~~INTELLIGENCE SUMMARY.~~

(Erase heading not required.)

132nd Field Ambulance — Army Form C. 2118.

Vol 3

May. 1916 — Map References: — BETHUNE (Combined Sheet) —

Place	Date	Hour	Summary of Events and Information	Remarks and references to Appendices
ROBECQ	1/5/16		Arrangements satisfactory & working well —	
"	3/5/16		Lieut. K.T. LIMBERY, RAMC, proceeded to take over medical charge of 184th Brigade RFA temporarily —	
"	8/5/16		Lieut. C.D. COYLE. RAMC took over temporary medical charge of 6th Cheshire Regt. (T) —	
"	12/5/16		Lieut. A.E. SUTTON, RAMC, proceeded to WITTES H4d.1.0 (Sheet 36A) to take over medical charge of XI Corps Cyclist Battalion, and was struck off the strength of 132 Fld Amb from this date — Bearer division of the unit was ordered at 1.15pm to rendezvous at the Crossroads at W14b. (Sheet 36A) at 3.30pm (App 20): they were there inspected by D.D.M.S. XI Corps — and returned to billets afterwards —	App 19 & 19.a Orders re Lt Sutton. App 20. Orders re Bearer division
"	18/5/16		Unit inspected by D.M.S. 1st Army —	
"	21/5/16		Lt. C.D. COYLE. RAMC rejoined headquarters —	
"	22/5/16		Lt. K.T. LIMBERY posted to medical charge of 184th Brigade RFA & struck off the strength of the 132nd Fld. Amb. from this date —	
"	31/5/16		"A" & "B" Sections of unit moved to BOIS DE PACAUT (Q33.b.6.5) — after handing over the site at ROBECQ (P29b.6.4) to 2/3 South Midland Fld Amb —	
			Total admissions for month — 354. Of whom 113 were transfers: total cases of scabies dealt with = 223 —	

A. Kettlewell? Major RAMC
O.C. 132nd Fld. Amb —

T2134. Wt. W708—776. 500000. 4/15. Sir J. C. & S.

June 1916.

No. 132 F. A.

FA. 449.

D.A.G.
G.H.Q 3rd Echelon –

132nd FIELD AMBULANCE –

War Diary for June 1916 herewith –

A. Whittington-Jones –
Major –

4/7/16 –

R.A.M.C.
O.C. 132ND FIELD AMBULANCE.

Instructions regarding War Diaries and Intelligence Summaries are contained in F. S. Regs., Part II. and the Staff Manual respectively. Title pages will be prepared in manuscript.

WAR DIARY
or
~~INTELLIGENCE SUMMARY.~~
(Erase heading not required.)

132nd FIELD AMBULANCE –

Reference BETHUNE (Combined Sheet) Army Form C. 2118.

June – 1916 –

June 132. F Amb (1) Vol 4

Place	Date	Hour	Summary of Events and Information	Remarks and references to Appendices
BOIS DE PACAUT Q 33.b.6.5 –	2.6.16		Lieut W.S.T. CONNELL RAMC proceeded to take over charge of 11th Sussex Regt	App: 21 – ADMS order re Lieut Connell
"	9.6.16		Lieut G.W.D. CARLETON RAMC joined + was taken on the strength of 132nd Field Ambulance	
"	10.6.16		Lieut E.F. NIVEN RAMC taken on the strength of the unit –	
"	14.6.16		Instructions received to be prepared to move to VIEILLE CHAPELLE R.34 a.9.9 at an early date. Lieut C.J. MacDOUGALL + 10 other ranks sent on as an advance party –	App 21. ADMS Orders
"	16.6.16		Advance party, in addition, consisting of Lieuts C.E. TUCKER + F.G. MARTIN + tent subdivision of "A" Section + 26 other ranks sent to VIEILLE CHAPELLE to take over A.D.S. at ST VAAST (M.32.d.8.6) + main site at R.34.a.9.9 –	App: 22 ADMS order re ADS
"	17.6.16		Remainder of 132nd Field Ambulance moved to VIEILLE CHAPELLE (R.34.a.9.9) and relieved 105th Field Ambulance – Evacuation of wounded + sick from the front line through Regimental Aid Posts at PLUM STREET (S10.a.8.4) + FACTORY POST (S.9.d.1.7) via Advanced Dressing Station, composed of dugouts, at ST VAAST (M.32.d.8.6) + thence to main site at R.34.a.9.9 – Scheme of evacuation (App: 24) attached. Collection of wounded + sick from surrounding area East of LOCON–LESTREM Road (exclusive) + North of LE TOURET (X16.b.1.9) (App: 25) –	App: 23 – ADMS order re move – App: 24 – Scheme of Evacuation App: 25 – Div'l medical arrangements
VIEILLE CHAPELLE	24.6.16		All arrangements working satisfactorily –	

T2134. Wt. W708–776. 500000. 4/15. Sir J. C. & S.

Instructions regarding War Diaries and Intelligence Summaries are contained in F. S. Regs., Part II. and the Staff Manual respectively. Title pages will be prepared in manuscript.

WAR DIARY
or
~~INTELLIGENCE~~ SUMMARY.
132nd FIELD AMBULANCE. (Erase heading not required.)

Reference BETHUNE (Comb. Sheet) – June 1916 – ② –

Army Form C. 2118.

Place	Date	Hour	Summary of Events and Information	Remarks and references to Appendices
R 34.a.9.9. VIEILLE CHAPELLE.	25/6/16.		Orders received to be prepared to move at 48 hours notice – (App: 26) –	App 26. A.D.M.S. Orders.
" "	28/6/16		Orders to be prepared to receive considerable casualties (App: 27, 28 & 29) – All necessary steps taken to cope with these, personnel at A.D.S. augmented & additional stretchers provided –	App 27.28 & 29. A.D.M.S. Orders re forthcoming Operations.
" "	29/30		Expected Operation took place – 21 Officers & 634 N.C.Os & men passed through the A.D.S. & Main Dressing Station – Work was heaviest between 6 AM & 5 PM on 30/6/16, during which time most of the casualties came through – From 10 AM onwards large numbers of motor ambulances of No: 2 M.A.C. were available to clear – Evacuation proceeded very satisfactorily all day – Additional assistance from 133rd & 134th Field Ambulances, who supplied Officers & stretcher squads, was very welcome & gave us great assistance – The bearers performed very good work in the Front line & between it & the Regimental Aid Posts, & from the latter to the A.D.S. – Motor ambulances of the unit, and some from 133rd & 134th, cleared the A.D.S. to the Main Dressing Station at VIEILLE CHAPELLE – All arrangements worked well, and all ranks did their utmost – By 5.30 pm the main dressing station was clear, and further cases were evacuated at once as they came down – Lieut. E.F. NIVIN. R.A.M.C. was slightly wounded in the head, but continued to work for two hours at the A.D.S. – Ten other ranks wounded –	Total Admissions for the month. Wounded – 682. Sick – 230 – Total 912 –

A. Littlejohn – Major R.A.M.C.
O.C. 132ND FIELD AMBULANCE.

T2134. Wt. W708–776. 500000. 4/15. Sir J. C. & S.

39th Division

July 1916

132nd Field Ambulance

39 July

Vol 5

Instructions regarding War Diaries and Intelligence Summaries are contained in F. S. Regs., Part II. and the Staff Manual respectively. Title pages will be prepared in manuscript.

WAR DIARY
or
~~INTELLIGENCE SUMMARY.~~
(Erase heading not required.)

July. 1916 –

132nd FIELD AMBULANCE – Army Form C. 2118.

Map References – BETHUNE. (Combined Sheet) –

Place	Date	Hour	Summary of Events and Information	Remarks and references to Appendices
VIEILLE CHAPELLE. R34.a.9.9.	3/7/16		App (29 a). Report on collection, reception & evacuation of Casualties during the recent operations –	App: 29.a. Report –
"	6/7/16		Orders to be in readiness to move at 24 hours notice.	App 29. & 30.
"	6/7/16	5pm	Orders by ADMS to move to BETHUNE & take over the Field Ambulance site at the Civil & Military Hospital BETHUNE (E.10.d.8.8.) – An advance party consisting of Lieut. C.E. TUCKER & 6 other ranks proceeded, & was joined during the night of the 6/7 by "C" Section Tent Subdivision – This party then took over the Advanced Dressing Station at HARLEY STREET at A 20.d.2.9 –	Orders ADMS to move to new site –
BETHUNE.	7/7/16		The remainder of the Field Ambulance arrived at BETHUNE & took over the Main Dressing Station at E10.d.8.8. The site is a fairly good one, but its chief drawback is that the wards, which are good & large, are at the top of the building –	
"	11/7/16		Arrangements are satisfactory – Report on them in App 32 –	App: 32. Report on medical arrangements.
"	14/7/16		Orders to proceed to MESPLAUX (X14.a.9.6) on 15/7/16 (App 33) –	
"	15/7/16		"B" Section Tent Subdivision marched to ST VAAST and established an Advanced Dressing Station at M32.d.8.6: remainder of unit at BETHUNE, having handed	App 33. A.D.M.S. Orders to move to MESPLAUX –

Instructions regarding War Diaries and Intelligence Summaries are contained in F. S. Regs., Part II. and the Staff Manual respectively. Title pages will be prepared in manuscript.

WAR DIARY
or
~~INTELLIGENCE SUMMARY.~~
(Erase heading not required.)

Army Form C. 2118.

132nd FIELD AMBULANCE.

JULY 1916 –

Map Reference:– BETHUNE Combined Sheet – (2)

Place	Date	Hour	Summary of Events and Information	Remarks and references to Appendices
BETHUNE.	15/7/16		over the Civil & Military Hospital Field Ambulance Site to the 26th Field Ambulance, proceeded to MESPLAUX & opened a Main Dressing Station at X.14.a.9.6 –	App: 33(a)(b). A.D.M.S. Order No: 3. & Medical Arrangements
			The HARLEY STREET A.D.S. party (at A.20.d.2.9) left HARLEY STREET at 10pm & rejoined Headquarters at MESPLAUX at 1.30 AM on 16/7/16 –	
MESPLAUX.	17/7/16.		Arrangements working satisfactorily – Extract from Corps Routine Order 409 dated 16/7/16 is as follows:– Under Authority delegated by the General Officer Commanding-in-Chief, the Corps Commander, on the 14th instant, awarded the MILITARY MEDAL to the undernamed N.C.Os & men for gallantry and devotion to duty in action:– RAMC 132nd Field Ambulance, No: 65863. S.Sgt. F.A. HODGES, No: 65868 Pte. W. DANIELS, and No: 65884 L/Cpl E.T. FAIRBROTHER –	
"	23/7/16		Orders (App 34) received to hand over A.D.S. at ST VAAST to a 31st Div'l Fld Amb. and to take over the A.D.S. in the RUE DE BOIS at X17.d 5.8 – The ST VAAST ADS was handed over during the night of the 23rd inst –	App: 34. +34(a). A.D.M.S. Order No. 4 and Medical Arrangements
"	24/7/16		The A.D.S. in RUE DE BOIS was taken over during the morning from 133rd Fld Amb & work on their dug out at this site continued – Evacuation from the Front Line through R.A.Ps at PATH HOUSE S.14.b.6.4. & RUE DE CAILLOUX S20.d.8.1. (App 34.b)	App: 34(b) – Evacuation Scheme –

T2134. Wt. W708–776. 500000. 4/15. Sir J. C. & S.

Instructions regarding War Diaries and Intelligence Summaries are contained in F. S. Regs., Part II. and the Staff Manual respectively. Title pages will be prepared in manuscript.

WAR DIARY
or
~~INTELLIGENCE~~ SUMMARY.
(Erase heading not required.)

JULY. 1916 –

132nd FIELD AMBULANCE. –

Map Reference: – BETHUNE (Combined Sheet) –

Army Form C. 2118.

(3)

Place	Date	Hour	Summary of Events and Information	Remarks and references to Appendices
MESPLAUX	29.7.16		All arrangements working satisfactorily – Captain M.J. REES RAMC reported his arrival and is taken on the strength of the unit from this date. –	
"	31.7.16		Lieut S.A. WALKER RAMC proceeded to take over medical charge of the 6th Cheshire Regt. + is struck off the strength from today's date –	
			Admissions for the month –	
			Officers – Wounded 10.	
			Sick 18.	
			Other Ranks. Wounded. 148.	
			Sick 355 –	
			Total 531 –	
			1/8/16 –	
			[signature] – Major R.A.M.C. O.C. 132nd FIELD AMBULANCE.	

T2134. Wt. W708–776. 500000. 4/15. Sir J. C. & S.

34(b)

FA.557.

A.D.M.S.
Big Div –

Scheme of evacuation from the front line to A.D.S. RUE DE BOIS at X17 d.5.8 –

(1) PATH HOUSE. R.A.P. S.14.b.6.4 – In response to request for assistance by M.O. i/c Bn. 31st Div. 4 RAMC. personnel, two stretchers & two wheeled stretcher carriers have been supplied to this R.A.P. and cases are brought down on wheeled stretcher carriers by the RUE DE BOIS

(2) RUE DE CAILLOUX. S20 d.8.1. lying down cases by tramway car

(3) Any wounded from surrounding batteries etc as required –

Collection of Sick

By horse ambulance which visits LE TOURET daily –

A Littlejohn –
Major
R.A.M.C.
O.C. 132ND FIELD AMBULANCE.

27/7/16 –

Secret

Medical arrangements, 39th Div. (Amended 24.7.16)

MEDICAL UNIT	MAIN DRESSING STATION.	ADVANCED DRESSING STATION.	AID POSTS.	SECTION
132 FLD. AMB.	MESPLAUX (X.14.a.9.6.)	RUE DU BOIS (X.17.d.5.8.)	RUE DE CAILLOUX (S.20.d.8.1.)	FESTUBERT
134 FLD. AMB.	ANNEZIN. (E.9.b.2.8.)	MARAIS (F.5. central.)	RUE DE CAILLOUX (S.20.d.8.1) BARNTON ROAD (A.2.b.3.2.) FESTUBERT COLLECTING POST (S.25.d.5.4.)	FESTUBERT
133 FLD. AMB.	BETHUNE Ecole Maternelle [illegible] at WHITE HOUSE W 30.a.8.8.	LONE FARM (A.7.d.1.3.)	SOUTHMORE (A.8.d.7.4.) LAMBETH ROAD. (A.8.c.8.3.) QUEENS ROAD. (A.8.c.9.0.)	GIVENCHY.
82nd Sanitary Section – Headquarters, MESPLAUX (X.8.c.2.0)				

COLLECTION OF SICK – 132 Fld. Amb. LE TOURET, MESPLAUX and LOCON area.
133 Fld. Amb. BETHUNE, ESSARS, LE HAMEL and LES CHOQUAUX area.
134 Fld. Amb. GORRE, TUNING FORK and LOISNE area.

C. R. Millar
Major
for A.D.M.S. 39th Division

24.7.16.

84 (a)

Secret (34) Copy No 9

R.A.M.C. Order No. 4
by
Colonel G.W. Brazier-Creagh C.M.G.
A.D.M.S. 39th Division

Reference Map.
BETHUNE Combined Sheet
1/40.000.

1. ~~Information~~
The 39th Division is to hold the front from LA BASSEE CANAL to LA QUINQUE RUE crossing
2. The Main Dressing Stations of Field Ambulances will remain in their present sites
3. O.C. 132 Fld. Amb. will hand over A.D.S. ST. VAAST (M.32 d.8.6.) and KING GEORGE'S Collecting Post (X.5.d.5.2) to a Field Amb. of the 31st Division. Advanced parties will arrive on the evening of the 23rd July.
4. O.C. 133 Fld. Amb. will hand over A.D.S. RUE DU BOIS (X.14.d.5.8) to 132 Fld Amb. and will take over A.D.S. LONE FARM (A.4.d.1.3) from 134 Fld. Amb.
These reliefs to take place on 24th and night 24/25th July and will be carried out by mutual arrangement between the Field Ambulance Commanders concerned.
5. One Section of 133 Fld. Amb. will take over WHITE HOUSE (W.30.a.8.8.)
6. After the readjustment, the following will be the locations of the Medical Units
132 Fld Amb. MESPLAUX (X.14.a.9.6)
A.D.S. RUE DU BOIS (X.14.d.5.8)
133 Fld Amb. BETHUNE. ECOLE MATERNELLE
A.D.S. LONE FARM (A.4.d.1.3)
One Section at WHITE HOUSE (W.30.a.8.8)

134 Fld Amb. ANNEZIN (E.9.b.2.8)
A.D.S. MARAIS (F.5 central)

82nd San. Sect. MESPLAUX (X.8 c 1 0)

7. Baths - The RICHEBOURG ST.VAAST Baths will be handed over to the 31st Div.

8. Completion of reliefs to be reported to A.D.M.S.

C. R. Millar
Major
for A.D.M.S. 39th Division

23.7.16

Copies to.
G — 132 Fld. Amb
A.Q. — 133 "
Div RA — 134 "
Div RE — 82nd San. Sect
116 Inf Bde — A.D.M.S. 31st Div
117 " — D.D.M.S. XI Corps
118 " — War Diary
13 Glosters

Secret

39th Division Medical Arrangements (Amended 15.7.16).

MEDICAL UNIT	MAIN DRESSING STATION	ADVANCED DRESSING STATION	AID POSTS.		
132 FLD AMB	MESPLAUX X.14.a.9.6.	ST. VAAST (M.32.d.8.6)	PLUM STREET (S.10.a.8.4.) FACTORY POST (S.9.d.1.7.) KING GEORGES POST (X.5.d.5.2.)		
133 FLD AMB	ECOLE MATERNELLE, BETHUNE	RUE DU BOIS (X.17.d.5.8.)	PATH HOUSE (S.14.b.6.4) TUBE STATION (S.21.a.5.8)		
134 FLD AMB	ANNEZIN. (E.9.b.2.8.)	MARAIS (F.5.central) LONE FARM (A.7.d.1.3.)	RUE DE CAILLOUX (S.21.c.0.4) BARNTON ROAD (A.2.b.3.2) SOUTHMORE (A.8.d.7.4) LAMBETH ROAD (A.8.c.8.3.) QUEENS ROAD (A.8.c.d.0.)		
82ND SAN SECT	Headquarters. MESPLAUX X.8.c.2.0.				

33(b)

Dental Surgeon attends at 134 Fld. Amb. on Mondays from 9 am to 4 pm.

Evacuation Cases from 132 Fld. Amb. by No.2 M.A.C. Cases from 133 & 134 Fd. Ambs. by No.12 M.A.C.

Collection of Sick 134 Fld. Amb. GORRE and adjacent area: 133rd Fld Amb. ESSARS, LE HAMEL
BETHUNE-LOCON ROAD, exclusive of LOCON, and adjacent areas.
132 Fld. Amb. North of line LOCON (inclusive) MESPLAUX (inclusive) and LE TOURET (exclusive).

C. R. Millar

Major

for A.D.M.S. 39th Division

33 (a)

Secret. Copy No 13

R.A.M.C. Order No. 3
by
Colonel G.W. Brazier-Creagh C.M.G.
A.D.M.S. 39th Division

July 14 · 1916

Ref. Map
BETHUNE (Combined sheet)

1. Information – The 39th Division will take over the front from LA BASSEE CANAL (exclusive) (A.15.d.10.6½) to OXFORD STREET (S.5.C.4.4.)
Reliefs will be completed by 6am. 16th July.

2. The 132nd Field Ambulance will be relieved on the 15th inst. by a Field Ambulance of the 8th Division and will take over the site at MESPLAUX (X.14.a.9.6) An advance party will be sent on the morning of the 15th inst. to take over A.D.S. ST. VAAST (M.32.d.8.6.) and KING GEORGES POST (X.5.d.5.2.) from the 61st Division.
The A.D.S. HARLEY STREET (A.20.d.3.9½) and Fld. Amb. advanced posts will be taken over by the 8th Division on the night 15/16th July.
The Section of the 132nd Fld. Amb. at this A.D.S. will rejoin headquarters at MESPLAUX on the 16th July.

3. The 133rd Field Ambulance will remain at its present site ECOLE MATERNELLE, BETHUNE. The A.D.S. at CAMBRIN CHURCH (A.26.a.1½.8.) and advanced Fld. Amb. posts will be taken over by the 8th Division on the night 15/16th July – personnel of 133rd Fld Amb. to rejoin headquarters on the 16th inst.
The A.D.S. RUE DU BOIS (X.17.d.5.8.) will be retained by the 133rd Fld. Amb.

4 The 134th Field Ambulance will remain at its present site ANNEZIN (E.9.b.2.8.) with advanced Dressing Stations at MARAIS (F.5. central) and LONE FARM (A.7.d.1.3)

5. The 82nd Sanitary Section will move from BETHUNE to MESPLAUX (X.8.C.2.0.) on the 15th July.

6. Baths – The Baths at BETHUNE, BEUVRY, LE PREOL and ANNEQUIN, and the Divisional Laundry at BETHUNE will be handed over to the 8th Division.
The Baths and Divisional Laundry at LOCON will be reopened.

7
The Office of the A.D.M.S. will close at BETHUNE at 10am on the 15th July and will open at LOCON at the same hour.

C. R. Millar
Major
for A.D.M.S. 39th Division

Copies to:-			
	G.	116 I. Bde	134 Fld Amb
	A.Q	117 " "	82 San. Sect.
	D.A.D.O.S.	118 " "	A.D.M.S. 8th Div.
	A.P.M.	13 Glosters.	A.D.M.S. 61st.
	Signals	Div Train	D.D.M.S. XI Corps
	Div. R.A	132 Fld Amb	War Diary
	Div. R.E	133 "	

(32)

F.A. 479.

A.D.M.S
39 Div.

Accomodation & distribution of Personnel at present are as follows:—

(1) A.D.S. HARLEY STREET. A 20. d. 2.9.

(a) accomodation.
Three concrete dug-outs which will accomodate 22 stretchers each. Gas proof curtains.

(b) Personnel.
2 Officers.
40 Other ranks.
Two motor-ambulances.
One water cart.

(2) BEUVRY. Collecting Station. F 14. C. 3½. 3.
1 Sergeant.
6 Other ranks.
1 Motor Ambulance Car.
1 Horse " wagon.
1 Limbered wagon.
1 Water Cart.

At the Baths F. 14. a. 8.1.
5 men.

(3) LE PREOL Baths F 10. C. 6. 2.
4 men.

F.A. 479 -
(Contd)

(4) <u>Main Dressing Station</u> - E 10. d. 5.8.
The rest of the personnel, of whom, one Sergeant + 8 other ranks are employed at the ANNEXE. E 10. b. 7.3.
The two big wards at the Main Dressing Station would take about 100 stretcher cases each if required - (200 in all) -
In the billets of the men, about 250 sitting cases could be accommodated -
Tents would provide accommodation for about a further 150 sitting or 80 lying cases -
<u>Scheme of Evacuation</u> -
Cases are brought from the Front Line to the Regimental Aid Posts at A 21. a. 6. 7½ + A 21 c 6. 6½ -

(1) <u>R.A.P. at A 21. a. 6. 7½</u> - Near by is a Field Ambulance Post at A 21. a. 5. 6. There are four bearers: they bring lying down cases back by special stretcher on the overhead mono-rail to the HARLEY STREET ADS. Walking cases come down along the same trench, which is called HERTFORD STREET.

(2) <u>R.A.P. at A 21 C 6. 6½</u> -

Bearers clearing this R.A.P. are in two dug outs at A 20. d. 8½. 4 - called

(3)

F.A. 479.
(Contd)

COOMBES + ROTUNDA dug outs – I have instructed the O/C A.D.S. HARLEY STREET, to arrange for their bearers to carry the lying down cases from the R.A.P. to the LA BASSEÉ Road (along THE LANE trench) near BRADDELL CASTLE at A 20.d.9.5½: hence they are taken by wheeled stretcher carrier down the LA BASSEÉ Road + so to HARLEY STREET A.D.S. – There is a trench, not shown on the Trench Map, running from THE LANE across the LA BASSEÉ Road + thence to HARLEY STREET A.D.S. from about point A 21.C. 1½.6 just above THE FOUR HUNDRED, crossing the LA BASSEÉ Road at BRADDELL CASTLE + thence to HARLEY STREET A.D.S. which walking cases would follow, + stretchers could also be carried that way, if the wheeled stretcher carrier could not be used with safety on the LA BASSEÉ Road –

A Whitteyham – Major

11/7/16 –

O.C. 132 F.A

(31)

Secret

O.C. 132 Fd. Amb.

1. The 132nd Field Ambulance will proceed to BETHUNE tomorrow the 7th inst. marching at an early hour.
You will take over the Fd. Amb. site at Civil and Military Hospital, Bethune, from the 99th Fd. Amb. and also A.D.S. at HARLEY STREET.
You will take over Div. Laundry.

2. You will proceed yourself at Earliest possible moment to BETHUNE and put yourself in touch with O.C. 99th Fd. Amb. You will take with you one Officer, your Quartermaster, 1 N.C.O. and 6 R.A.F. (2 for the laundry) The Qr. Mr. will take over the laundry. Your Qr Master & you will return to complete your move which must be completed within the 24 hours. No fixtures of any sort are to be removed from present site.

3. All patients, that cannot be evacuated to be left at VIELLE CHAPELLE and

handed over to the incoming Fd. Amb.

4. You will hand over VIELLE CHAPELLE + RICHBOURG Baths to 61st Div.

Acknowledge

S. Brazier Creagh
Colonel
ADMS 39th Div

A. D. M. S.
No. 4/102
6.7.16
39th DIVISION

(30)

Secret

O.C. 132 Fd. Ambulance

You will hold your unit in readiness to move to a new site at 24 hours notice.

Acknowledge.

A.D.M.S.
No. 4/92
6.7.16
39th DIVISION

C. [illegible]
Major
for A.D.M.S.
39th Div.

(29 (a))

F.A.444 –

A.D.M.S.
39 Divn.

I have to report that in expectation of active operations on the 29/30 of June 1916 ~~each~~ steps were taken for the reception of wounded as follows –

(1) Advanced Dressing Station –

(a) Twelve bearers & ~~eighteen~~ sixteen additional Stretchers were sent to PLUM STREET R. Aid Post to carry out evacuation by trolley line to A.D.S –

(b) Twenty four bearers & 22 extra stretchers were sent to the FACTORY POST R. Aid Post: in this case six squads of bearers were provided to work between the front line & the regimental Aid Post; the number of wheeled stretcher carriers was brought up to six, and twelve further bearers were detailed to evacuate the wounded by means of wheeled stretcher carriers between FACTORY POST & the A.D.S –

(c) At the A.D.S. arrangements were made for dressing patients in the new dug

cupola dug outs on the WESTERN side of the compound – hot drinks were prepared – At the A.D.S. there were also six further squads of bearers, in reserve, who were needed as soon as operation had commenced –
From about 5 A.M. on the 30th June 1916 wounded were coming in in large numbers for several hours, were given refreshments, and necessary dressings were carried out as expeditiously as possible, & cases evacuated to the Main Dressing Station by means of Motor Ambulances as rapidly as possible – Between 8 & 9 AM the A.D.S. was shelled. 14 shells dropped in the compound, & 18 outside within a hundred yards of the A.D.S. compound – There was a direct hit on the cupola dug out, in which dressings were being performed, by a 5.9" shell, which bent in one of the plates but did not penetrate it – Lieut. E.F. NIVEN who was working just beneath this point of impact was wounded in the head not severely, as the result of this but continued to perform his duties – When this occurred, all urgent cases

FA 444.

had their dressings completed & were removed to the longer dug outs South of the dug outs which had been hit. The other cases had meanwhile been placed under cover in the long dug outs, & the dug outs on the Eastern side of the compound. The dressing room was also shifted over to that side of the compound. Shelling ceased soon after this, and there was no recurrence. Work went on at high pressure through the whole day until about 4 p.m., when the rush had ceased. Many more casualties came in during the evening up to about 7 P.M. and a few at intervals through the night.

(2) At the main Dressing Station.
All preparations for a large number of casualties had been made. The rush commenced at about 6 AM & continued uninterruptedly until about 5 pm. All ranks worked at high pressure throughout this time. There were ample provisions made for the supply of food & hot medical comforts. It was early seen that additional help would be required and in response to a message to O.C.

133 Field Ambulance, two medical officers arrived to help in the dressings – Further assistance here and at the ADS was presently provided by the ADMS 39 Divn – In response to urgent messages from HQ 116 Brigade six further squads of bearers with stretchers from 133 FA went up, and also six additional stretchers – No further demands for personnel or stretchers were made on me – No 2 MAC started to clear the main dressing station at about 10 AM, & in a short space of time afterwards, by 11 AM there were a large number of cars available: evacuations were speedily carried out throughout the rest of the day until the whole place was cleared, & from 6 pm onwards through the night cases were removed as required by No 2 MAC, who kept cars at our disposal throughout the night –

The total casualties which passed through the Field Ambulance during the period under review amounted to:–

(5) FA 444.

21 Officers and 634 Other ranks

I am satisfied that all ranks did their utmost throughout this time for the wounded, and this being so it is extremely difficult to pick out any individuals for special mention —

I gratefully acknowledge the splendid assistance given to us by the personnel of O.C.s 133 & 134 Field Ambulances, which was as [illegible] at once —

I desire to bring the undermentioned to your notice —

(1) Temp Lieut. D. J. MacDOUGALL. who was responsible for the equipment of the Regimental Aid Posts with their extra personnel etc & for the arrangements at the A.D.S. he had a period of great anxiety during the time prior to the Operation, & carried out all his instructions in a most praiseworthy manner, and I consider that the results on the day were a great credit to him —

2) Temp. Lieut. E.F. NIVIN. for the plucky way in which he continued to carry on his duties for two hours, after he had been wounded & partially stunned, when the dug out in which he was working had been struck, by a direct hit of a 5·9" H.E. shell -

(3) No: 65863 Staff Sgt: F.A. HODGES for his good all round work at the A.D.S: when all the officers had their hands full attending to the wounded, this N.C.O. did excellent work in the supervision of the reception & evacuation of wounded and in all round general supervision -

Amongst the bearers, where all behaved with great credit to the Corps, the following have been brought to notice:-

(1) No: 65868 Pte W. DANIELS. who, although himself wounded in the leg, refused to be removed from a dug out where there were four other wounded men, until they had all been taken back, and himself helped to place the other wounded men on the stretchers, working on his hands & knees -

(7)

FA. 444 –

(2) For coolness under fire & good work all through the day: –

No: 65884 L-Cpl E.T. FAIRBROTHER –
No: 65849 Pte. J.F. PULMAN –
No: 69033 " J.H. BOWERS –
No: 65867 " H. EVERALL –

At the main Dressing Station all worked untiringly & I hope that on a future occasion there may be an opportunity of bringing some names forward for reward. –

[illegible] –
Major
O.C. 132 Fd. Amb.

3/7/16.

(33)

Secret

O.C. 132 Fd. Amb

The 132nd Fd. Amb. will move from BETHUNE to MESPLAUX (X.14.a.9.6) and take over the A.D.S. at ST VAAST M.32.d.8.6. and KING GEORGES POST X.5.d.5.2

Advanced parties to be sent on early on the morning of the 15th inst. to take over these posts.

The main body will move by sections on the 15th inst. and establish the Main Dressing Station at MESPLAUX.

C. Bhullar
Major
for ADMS 39th Dn

A.D.M.S.
No. 4/252
14.7.16
39th DIVISION

Instructions regarding War Diaries and Intelligence Summaries are contained in F. S. Regs., Part II. and the Staff Manual respectively. Title pages will be prepared in manuscript.

WAR DIARY
or
~~INTELLIGENCE SUMMARY.~~
(*Erase heading not required.*)

AUGUST 1916 – 132nd FIELD AMBULANCE – Army Form C. 2118.

(1)

Map Reference – BETHUNE Combined Sheet – HAZEBROUCK Sheet 5A

Vol 6.

Place	Date	Hour	Summary of Events and Information	Remarks and references to Appendices
MESPLAUX 1/8/16 X.14.a.9.6.	1/8/16	12 noon	Captain J. MORRIS. RAMC (T) reported his arrival & was taken on the strength of the unit — and took over command of "B" Section –	
"	2/8/16	12/Noon	Orders from ADMS 39 Div. re relief of 39 Division –	App: 35 – ADMS Orders re move –
"	3/8/16	12.15pm	Instructions received from ADMS re Situation of Casualty Clearing Station in region of concentration of 39 Div. on relief in GIVENCHY & FESTUBERT Sections –	App: 36 a. ADMS orders re C.C.S.
"	7/8/16	10.30AM	ADMS Preliminary Order received for the Fld Amb. to march from MESPLAUX (X.14.a.9.6) to ALLOUAGNE (Sheet 5.A.) (Q6.)	App. 35 b. ADMS orders re move –
"	"	3PM	RAMC Operation Order No 5. received –	App. 35 (c) ADMS Operation Order No 5.
"	"	5 PM	ADMS order detailing Lieut. G.W. CARLETON. RAMC to take over medical charge of the 12th Bn Royal Sussex Regt – Lt CARLETON proceeded forthwith & is struck off the strength of the 132nd Field Ambulance from today's date – New Dugout at A.D.S. at RUE DE BOIS X 17 d 5.8. completed –	App. 36. Detail of Lt CARLETON
"	8/8/16	7.30PM	Relieving party from 30th Div. Field Ambulance arrived at RUE DE BOIS A.D.S. –	
"	9/8/16	7.30AM	Party at A.D.S. RUE DE BOIS rejoined Headquarters at MESPLAUX, having handed over the A.D.S. to the relieving party – At 3pm Operation Order No. 6 by ADMS (App. 37) received –	App. 37 & 37 a. ADMS Operation Order No. 6 & amendment
"	10/8/16	12.30PM	98th Fld. Amb. of 30th Division arrived at MESPLAUX and took over M.D.S. there –	
"	"	3.15PM	132nd Fld. Amb. marched from MESPLAUX to ALLOUAGNE, arriving at the latter place	

132nd FIELD AMBULANCE 5 SEP 1916

Instructions regarding War Diaries and Intelligence Summaries are contained in F. S. Regs., Part II. and the Staff Manual respectively. Title pages will be prepared in manuscript. AUGUST 1916

WAR DIARY
132nd FIELD AMBULANCE or ~~INTELLIGENCE SUMMARY~~.

(Erase heading not required.)

Map Reference: — HAZEBROUCK Sheet 5A, LENS Sheet 11., Sheet 51C.

Army Form C. 2118.

(2)

Place	Date	Hour	Summary of Events and Information	Remarks and references to Appendices
ALLOUAGNE.	10/8/16.	8pm.	at 8pm. having crossed the LA CLARENCE River at CHOCQUES at 6.30 pm. The march was carried out without any untoward incident, men + horses marching well. The day was cloudy + fairly cool.	
"	11/8/16	7.30 AM	117th Infantry Brigade Order No: 45 received (App 38). Very hot + bright day. The unit marched out of ALLOUAGNE at 4.45 pm. and proceeded via AUCHEL, CALONNE RICOUART, DIVION, OURTON, DIEVAL, LA THIEULOYE to MAGNICOURT-EN-COMTÉ: a long + trying march, with several very steep hills; men + horses marched splendidly. Halted for 45 minutes at DIVION from 8-8.45 P.M. A few cases were picked up on the road at OURTON. MAGNICOURT-EN-COMTÉ was reached at 2 AM. on 12/8/16.	App. 38. 117 Inf Brigade Order No: 45. re march.
MAGNICOURT-EN-COMTÉ.	12/8/16	1AM.	117th Infantry Brigade Order No 46. received (App 39). Unit left MAGNICOURT-EN-COMTÉ at 9AM	App. 39. 117 Inf Brigade Order No. 46 re march.
		9AM.	+ marched to TINCQUETTE in good order, reaching there at 12 noon. (Sheet 51C. C.a.) Tent hospital erected at C 4.6.2.3 (Sheet 51.C). Very hot day.	
TINCQUETTE	13.8.16	10.30AM.	A.D.M.S. inspected site.	
"	15.8.16		Wet weather. Orders (App 40) received re treatment of Scabies Cases of the Division.	App 40. ADMS order re Scabies.
"	17.8.16	1PM.	ADMS order (App 41) received to be prepared to move at 8½ hours notice. Still wet weather.	App 41. ADMS Order re move.

T2134. Wt. W708-776. 500000. 4/15. Sir J. C. & S.

132nd FIELD AMBULANCE 5 SEP. 1916

Instructions regarding War Diaries and Intelligence Summaries are contained in F. S. Regs., Part II. and the Staff Manual respectively. Title pages will be prepared in manuscript.

132nd Field Ambulance

AUGUST 1916.

WAR DIARY
or
~~INTELLIGENCE SUMMARY.~~
(Erase heading not required.)

Map reference:— Sheets {51 C. {57 D.

Army Form C. 2118.

(3)

Place	Date	Hour	Summary of Events and Information	Remarks and references to Appendices
TINCQUETTE	19.8.16	—	Still showery —	App. 42. Movement Orders 42a + 42b. orders re Advance Party + Evacuation Scheme
"	21.8.16	12.30 PM	Finer weather — A.D.M.S. orders received re move under Orders of "C" Group Commander & orders re Advance party to be sent to ACHEUX on 22/8/16 — Evacuation scheme in new area received also —	
"	22.8.16	7 AM.	116th Brigade Order No: 40 re moves on 23 & 24th inst. received (App. 43) — Lt. C.E. TUCKER, one NCO & 4 men, one motor ambulance with two drivers & car orderly left for ACHEUX at 1.30 pm — Fine dry weather — Sick Cases transferred to 2/5 London Fd. Amb. & ordinary cases to 30 C.C.S. — Camp struck & wagons packed in readiness for move —	App. 43. 43a & b. 116 Brigade Order 40.
HONVAL.	23.8.16	5.15 AM.	Unit marched to HONVAL via AVERDOINGT, GOUY-EN-TERNOIS, MONTS-EN-TERNOIS, MONCHEAUX, HOUVIGNEUL, HONVAL: headquarters at latter place at G 23 d. 2.5: HONVAL reached at 10 A.M. cool march — At 10.30 PM. 116th Infantry Brigade Order No: 41 received (App. 44) & 44. (a))	App. 44. 116 Brigade + 44a. Order No 41.
SUS ST LEGER	24.8.16	6 AM	Unit marched via REBREUVIETTE, IVERGNY, to SUS-ST-LEGER, which was reached at 10 A.M. after a cool march: headquarters at N 24. c. 3.3.	
"	{24.8.16 {25.8.16	12. MN.	Amendment to 116 Inf Brigade Order no 41 received. (App. 44 b) —	App. 44. b. Amendment to 116 Inf. Brigade Order no 41 —
"	25.8.16	7.30 AM.	Unit marched via LUCHEUX, HALLOY, ORVILLE, THIEVRES, AUTHIE, to BOIS DU WARNIMONT which was reached at 3 pm. headquarters established at I 24. d. 9.9. (Sheet 57 D) — A very hot & tiring march: unit	

Instructions regarding War Diaries and Intelligence Summaries are contained in F. S. Regs., Part II. and the Staff Manual respectively. Title pages will be prepared in manuscript.

WAR DIARY

132nd FIELD AMBULANCE ~~or INTELLIGENCE SUMMARY.~~

(Erase heading not required.)

AUGUST 1916 –

Map Reference Sheet 57D –

Army Form C. 2118.

(4)

Place	Date	Hour	Summary of Events and Information	Remarks and references to Appendices
BOIS DU WARNIMONT	25.8.16	3 PM	Marched well, only one man, who had only just recovered from Trench fever, failing to complete the distance: one ambulance wagon (horsed) had been detached to 13 Bn. Gloster Regt for this march, one marched in rear of column, whilst the third marched with the Field Ambulance: the wagons were taxed to their full capacity, but those picked up were able to rejoin their units on arrival at destination –	
		3 PM	RAMC Operation Order No 7 received. (App. 45).	App. 45. ADMS RAMC Operation Order No: 7 –
ACHEUX	27.8.16	10.30 AM	Unit marched to ACHEUX & parked at P13.a.3.2. – Very wet weather. –	
	28.8.16	4 PM	Orders received to form Divisional Collecting Station at P23.d.9.2. – Accompanied DDMS V Corps who indicated site. Six Soyer stoves were obtained during the course of the evening, and C.R.E. 39 Div. approved erection of temporary shelter by one of the Field Companies R.E.	App. 46. ADMS Medical arrangements active operations –
	29.8.16	10 AM	Saw O.C. 225 Coy R.E. & arranged for temporary shelter of wood & felt, 100 ft by 20 ft to be completed during day: transported stoves & tents to site, two operating tents & five bell tents being pitched. – Necessary supplies were indented for. –	
	30.8.16	3 PM	Made reconnaissance of routes by which wounded walking cases are to come to D.C.S. dreadful weather & very bad going in places: rejoined my Headquarters at 9 pm –	

A.D.M.S. indicated a site agreed on with D.D.M.S. & A.D.M.S. availed of by OC 132 FA of [illegible] suitable B-C

T2134. Wt. W708–776. 500000. 4/15. Sir J. C. & S.

Instructions regarding War Diaries and Intelligence Summaries are contained in F. S. Regs., Part II. and the Staff Manual respectively. Title pages will be prepared in manuscript.

132nd FIELD AMBULANCE

WAR DIARY
or
~~INTELLIGENCE SUMMARY.~~
(Erase heading not required.)

132nd Field Ambulance

AUGUST 1916.

Map Reference Sheet 57.D.

Army Form C. 2118.

(5)

Place	Date	Hour	Summary of Events and Information	Remarks and references to Appendices
ACHEUX	30.8.16	12 NOON	Orders (App 47) received whole Bearer Division in readiness to move at a moment's notice.	App. 47. Army Order re Bearer Division
"		12.30 PM	Operations postponed 24 hours.	
"	"	2 PM	Attended conference at ADMS's office. At 5 PM visited D.C.S.: roof of shelter had been practically destroyed saw O.C. 225 Coy R.E. who promised to complete shelter by night of 31st inst + put in two hundred gallon water tanks for storage of a reserve of water. Weather has wet.	App. 47. a. b. c Orders re Operations.
"	31.8.16	12 NOON	Notified that operations will take place on 1/9/16.	
"	"	12.15 PM	Notified that operations are postponed until 2/9/16.	
"	"	2 PM	Visited site of D.C.S. + found all complete + everything ready. D.D.M.S. V Corps had just seen the arrangements + expressed his satisfaction to the officer in charge of advance party at D.C.S. Later visited the Intermediate Post at Q.32.a.2.0. + found all ready: there were here two Bell tents + two Soyer Stoves. One hundred gallon water tank installed by O.C. 225 Field Coy R.E. who gave me splendid assistance throughout.	

A Whittingham
Major RAMC.
O.C. 132nd F.A. Amb.

In The Field 5/9/16.

T2134. Wt. W708-776. 500000. 4/15. Sir J. C. & S.

8.1.1916

140/1734

39th Div.

132nd Field Ambulance

Instructions regarding War Diaries and Intelligence Summaries are contained in F. S. Regs., Part II. and the Staff Manual respectively. Title pages will be prepared in manuscript.

132 Fd Amb

Army Form C. 2118.

WAR DIARY
or
~~INTELLIGENCE~~ SUMMARY.
(Erase heading not required.)

SEPTEMBER 1916 –

Map References:– Sheet 57D.

132nd FIELD AMBULANCE Sept 1916

(1)

Place	Date	Hour	Summary of Events and Information	Remarks and references to Appendices
ACHEUX	1.9.16	10AM	Notification of date of operation received (App. 47d). Fine weather –	App. 47.d. re Operations –
"		10.30AM	Visited D.C.S. + Intermediate Post + found all in good order –	
"	2.9.16	11AM	Notification of time of Commencement of operations received (App. 47.e) – Bearer Division was moved up to Divisional Collecting Station (P23.d.9.2) forthwith –	
"	"	2PM	Remainder of available personnel moved up to D.C.S. – Capt. M.J. REES left for A.D.S. at COOKERS	
"	"	4.45PM	Headquarters of Fd Amb. moved to D.C.S.	
		5PM	Bearer Division left for A.D.S. at MESNIL: Lieut C.E. TUCKER in Command, accompanied by Lieuts. D.J. MACDOUGALL + D.W.F. JONES –	
Divisional Collecting Station	3.9.16	8AM.	Walking wounded began to arrive + continued to come in all day until 9 P.M. the busiest time was from 9AM to 3P.M.: 12 officers + 679 other ranks were admitted, redressed if necessary, registered, fed + evacuated to Corps Collecting Station in motor charabancs, motor lorries, horsed ambulance wagons + G.S. wagons – The arrangements worked without a hitch of any kind – A detailed report forms the subject matter of App. 47.f – During the operation Lt C.E. TUCKER was wounded, Other ranks 2 Killed 23 wounded –	App. 47.f – Report on Divisional Collecting Stn –
"	4.9.16	4PM	Orders received to close down D.C.S. + return to ACHEUX: moved completed by 7.45 P.M. –	App. 48. Re closing of D.C.S. –

T2134. Wt. W708–776. 500000. 4/15. Sir J. C. & S.

Instructions regarding War Diaries and Intelligence Summaries are contained in F. S. Regs., Part II. and the Staff Manual respectively. Title pages will be prepared in manuscript.

WAR DIARY
or
~~INTELLIGENCE~~ SUMMARY.
(Erase heading not required.)

SEPTEMBER 1916

Map Reference:- Sheet 57D.

Army Form C. 2118.

②

Place	Date	Hour	Summary of Events and Information	Remarks and references to Appendices
ACHEUX.	4/9/16	10 PM.	Lts D.W. JONES & D.J. MACDOUGALL & A & C Sections bearer subdivisions rejoined Headquarters, "B" Section bearer subdivision remaining at the A.D.S. at MESNIL.	App. 49. OC Bearer Division Report
"	6/9/16	10 AM	Lt D.W. JONES's Report on Bearer Division work during Operations received & forwarded to A.D.M.S. 39 Div. Lt D.W. JONES's Report (App 49) shows that the Bearer Division worked splendidly under very arduous trying circumstances. My recommendations form the subject of App. 50.	App. 50. O.C. 132 Fld. Amb. Recommendations
"	"	1.45 PM	Orders received to take over Fld. Amb: site at BERTRANCOURT (J33.a.7.2) & A.D.S. at MAILLY MAILLET (P12.d.9.7.) on 7th inst. I accompanied Advance Party & saw the M.D.S. & A.D.S. Lt D.J. MACDOUGALL proceeded to take over medical charge of 13 Royl Sussex Regt.	App. 51. Orders re BERTRANCOURT.
BERTRANCOURT	7/9/16	12 Noon	M.D.S. & A.D.S. taken over: main body of Fld. Amb: arrived at BERTRANCOURT as arranged with O.C. 1/3 South Midland Field Ambulance.	
"	"	4 PM.	Visited A.D.S. & advanced Posts at AUCHONVILLERS Q9.a.1.1. and THURLE'S DUMP Q9.d.9.5. Reports on M.D.S. A.D.S. advanced Posts & lines of evacuation are attached & form Appendices 52 & 52a.	App. 52 & 52a Reports on Advanced Posts A.D.S. & M.D.S.
"	"	10 P.M.	Lieut: D.W.F. JONES proceeded to take over medical charge of 17 K.R.R.C. & was struck off strength of the unit: this officer has rendered invaluable services to the unit,	

T2134. Wt. W708-776. 500000. 4/15. Sir J. C. & S.

Instructions regarding War Diaries and Intelligence Summaries are contained in F. S. Regs., Part II. and the Staff Manual respectively. Title pages will be prepared in manuscript.

WAR DIARY
or
~~INTELLIGENCE SUMMARY.~~
(Erase heading not required.)

SEPTEMBER 1916

Map Reference Sheet 57 D.

Army Form C. 2118.

132nd FIELD AMBULANCE Sept. 1916.

(3)

Place	Date	Hour	Summary of Events and Information	Remarks and references to Appendices
BERTRANCOURT	7/9/16		and I lose his services with deep regret, but hope that he may rejoin the unit later.	
"	8/9/16	12.45 PM	Village shelled: all patients removed + placed in open fields away from line of fire. no shells fell in Fd. Amb. site.	
"	9/9/16	3 PM	Inspected RAPs + FAPs of line on our left + their lines of evacuation, a report on these is included in App: 53. Weather fine.	App. 53. Report of RAPs etc.
"	10/9/16	2 PM	Village shelled: patients removed to fields: no shells fell in Fd. Amb. site.	
"	14/9/16	1.30 PM 8 PM	Orders (App. 54) to move Headquarters of Fd. Amb. + "A" section to ~~BERTRANCOURT~~ BUS: move completed + site taken over at J 26.c.2.7. Patients were transferred during the course of the night. "B" section remained in charge of BERTRANCOURT site. A.D.S. at RED HOUSE Q1.d.2.3 taken over + equipped.	App. 54. ADMS. Orders re move to BUS.
BOS-LES-ARTOIS.	18/9/16	8 AM.	Orders received to be in readiness to take over the evacuation of a further part of the line.	
"	19/9/16	1.55 PM	Orders received re taking over of the ADS at COLINCAMPS at K 25.c.2.8. advanced party sent up to learn lines of evacuation.	App. 55. ADMS. Orders re COLINCAMPS.
"	20/9/16	11 AM	A.D.S. COLINCAMPS + Field Ambulance Posts at EUSTON (K 33.a.2½.4) + VIEW POST K 33.d.1.5.	

T2134. Wt. W708—776. 500000. 4/15. Sir J. C. & S.

Instructions regarding War Diaries and Intelligence Summaries are contained in F. S. Regs., Part II. and the Staff Manual respectively. Title pages will be prepared in manuscript.

WAR DIARY
or
~~INTELLIGENCE SUMMARY.~~
(Erase heading not required.)

SEPTEMBER 1916.

132nd FIELD AMBULANCE Sept 1916 Army Form C. 2118.

Map Reference — Sheet 57D.

(4)

Place	Date	Hour	Summary of Events and Information	Remarks and references to Appendices
BUS-LES-ARTOIS.	20/9/16	11 A.M.	taken over + staffed, and bearer squads placed in two RAPs Q4.a.6.9 MOUNTJOY, K34.a.6.4 BOWSTREET, K34.b.2.8 FLAG AVENUE and OBSERVATION WOOD K28b.3.3. Personnel + equipment found by "B" Section who vacated BERTRANCOURT, one officer + 8 other ranks remaining at the latter place which is being used as a reception station from both A.D.S. at RED HOUSE + COLINCAMPS. BERTRANCOURT was heavily shelled between 4 + 5 P.M. two soldiers +	
		10 PM	one woman being killed + one soldier wounded. Orders were received at 11 PM to withdraw party there with the exception of two O.R to remain in charge of the site.	
"	21/9/16	10 A.M.	Visited A.D.S. COLINCAMPS + FAPs at EUSTON + VIEW POST + RAP at MOUNTJOY + BOW STREET + went over routes of evacuation from these posts to EUSTON, whence cases are transferred by motor ambulance to the A.D.S. at COLINCAMPS. Report forms subject of App. 56. The Field Ambulance is now working behind seven Battalions in the line.	App. 56. Lines of Evacuation. App. 56a. Lines of evacuation.
"	24/9/16	4 PM.	Visited RAPs at FLAG AVENUE + OBSERVATION WOOD and lines of evacuation from them which are described in App. 56.a.	
"	28/9/16		No: 65812 Cpl. F.H. MANN awarded the MILITARY MEDAL by G.O.C. V Corps for gallantry + devotion to duty.	
"	30/9/16		Total Admissions for September:— Officers WOUNDED 16. SICK 24. Other Ranks WOUNDED 942. SICK 729. Total = 1711.	

A. Whittington, Major RAMC. O.C. 132nd Fd Amb.

Very Secret App 47.d.

5/112

O.C. 132 Fd. Amb.

The date of the operations will now be Sept. 3rd

Acknowledge.

C. R. Miller
Major
for ADMS 39th Div.

H.Q. 39th Div
1.9.16

Very Secret   App 47 e.   5/146

O.C. 132 Fd. Ambulance

The operations on the 3rd Sept. will commence at 5.10 a.m.

C. [illegible]
Major
for ADMS
39th Div.

2/9/16

O.C. 132 Field Ambulance

Two bearer subdivisions and 16 men of C Section - to complete the reserve bearer subdivision - left the Divisional Collecting Station at 5 pm 2.9.16. with Lt C E Tucker RAMC in Command. Lt Tucker reported his arrival to the M.O in charge of the A.D.S at Mesnil and shortly afterwards moved to the Field Ambulance Aid Post at Knightsbridge Barracks with the two bearer divisions, the reserve bearer subdivision in charge of Lt D. J MacDougall remained at Mesnil pending further instructions from the M.O in charge there.

The two bearer divisions were placed in a dugout in Knightsbridge which was partly occupied by troops.

Lt Tucker reported to the Brigade Major from whom he received instructions that Gabion Avenue & Piccadilly Trench were the 'up' trenches to be used. Neither of these trenches could be entered until 5.10 am on the 3.9.16. The use of Knightsbridge Trench leading from the evacuating Trench via Constitution Trench, to the Aid Post was forbidden.

Lt MacDougall arrived about 10 pm with the reserve bearer subdivision to take charge of the Fd. Amb. Aid Post.

Lt Tucker decided to take the two bearer subdivisions up Gabion Avenue to the front line.

At 5.10 am Lt Tucker entered Gabion Avenue

followed by all the bearers, myself bringing up the rear. The going was very laborious owing to conditions underfoot and blocking of the trench by carrying parties etc.
The shelling of this trench was very severe & before Victoria Street was reached there were seven casualties amongst the bearers. Evacuation of these was impossible backwards and as they were not severely wounded they were left in a small communication trench & they eventually reached the Fd. Amb. Aid Post some hours later.
About 6.30 am Lt Tucker was struck by sharpnel in the leg and could not proceed. He refused aid and ordered me to carry on. I moved the head of the bearers into Victoria St and Bedford St to the junction of Long Sap and Robert's Trench and up into Long Sap. The bearers were ordered back by a staff officer from Long Sap owing to the movements of troops.
Seeing the impossibility of reaching the front line at that time I decided to attend & collect the many wounded lying in Robert's Trench and the vicinity. At this stage Lt MacDougall joined me, with the reserve bearers, to replace Lt Tucker.
As it was still impossible to progress into the front line I decided to lead the bearers with many wounded towards Constitution Trench.
The Communication trenches were severely shelled

and in many points were blown in, the wounded having to be carried over the 'blocks' in the trenches. At one of these points there were more casualties among the bearers – one being killed and another severely wounded. Lt MacDougall and myself being ahead seeing to other wounded did not actually see this incident.

The wounded were brought down Constitution Trench & from there in the open under heavy fire to the Fd. Amb. Aid Post where Lt Linderman M.O. Notts & Derby was in charge in Lt MacDougall's absence – The whole journey took six hours to complete.

Lt MacDougall & myself took the bearers again immediately up Gabion Avenue and distributed the bearers in various parts in Roberts Trench – Tong Sap and Regent St. From this time (12 noon) onwards wounded were allowed to be evacuated along other trenches.

At about 3pm Lt MacDougall returned to take charge of the Aid Post and as our troops were back in the front line and the bearers knew their way I also went to the Fd. Amb. Aid post to work as a great number of wounded had accumulated there.

About 6pm the line between the Fd. Amb. Aid Post & the ADS was smashed by shell fire at several places & in consequence two of our stretcher squads were detailed to help carry the wounded to the A.D.S.

At the request of Regimental M.Os bearer squads were dispatched to various ~~& various~~ points to take over wounded.
Throughout the whole night work went on at high pressure and wounded were brought in from all positions of the line by the bearers.
The following day (4.9.16) up to the time of our departure from the 9th Amb. Aid Post exhaustive searches were made of the trenches & dugouts to bring back fresh and to recover any wounded missed during the night.
During the whole of the operations under constant and at times particularly heavy firing the bearers behaved splendidly, and showed great efficiency not only in the transport of the wounded but in the skilful rendering of first aid.
At times this was particularly trying especially at night when the enemy used gas shells which necessitated the bearers wearing their gas helmets.

I wish to bring to your special notice the very good work done by Corporal Mann. This N.C.O did excellent work in bearing and leading stretcher squads to all parts of the line, his behaviour and courage were a magnificent example to the men & his help to me was most valuable.

The following N.C.Os and men were also conspicuous by their excellent work:-

Corporal Harvey.
" Henderson.
Private Dilley
" Everall
Harris
" Lockyer
" Leigh

D.W.A. Jones.
Lt. RAMC
132 Field Ambulance

F.A. 854.

A.D.M.S.
3rd Div.

War Diary (September) in duplicate herewith please, together with Appendices.

A. Whittle-Johnson
Major
O.C. 132 Fd. Amb.

1/10/16.

App. 56 a.

FA 875

A.D.M.S.
3rd Div.

Beg to submit further report on evacuation from Front Line:—

① Flag Avenue R.A.P. via SACKVILLE STREET trench, SOUTHERN AVENUE as far as WATERLOO BRIDGE & thence by road to EUSTON. I regret that not having Trench map I am unable to give map references. My map is with the Officer i/c ADS COLINCAMPS.

Should the road route be unsafe from WATERLOO BRIDGE on account of shelling, bearers can continue on on the SOUTHERN AVENUE trench which comes out quite near EUSTON.

② OBSERVATION WOOD R.A.P. evacuation via SAPPER TRENCH (this trench is the unnamed trench on Trench map LA ~~[illegible]~~ FARM) to SOUTHERN AVENUE & so to WATERLOO BRIDGE & then as before: there is another

F.A. 515
(Contd)

route which I intend to investigate at my next visit viâ CENTRAL AVENUE, RAILWAY AVENUE & BLACKFRIARS BRIDGE which is situated at the bend in the road coming from WATERLOO BRIDGE (shown as dotted line road on trench map) to EUSTON.

I am having two wheeled stretcher carriers placed at WATERLOO BRIDGE, which will I think be a great help in the evacuations from these R.A.Ps.

(3) Improvements are being carried out in the dugouts at A.D.S. COLINCAMPS as regards overhead cover & rendering them watertight, with the assistance of O.C. 226 Field Coy R.E. at COURCELLES: an engineer officer has visited the A.D.S. & materials have been transported today for this work.

(4) 1 officer + 20 O.R. Gloucester Rgt. arrived today, & materials have been drawn: work on the new huts will commence tomorrow. The officer has surveyed & marked out the ground.

A Chattleys [illegible]
Major
O.C. 132 Fd. Amb

25/9/16

App. 56. F.A. 77[2]

A.D.M.S.
Div.

I have visited the A.D.S. EUSTON. VIEW POST.

& the R.A.P.S at MOUNTJOY (about Q 4. a. 6. 9. Map [illegible] Contour ridge) and BOW STREET (about K 34. a. 6. 4).
I now forward preliminary report:—

Evacuation.

(1) MOUNTJOY. R.A.P. should by day in my opinion be carried out via MOUNTJOY & 6th AVENUE trenches to F.A.P. at VIEW POST, as it is not safe to cross the open (there is a danger flag post which troops are not allowed in daylight): after dark I think the open country route should be used — From VIEW POST a new set of bearers take the cases on to AUCHONVILLERS HEBUTERNE Road — thence via SUCRIE on K 33 C to EUSTON — Here cars are called up from ADS at COLINCAMPS as required by cyclist orderly —

(2) BOWSTREET. Evacuation by CHEEROH AVENUE trench which comes out near EUSTON I think is the best way —

I shall render a further report on the evacuation of the new line after further inspection — also details as to Posts —

21/9/16 —

A. Huttley [illegible]
Major
O.C. 132 Fd Amb.

App. 52a. FA. 67

ADMS
39 Div.

Accommodation at M.D.S. at BERTRANCOURT is as follows —
Two barns & 5 huts capable of accommodating 126 lying down cases completely, & about 150 in case of necessity — Stretcher trestles, Stretchers & paillasses available for all these beds —
The accommodation is good & ample, surroundings are being improved rapidly —
Two good rooms for reception & operating rooms —

[illegible]
Major
OC 132 Fd Amb

9/9/16 —

SECRET – App. 53. Pk 191.

ADMS
39 Div

Reference your S/263 of today's date, I have reconnoitred the ground & beg to report as follows: –

RAP. of Right Bn is SPIROCHAETE CORNER situated at Q.9.b.9.5: dug out is protected from gas, will accommodate about 8 stretcher cases, entrance is down several stairs but could be used with care – evacuation by trench, 2nd AVENUE, alongside sunken road to Q 9.a.9.1. where a wheeled stretcher will be retained to take on lying down cases to our post in AUCHONVILLERS at Q.9.a.1.1 –

RAP. of Left Bn: is WHITE CITY situated at Q.4.a.5.3: protected from gas, will accommodate six stretcher cases: well protected from shells – Fd Amb bearers in next dug out – Evacuation by trench 5th Avenue AVENUE entered about 80 yards from RAP: a long carry of about 1000 yds to

Field Ambulance Post, SUNKEN ROAD POST, at Q.3.a.8.3: this is a very deep

F.A. 691.
(Contd)

dug out, down many steps, but quite protected: as a rule cases would be going straight on: two wheeled stretcher carriers here; route is along Sunken Road through Q3.C. to AUCHONVILLERS to our post at Q.9.a.1.1 – Road fairly good, but badly shelled in parts near AUCHONVILLERS –
The trenches used for evacuation from both RAPs are good & broad, & dry –

Personnel required will be 4 bearers in SPIROCHAETE CORNER RAP. 2 WHITE CITY RAP an NCO & 8 men, half of whom are accommodated in the dug out next RAP, & the rest in a dug out TENDERLOIN at Q.4.c.6.8; this dug out may have been used as a RAP at times –

From AUCHONVILLERS Post, cases are evacuated by Ford car to ADS. MAILLY.

Present unit having an ADS. at Q1d.2.3 RED HOUSE: we should not need to use this at all as an ADS, but could put in a holding party if required –

9/9/16 –

[illegible] Major
O.C. 132nd Fd. Amb

App. 55

Secret

O.C. 132 Fd. Amb.

A.D.M.S.
No 5/472
Date 18.9.16
39th DIVISION

In connection with the new part of the line to be taken over by the 39th Div. You will :-

1. Detail an advance party to proceed to A.D.S. COLINCAMPS K.25.c.2.8. tomorrow the 19th inst. to arrive at 12 noon. The party to consist of 1 Officer and 20 O.R. & will learn the lines of evacuation etc.

2. You will take over the A.D.S. COLINCAMPS and subsidiary posts from No. 6 Field Ambulance on the 20th inst.
A certain amount of Equipment will be taken over at the A.D.S.

3. Personnel required.
4 men in VIEW POINT (6th Avenue) about K.32.d.1.5.
4 men for Centre battalions R.A.P.s at K.34.b.2.8. and K.34.a.6.4.
4 men Observation Wood K.28.b.3.3.

12 men at Fd. Amb. Post (EUSTON)

(2)

K. 33. a. 4. 3. This post takes all casualties from above. Cars come up when required from A.D.S. (push bike kept to send message)

A.D.S. COLLINCAMPS 2 O. 15 O.R.

4. Acknowledge.

H.Q. 39th Dn.
18.9.16

C. ? Chiller
Major
for ADMS 39th Dn

Urgent

AH 54

O.C. 132 Fd. Ambulance

You will make the following changes in your arrangements forthwith.

1. Headquarters of Fd. Amb. with headquarters Section to move to BUS.

2. One Section to remain at BERTRANCOURT – which will be used as a receiving station for cases from A.D.S. All patients for retention in Field Ambulance to be kept at BUS.

3. A.D.S. at RED HOUSE to be staffed & equipped and taken into use as your Advanced Dressing station. A detachment will remain at A.D.S. MAILLY MALLET.

4. You will see that no troops or transport lines encroach in any way under any circumstances on the Field Ambulance site at BUS.

5. Acknowledge & report compliance.

H.Q. 39th Div.
14.9.16

[signature]
Colonel
A.D.M.S. 39th Div

App. 52. 7A 679

A.D.M.S.
39 Div.

I beg to report on the various Posts taken over —

Q.9.d.9.5

(1) THURLES DUMP Field Amb Post is a dug out which will accommodate an N.C.O. & 4 men of the Fld Amb. It is only suitable for this purpose, but as it is near down to the R.A.P. it is not required to accommodate patients — requires more gas protection & roof is not very strong —

(2) R.A.P. at Q.9.d.9.5. is a good dug out, & would take 12 stretchers on the floor. I think the protection appears good, & gas protection satisfactory — Large & roomy, about 30 ft by 10 ft —

Evacuation —
Cases are taken over at RAP by Fld Amb bearers posted at THURLES DUMP F.A.P. — lying down cases come down on wheeled stretcher carriers along HAMEL — AUCHONVILLERS road through Q.9.b.c.7.0 to

F.A.P. at AUCHONVILLERS at Q.9.a.1.1.
Walking cases can leave the above mentioned road at Q.9.a.9.0 & take

FA 79
(Cont.)

a path through the wood which brings them out a few yards from the AUCHONVILLERS post at Q9.a.1.1.

<u>FAP at AUCHONVILLERS</u> – Q9.a.1.1. Consists of a cellar; hardly thought a shelter; could be put into it, but if sitting cases could be accommodated. This would not often be required probably, as a Ford Car stays at this post & brings cases on at once to ADS at MAILLY. There are big stables in the yard of the F.A.P. and yet very little damaged by shell fire. There is practically no added protection of sandbags at present. I think this Post if strengthened could be made into a good intermediate post between THURLES DUMP and ADS MAILLY. No gas protection in the AUCHONVILLERS post.

<u>Evacuation.</u>
Carried out at once from here by Ford Car to MAILLY ADS. along AUCHONVILLERS – MAILLY road.

Condition of roads from THURLES DUMP to MAILLY ADS is very fair considering that the roads are often under shell fire: there were no bad holes in the road when I went over them last night – Evacuation will be speedy as the distances are not great & the Ford car at AUCHONVILLERS is probably under 1000 yds from the RAP at Q.9.a.9.5 –

ADS MAILLY MAILLET P.12.c.9.7 in a large building as yet practically undamaged by shell fire – but likely to become so – the ground floor has good accommodation for dressing cases – there is no protection from shells or gas – Underground however there is very spacious cellar accommodation which would take something like a hundred stretcher cases – There is no added protection to these cellars, but they appear strong ones with 5 layers of brick in the roof – They could be made enormously strong, I think, whilst protection of the ground floor would be desirable – Dressing etc can be done underground if MAILLY is being shelled – The cellars are rather wet in places – They are situated under the large courtyard in front of the ADS & under the buildings –

FA [illegible]
[illegible]

Two Sunbeam Cars are stationed at the A.D.S. & then run back to the M.D.S. at BERTRANCOURT via BEAUSSART. The road is pretty good, save where road metal is being laid down –

The R.A.P. at Q.9.d.4.5. is the R.A.P. of our left Battalion –
The [illegible] R.A.P. down towards KNIGHTSBRIDGE [illegible] & I presume its cases go back through KNIGHTSBRIDGE F.A.P. & this would appear to be the best way as the road from KNIGHTSBRIDGE to the R.A.P. at Q.9.d.4.5 is very exposed & I was informed by the O i/c MAILLY A.D.S. of the [illegible] [illegible] [illegible], [illegible] [illegible] for cases to come along –

M.D.S. at BERTRANCOURT will form the subject of a later report –

[illegible]
Major –

8/9/16 –

Urgent

App (51)

No. 5/204
Date 6.9.16

O.C.
132 Fd Amb

Please send 1 officer + 10 O.R. to take over Fd. Amb. at BERTRANCOURT + A.D.S. at MAILLY-MAILLET. The H.Qrs. of your unit will proceed to BERTRANCOURT on the 7th inst.

You will also take over the Baths situated in the A.D.S. at MAILLY-MAILLET. The 4 T.U. men now at 134th Fd. Amb. previously at these Baths should be taken on by your advance party this afternoon.

Cecil W. Cozhe
Lieut.
for A.D.M.S.

6.9.16

— Confidential (App 50)

F.A. 666 –

A.D.M.S.
 [illegible] Div.

I forward herewith the report of Lieut. D.W.F. Jones RAMC who took over command of the Bearer Division during the operations, after Lieut. C.E. TUCKER had been wounded –
In connection with this report I beg to bring to your notice the undermentioned, whom I consider deserving of special recognition for their splendid work under very arduous & trying circumstances –

(1) Lieut. D.W.F. JONES – who took over command of the Bearer Division at 6.30 AM on the 3rd inst, when his O.C. was wounded; he supervised the collection of the wounded under very heavy fire, and by his coolness & devotion to duty set a splendid example to his men – I recommend him for the MILITARY CROSS –

(2) No. 65812 Cpl. F.H. MANN – The OC Bearer Division says of him: – "This NCO did excellent work in "bearing & leading stretcher squads to all parts of the "line, his behaviour and courage were a magnificent "example to the men & his help to me was most "valuable –" I recommend him for the DISTINGUISHED CONDUCT MEDAL –

FA. 660 –
(Contd)

(3) The following NCOs + men of the Bearer Division were conspicuous by their excellent work:—

No. 1909 Cpl. H.A. HARVEY. (Territorial Force) – ①
" 72157 Cpl T. HENDERSON – ②
" 65580 Pte. H. DILLEY – ②
" 65867 Pte. H. EVERALL – ①
" 65818 Pte. H.G. HARRIS – ③
" 65901 Pte. H.W. LOCKYER – ④
" 72197 Pte. A. LEIGH – ⑤

For courage & devotion to duty in action I recommend all the above for the MILITARY MEDAL: the figures in the margin indicate the order of merit in the different ranks –

II. Divisional Collecting Station –

In connection with this I desire to bring the undermentioned to your notice for their devotion to duty, zeal, self sacrifice & the cheerful & kindly manner in which they do all in their power to alleviate the sufferings of the wounded –

1) Lieut. F.G. MARTIN, who has rendered striking service now as on all other occasions since joining the Field Ambulance – His skill and kindliness in dealing with the

FA 66 6.
(Contd) –

patients & his never failing patience are worthy of all admiration & reward –

(2) No: 38943. Sgt Major B.G. SHARPE.
for his invaluable assistance at all times in the performance of all duties –

(3) No: 65873 Sgt G. PELLETT.
No: 658 55 Sgt. J.A. GRANSBY.
No: 59471 Sgt J.W.J. ROSSIE
No: 41382 Cpl H. WALLACE.
No: 72142 Pte L.G. COXHEAD.
No. 65881 Pte H.F. LOVATT

For zeal & devotion to duty on this occasion & at all times –

A. Whittyshaw –
Major RAMC
O.C. 132nd Fld Amb

6/9/16 –

App. 47.f.

EA. 166.

ADMS
39 Div.

Beg to report that all arrangements had been made for the reception of the Casualties at the Divisional Collecting Station at P.23 d 9.2 during the Operations of 21/9/16 – At 7.30 A.M. the ADMS 39 Div. arrived & [illegible] up from DCS to ADS at [illegible] and [illegible] MM WOODS [illegible] and at [illegible] 8 AM onwards [illegible] cases began to arrive & ambulances to [illegible] the [illegible] the day till 9.30 AM – [illegible] [illegible] [illegible] DCS [illegible] ADS at [illegible] & brought back other cases [illegible] also arrived from the front by [illegible] the [illegible] [illegible] DCS [illegible] [illegible] wounded [illegible] passed through [illegible] [illegible] were made & ATS given the [illegible] [illegible] for redressing [illegible] [illegible] to the [illegible] [illegible] refreshments were provided [illegible] waiting their turn [illegible] [illegible] [illegible] [illegible]

whilst awaiting their turn for registration etc –
Cases were evacuated to Corps Collecting Station at ACHEUX in motor charabancs, motor lorries, horsed ambulance wagons, G.S. wagons, each vehicle leaving as it was filled – At no time was there any congestion or delay, and the arrangements worked smoothly –
At 12 noon application for reinforcement for M.O. i/c A.D.S. MESNIL to replace battle casualty was received and Capt. J. MORRIS RAMC(T.F) went forward – I had now two officers available for dressing cases, & for the next three hours I carried out A.T.S. inoculations personally: the ADMS 3 Div brought Lt. C.D. COYLE over to effect & took over the A.T.S. inoculations –
At about 10AM the DDMS 5th Corps visited the FCH: he very kindly expressed his satisfaction with the arrangements –
The busiest time was from 9AM to 3PM –
Total number of wounded cases dealt with was – Officers 12 . Other Ranks 679 –

[illegible]

4/9/16 –

Urgent.

App. 48-

O.C. 132 Fd. Amb.

1. You will close down the Divisional Collecting Station this evening and return to Headquarters.
Report accordingly.
2. You will send back the two Char-a-bancs to report to this office.

3. Two of your bearer sub-divisions will be brought back to ACHEUX today. And Capt Rees from the Cookers. Lts. MacDougall & Jones will also come back.
One bearer sub-division will be left at Mesnil.

C. R. Millar
Major
for ADMS
39th Div

4.9.16

F.A. 880

A.D.M.S.
3rd Div

If 132nd Fd. Amb. War Diary for September has not yet left your office, will you please place attached report among the appendices at the early part of the month & these duplicate reports for the War Diary ~~and~~ I had some difficulty in collecting owing to the officer rendering the report having left me.

A. Whittingham
Lt Col

4/10/16

R.A.M.C.
O.C. 132nd FIELD AMBULANCE.

Aug 1916

140/1949.

132nd F.A.

Oct 1916

140/1949

132nd F.A.

Instructions regarding War Diaries and Intelligence Summaries are contained in F. S. Regs., Part II. and the Staff Manual respectively. Title pages will be prepared in manuscript.

WAR DIARY
182nd FIELD AMBULANCE or ~~INTELLIGENCE SUMMARY.~~
(Erase heading not required.)

OCTOBER 1916.

(1)

Map Ref:- Sheet 57D -

Vol 8

Army Form C. 2118.

Place	Date	Hour	Summary of Events and Information	Remarks and references to Appendices
BUS-LES-ARTOIS	1-10-16	1 PM.	Orders received to be prepared to move within 36 hours –	
		5 PM.	Advanced Party of two Officers + 6 Other Ranks proceeded to ADS. LANCASHIRE DUMP Q.35.d.1.6 to become acquainted with evacuation from new area –	
"	2/10/16	2 PM.	ADS's at COLINCAMPS + RED HOUSE, + MDS. at BERTRANCOURT handed over to No:5 Fd. Amb.	App (1) Admin Operation Order No. 9.
"	3/10/16	2 PM.	M.D.S. at BUS LES ARTOIS handed over to 1/2nd Highland Fd. Amb – 182nd Field Amb. proceeded to FORCEVILLE and billeted at Fld Amb site at P21.c.7.8. but did not open –	App: (2)
FORCEVILLE	5/10/16	10 AM.	Fd. Amb site at FORCEVILLE handed over to 1st Field Amb. 63rd Divn + marched to Q.31.a.0.2 + went under canvas –	Admin Operation Order No: 10.
Q.31.a.0.2.	"	4 PM.	Two Officers + 50 Other ranks proceeded to LANCASHIRE DUMP ADS Q.35.d.1.6 + PAISLEY AVENUE ADS. Q.30.c.7.4: being followed by remainder of "B" + "C" Section Tent Subdivisions, and rest of Bearer Division during the night of 5/6 –	
Q.31.a.0.2	6/10/16	9 AM.	ADS at LANCASHIRE DUMP (Q.35.d.1.6) PAISLEY AVENUE (Q.30.c.7.4) AVELUY POST W.11.d.5.9 with subsidiary Posts WOOD POST (X.1.c.5.6) BLACK HORSE BRIDGE (W.6.a.1.1) ROSS CASTLE (Q.30.b.3.0)	

T2134. Wt. W708–776. 500000. 4/15. Sir J. C. & S.

Instructions regarding War Diaries and Intelligence Summaries are contained in F. S. Regs., Part II. and the Staff Manual respectively. Title pages will be prepared in manuscript.

WAR DIARY or ~~INTELLIGENCE~~ SUMMARY.

(Erase heading not required.)

132nd FIELD AMBULANCE

OCTOBER 1916.

Map Ref. Sheet 57D.

(2)

Army Form C. 2118.

Place	Date	Hour	Summary of Events and Information	Remarks and references to Appendices
Q.31.a.0.2.	6.10.16	9AM.	LEMBERG POST (R31.d.9.6.) THIEPVAL F.A.P. (R26.C.3.4.) were taken over from 18th Divisional Fld. Amb. Headquarters & wagon lines of unit remaining at Q.31.a.0.2.	
"	7.10.16.	10AM.	Visited all three A.D.Stations & found everything in good order.	
"	8.10.16	10AM	visited & went over route of evacuation from THIEPVAL via LEMBERG POST, WOOD POST ~~and~~ to AVELUY POST A.D.S.	
"	9.10.16	5.30AM	Went to AVELUY POST & up via WOOD POST to THIEPVAL: following a raid 100 cases passed through AVELUY POST A.D.S. and 20 through LANCASHIRE DUMP A.D.S. during the day. Evacuation through WOOD POST was as follows:- from THIEPVAL F.A.P. to LEMBERG POST, thence by peel bearers through BLIGHTEY VALLEY to point about X1.b.4.4. & thence by another relay of bearers to WOOD POST. From here by hand trolley to AVELUY POST A.D.S. Bearers worked well under shell fire. R.25.6.8.8	Aff. 3. Report on work on 9/10/16.
			Evacuation from the left come from R.A.P. at XX down through valley along East side of THIEPVAL WOOD & along Southern end of same wood to PAISLEY AVENUE A.D.S. at Q.30.d.0.5. thence by trolley to LANCASHIRE DUMP A.D.S. Report attached (Aff 3). Captain S. MILLER R.A.M.C. (S.R.) was taken on the strength of the Fd. Amb.	

Instructions regarding War Diaries and Intelligence Summaries are contained in F. S. Regs., Part II. and the Staff Manual respectively. Title pages will be prepared in manuscript.

WAR DIARY
or
INTELLIGENCE SUMMARY.
(Erase heading not required.)

132nd FIELD AMBULANCE
OCTOBER 1916.

(3)

Map Ref:- Sheet 57D.

132nd FIELD AMBULANCE 1 NOV. 1916

Army Form C. 2118.

Place	Date	Hour	Summary of Events and Information	Remarks and references to Appendices
Q 31.a.o.2.	10/10/16		Lieut. J.H.P. Barrett RAMC was evacuated sick and struck off the strength of the Fd. Amb.	
Q 31.a.o.2.	10/10/16	10AM	Headquarters of Fd. Amb. moved to LANCASHIRE DUMP ADS.	
LANCASHIRE DUMP	11/10/16	10AM	New route of evacuation from THIEPVAL to AVELUY POST ADS reconnoitred, & decided upon for immediate use: from RAP skirting round Eastern & Southern portions of ruins of THIEPVAL to top of THIEPVAL-AUTHUILLE-AVELUY road, where wheeled stretcher carriers have been placed: thence for about 400 yards down the road to CYCLIST POST (Q 36.b.9.5), at which point a cyclist summons Ford Car from AVELUY POST as required, & so by Ford Car to AVELUY POST ADS. This route greatly expedites the evacuation of wounded.	
"	12/10/16	Noon	Orders to prepare for active Operations (App. 4)	App: (4) Orders Re Operations.
"	14/10/16 to 16/10/16	2 PM / 10 AM	Active Operations took place. As soon as possible evacuation from the Front line commenced & continued for nearly 48 hours, during which time 167 lying & 418 walking cases passed through the Advanced Dressing Stations. Collection of wounded was carried out under most arduous & trying conditions, under heavy shell fire often, over ground completely churned up & pitted by crater holes, with great gallantry & devotion to duty by all ranks concerned. App: 5 forms the subject of their report on the operations in connection with the capture of the SCHWABEN REDOUBT.	App. (5) Report on Operations of 14/10/16. App. (6) Recommendation.
			Capt. J.J. FIELD RAMC was evacuated on 15/10/16 suffering from SHELL SHOCK (W) and struck off the strength of the unit.	

Instructions regarding War Diaries and Intelligence Summaries are contained in F. S. Regs., Part II. and the Staff Manual respectively. Title pages will be prepared in manuscript.

WAR DIARY
or
~~INTELLIGENCE SUMMARY~~.
(Erase heading not required.)

132nd Field Ambulance. ④ OCTOBER 1916. Map Ref: Sheet 57D.

Army Form C. 2118.

Place	Date	Hour	Summary of Events and Information	Remarks and references to Appendices
LANCASHIRE DUMP.	16.10.16	5 P.M.	Captains J.L. PERCEVAL & C.A. ROBINSON RAMC. reported their arrival & were taken on the strength of the Fd. Amb.	
LANCASHIRE DUMP.	18/10/16	10.15 A.M.	Orders received to prepare for active Operations on 19/10/16 (App: 7). All necessary action taken and everything was ready for the 19th inst. Two postponements occurred. Lieut M.M. WOODS RAMC. was evacuated sick, and struck off the strength of the unit.	App: 7. ADMS. Operation Order No: 12.
	21/10/16 to 22/10/16	11 A.M. 8.30 P.M.	All personnel in their allotted places. Attack on STUFF TRENCH commenced at 12.7 P.M. Collection of wounded expeditiously carried out under most arduous & trying conditions from SCHWABEN REDOUBT & STUFF TRENCH, often under very heavy shell fire: all ranks concerned did splendid work under command of Captain SINCLAIR MILLER RAMC (S.R.). By 10 P.M. 21/10/16 87 stretcher cases & 69 severe walking cases had passed through the A.D.S. & been evacuated direct from there to C.C.S.: in addition the lightly wounded walking cases had gone straight through to 134 Fd Amb at CAP STAND where they were admitted. Evacuation went on all through night of 21/22nd & 22nd inst, & by 8.30 P.M. 22/10/16 209 stretcher cases & 86 more severe walking cases had been evacuated to C.C.S. (App. 8 & 8a). Capt. M.J. REES was severely wounded while making a reconnaissance on 22/10/16 & evacuated to C.C.S. & struck off strength.	App. 8 & 8a. Report on Operations of 21/10/16. App: 9. Recommendations.
	23/10/16	10 A.M.	Orders re further Operations received. All preparations completed. The A.D.S. at AVELUY POST was handed over to 58 Fd. Amb:, evacuations from our	

T.2134. Wt. W708-776. 500000. 4/15. Sir J. C. & S.

Instructions regarding War Diaries and Intelligence Summaries are contained in F. S. Regs., Part II. and the Staff Manual respectively. Title pages will be prepared in manuscript.

WAR DIARY
or
~~INTELLIGENCE SUMMARY.~~
(Erase heading not required.)

132nd Field Ambulance (5)

OCTOBER 1916 –

Ref. Ref: Sheet 57D –

Army Form C. 2118.

132nd FIELD AMBULANCE 1 NOV 1916

Place	Date	Hour	Summary of Events and Information	Remarks and references to Appendices
LANCASHIRE DUMP	23/10/16		right through THIEPVAL now coming across BLACK HORSE BRIDGE W 6.a.1.1. & up to A.D.S. at LANCASHIRE DUMP – by Ford car from CYCLIST POST –	
"	24/10/16		Wagon lines moved to new D.C.S. site at Q 31 b.9.2 – Lieut. C.H.L. RIXON reported his arrival and was taken on the strength on 23/10/16 –	
"	26/10/16		Lieut. C.H.L. RIXON RAMC was evacuated to C.C.S. suffering from accidental injury to head, and struck off the strength of the unit –	App. 10. ADMS report.
"	27/10/16		Operations postponed –	
"	31/10/16		Some improvement in weather – Nothing further to report –	

1/11/16 –

[signature] – Lt Col
R.A.M.C.
O.C. 132nd FIELD AMBULANCE.

T2134. Wt. W708–776. 500000. 4/15. Sir J. C. & S.

Vol 9

140/80

Confidential

War Diary

of

132 Field Ambulance

from Nov. 1st 1916 to Nov. 30th 1916.

(Volume I).

39th Div

~~Nov. 1916~~

Instructions regarding War Diaries and Intelligence Summaries are contained in F. S. Regs., Part II. and the Staff Manual respectively. Title pages will be prepared in manuscript.

132nd Field Ambulance.

WAR DIARY
or
~~INTELLIGENCE SUMMARY.~~
(Erase heading not required.)

(1)

Army Form C. 2118.

NOVEMBER. 1916.

Map: Ref. Sheet 57D.

Place	Date	Hour	Summary of Events and Information	Remarks and references to Appendices
LANCASHIRE DUMP	1/11/16		Weather slightly improved, but still inclined to rain.	Ahh.
"	4/11/16	1PM	Orders received to resume normal conditions.	Ahh
"	6/11/16	9PM	Orders received to be in readiness for active operations on 9/11/16.	Ahh
"	7/11/16	9PM	Operations postponed to 10/11/16.	Ahh
"	8/11/16	12 Noon	Operations postponed to an indefinite date.	Ahh
"	10/11/16	1PM	Orders re Operations on 13/11/16 received.	Ahh
	13/11/16	5.45AM	Operations commenced. Evacuation from the Front line commenced as soon as possible and cases soon began to arrive at the ADSs at PAISLEY AVENUE & LANCASHIRE DUMP, where they were speedily dressed, fed & evacuated by 20 MAC cars to CCS. German prisoners were used to assist in collection of wounded & the majority of the wounded had been cleared from the Field by 12.30 PM. By 9PM 13/11/16, 153 stretcher cases & 77 [illegible] wounded sitting cases had been evacuated to CCS. and all were cleared. Reports on these Operations form the subject of App. 1.1a. & 1b. The evacuation was carried out with great devotion to duty by all ranks over very difficult ground.	App 1.1a.1b. Reports on Operations App 2 Medical Arrangements in connection with Operations Ahh.

Instructions regarding War Diaries and Intelligence Summaries are contained in F. S. Regs., Part II. and the Staff Manual respectively. Title pages will be prepared in manuscript.

WAR DIARY
or
~~INTELLIGENCE~~ SUMMARY.
(Erase heading not required.)

Army Form C. 2118.

132 Field Ambulance (2)

Nov. 1916 – Map Ref. Sheet 57D – & 27 –

Place	Date	Hour	Summary of Events and Information	Remarks and references to Appendices
			and often under heavy fire –	App. 3.
LANCASHIRE DUMP	15.11.16	1. AM	RAMC Operation Order No. 15 received: the A.D.S. & at PAISLEY AVENUE & LANCASHIRE DUMP & all subsidiary Posts were handed over to the 19th Division by 9 AM 15/11/16 –	RAMC Operation Order No. 15.
WARLOY	15.11.16		The 132 Fd Amb. concentrated at Q.31.b.9.5 & having handed this site over to an NCO & 4 men of 134 Fd Amb, marched to WARLOY & spent the night under Canvas at V19.c.6.8 –	App. 3.a. ADMS. Report on Operation 13/11/16. Alh.
WARLOY	16.11.16	10.40 AM	Unit left WARLOY in accordance with 115 Inf Brigade Order No 66. & marched via CONTAY, TOUTENCOURT, PUCHEVILLERS, BEAUQUESNE, TERRAMESNIL, HULEUX to BRETEL which was reached at 6 PM, a long march splendidly carried out by the unit – Unit then went into billets at A15 c 5.8.	App. 4. 115 Inf Brig Order No 66. Alh.
BRETEL	18.11.16		Unit entrained by 6.24 PM at DOULLENS & arrived and detrained at 4 AM 19.11.16 at HOUPOUTRE & marched to WATOU and occupied Fd. Amb. site at K4.b.6.6. in accordance with RAMC. Operation Order No. 16 (App 5) –	App. 5. RAMC Operation Order No. 16. Alh.

T.2134. Wt. W708–776. 500000. 4/15. Sir J. C. & S.

132nd F... AMBULAN...

Instructions regarding War Diaries and Intelligence Summaries are contained in F. S. Regs., Part II. and the Staff Manual respectively. Title pages will be prepared in manuscript.

WAR DIARY
or
~~INTELLIGENCE SUMMARY.~~
(Erase heading not required.)

Army Form C. 2118.

132 Fld. Ambulance (3)

NOVEMBER 1916 — Map Ref. Sheet 27.

Place	Date	Hour	Summary of Events and Information	Remarks and references to Appendices
				App. 64 6a. Recommendations in connection with Recent Operations
WATOU	21/11/16		New horse standings commenced —	
"	22.XI.16		LIEVT. J. STEEL R.A.M.C. (S.R.) and LIEVT. A. PORTER R.A.M.C. (TEMP).	JM
			reported for duty, and taken on the strength of the Ambulance from this date.	JM
"	23.XI.16		Conversion of barn into mens Dining Room commenced, also new	JM
			Pack Store in Cart Shed commenced.	
"	24.XI.16		Weather turned very cold & hard frost during the night.	JM
"	27.XI.16		Mens dining room completed. RAMC Operation order No 17. received.	App. 7. JM
"	30.XI.16		Pack-store completed. Considerable progress with Horse Standings, but	JM
			hampered by shortage of materials from R.E.	
			Admissions during November —	
			Wounded 610	
			Sick 449	

4/12/16

A. Littlejohns
Lt. Col. RAMC
O.C. 132 Fld Amb

v. App. 7

A.D.M.S. No. 4797 Date 27.11.16 38th DIVISION

SECRET.

Copy No. 8

R.A.M.C. OPERATION ORDER NO.17

by

COLONEL G.W. BRAZIER-CREAGH, C.M.G., A.D.M.S. 39th. DIV.

Ref. Map Sheet 28 N.W.
1/20,000

27th. November, 1916

1. The 118th. Infantry Brigade is relieving the French 79th. Territorial Regiment and one Battalion of the French 80th. Regiment on the 29th. and 30th. of November.

2. The A.D.M.S. 38th. Division is arranging to take over from the French the Regimental Aid Posts at BOESINGHE CHATEAU and BLUET FARM and also the Collecting Post at LARRY FARM.

3. O.C. No.132 Field Ambulance will arrange to clear all sick, and cases for the Divisional Rest Station of the 39th. Division from No.129 Fld.Amb. at A.23.c.2.9. daily at 2 p.m.

4. On the 28th. inst. all sick of the 118th. Infantry Brigade while on the march will be cleared to No.133 Field Ambulance, HERZEELE or to No.132 Field Ambulance WATOU, by two horse Ambulance wagons which have been detailed to accompany the Brigade and to remain with the Brigade until it reaches ELVERDIGNE.

5. On the morning of the 29th.inst. Ambulance Cars of the 38th. Division will clear from camps G. K. and F. occupied by two Battalions of the 118th. Brigade, One Field Coy. R.E. Machine Gun Coy. and Trench Mortar Battery.
O.C. No.132 Field Ambulance will arrange to clear on the morning of the 29th. any sick from the Battalion billeted in POPERINGHE on the night of the 28th.-29th. inst.

B H Odlum
Capt.
for A.D.M.S. 39th. Div.

Copies to:-
1. G.
2. A.Q.
3-7. 118th. Inf. Bde.
8. No.132 F.Amb.
9. " 133 " "
10. " 134 " "
11. " 82 San. Sect.
12. D.D.M.S. Vlll Corps.
13. A.D.M.S. 38th. Div.
14. C.R.E.
15. War diary
16. " "
17. Operation File.

Nov. App. 6.a.

~~Confidential~~

FA 2/283.

ADMS
34 Div –

In connection with the operations during the past four weeks I beg to bring to your notice the undermentioned for reward & mention other than "immediate" –

1) Captain JOHN MORRIS. RAMC T.F.
has rendered sterling services and given me invaluable assistance during the period since he joined the Field Ambulance in July last – All through recent operations he has been in charge of RAILEY AVENUE ADS & has carried out all his duties with the utmost energy & devotion to duty and I consider the evacuation through this A.D.S. to have been very successfully carried out – I strongly recommend him for the
MILITARY CROSS –

(2) Captain FREDERICK GEORGE MARTIN
is recommended for mention in Despatches: during his period of service with the Field Amb...

(2)

FA 2/2/3 (Contd)

he rendered most valuable services to the sick & wounded by his operating skill, & his kind & cheery personality was always a pleasure to see.

Other Ranks.

No: 38943 Sgt Major BERTRIC GEORGE SHARPE. He has always given me invaluable assistance at all times.

No: 65893 Sgt GEORGE PELLETT.
No: 65855 Sgt. JOHN ALEXANDER GRANSBY.
No: 59471 Sgt JAMES WILLIAM JOSEPH ROSSIE.
No: 72157 Cpl TOM HENDERSON.
No: 65787 LCpl JOHN SMITH.
No: 72148 Pte LESLIE GUY COXHEAD.
No: 65881 Pte WILLIAM FRANK LOVATT.
No: 43182 Cpl HARRY WALLACE.

All the above in their various duties have shown the utmost devotion to duty & self sacrifice and are deserving of recognition.

A Whittingham.
Lt Col.
OC. 13th Fld Amb.

20/11/16.

Confidential - Nov. App. 6. FA.2/202.

A.D.M.S.
39 Div.

In connection with recent operations I beg to bring to your notice the undermentioned :— for immediate Reward—

Captain SINCLAIR MILLER, RAMC SR + A.C.

MEECH again rendered distinguished services in connection with the evacuation of the wounded and their efforts met with remarkable success, which enhances their claim to the DSO + M.C for which they have already been recommended—

~~Captain~~

132nd Field Ambulance—

(1) ~~Sgt~~ No 65972 Sgt. ARTHUR GEORGE REEVE twice recommended for DCM is again brought to notice for conspicuous courage + devotion to duty during the whole period in which wounded were being evacuated—

FA 2/262
(Contd)

2) No: 65782 Sgt WILLIAM REEVE, already recommended for the DCM in connection with operations on 9th & 10th Oct 16 —

On the night of the 14/15 Nov. 1916, this NCO took up bearer squads to our new Front Line under heavy shell fire and succeeded in evacuating several stretcher cases for whom assistance had been asked — Through all the recent operations this NCO has rendered distinguished service and I again recommend him for the

DISTINGUISHED CONDUCT MEDAL.

3) No. 62063 Pte WILLIAM FREEMAN. }
4 No. 65580 Pte HERBERT DILLEY }
On 13/11/16 they showed very marked devotion to duty evacuating wounded from the Front Line under heavy shell fire —

They are recommended for the MILITARY MEDAL.

(3)

FA.2/2Pd(cont)

133 Fld Amb

(1) No 72003 Pte FRANK HODSON did excellent work for 12 continuous hours on 13/11/16, without food or rest, evacuating wounded from the Field amid very trying circumstances –

(2) No. 72028 Pte GEORGE WILLIAM BALCOMBE on 13/11/16 displayed very marked devotion to duty showing no regard for his own personal safety, and on several occasions brought in wounded under heavy shell fire –

Both recommended for the

MILITARY MEDAL –

(4)

FA. 2/282
Cuts.

134 Fld. Ambulance.

(1) No. 64637 Pte SAMUEL MASON worked all day under heavy shell fire carrying wounded over open + difficult ground without food or rest, + was always ready to do more. (on 13/11/16)

(2) No. 72161 Pte FOUNTAIN WILLIAMSON worked all day on 13/11/16 without food or rest carrying wounded over open + difficult ground showing no regard for his own personal safety.

Both recommended for the

MILITARY MEDAL.

A. Whittingham
Lt Col.
O.C. 132 Fld Amb.

20/11/16.

Nov. App. 5

SECRET

R.A.M.C. OPERATION ORDER No. 16 Copy No. 4.
by
COLONEL BRAZIER CREAGH, C.M.G., A.D.M.S. 39th DIVISION.

Map reference Sheet 27 N.W.
" 27 N.E.
1/20,000

17th November 1916.

1. The Division on arrival at the VIII Corps area will be distributed as follows :-
Headquarters - ESQUELBECQ.

PROVEN AREA.
Headquators - POPERINGHE.
116th Infantry Brigade - K.L.M.Y.
Machine Gun Co. - Z Camp.
132nd Field Ambulance.

WORMHOUDT and HERZEELE area.
Headquarters - WORMHOUDT.
118th Infantry Brigade (2 Batt. at WORMHOUDT.
(2 Batt. at HERZEELE.
Machine Gun Company - WORMHOUDT.
133 Field Ambulance
134 " " less one Section.

BOLLEZEELE AREA.
117th Brigade less) MERCKEGHEM.
one Battalion) VOLKERINCKHOVE.
Pioneer Battalion - ESQUELBECQ.
R.E. 2 Companies - LEDRINGHEM.

2. No.132 Field Ambulance will detrain at HOUPOUTRE at 23-58 on 18th instant and will march to WATOU and take over the Hospice and billets arranged for them. They will open and deal with the sick of the units in the PROVEN AREA.

3. No.133 Field Ambulance will entrain at ESQUELBECQ at 1-17 on the 19th instant and march to HERZEELE and take over the billets at HERZEELE CHATEAU. They will open to receive and deal with the sick of the units in the WORMHOULT and HERZEELE area.

4. No.134 Field Ambulance will detrain at HOUPOUTRE at 3-58 on the 19th instant, and march to WORMHOUDT and take over the Divisional Rest Station and Officers Hospital.
One Section of 134 F.A. complete with equipment and transport will be ready to move to the BOLLEZEELE AREA and open out at a site yet to be selected to receive the sick of the units in the BOLLEZEELE AREA.

5. 82nd Sanitary Section on arrival will be billeted at ESQUELBECQ.

6. Acknowledge.

B.A. Odlum
Captain,
for A.D.M.S., 39th Division.

Copies to :-
1. D.M.S.Second Army.
2. D.D.M.S.VIII Corps.
3. G.S., 39th Division.
4. O.C., 132 Field Amb.
5. O.C., 133 "
6. O.C., 134 "
7. O.C.82nd Sanitary Sect.
8. A.D.V.S., 39th Division.
9. War Diary.
10. Do.
11. Operation File.

Nov. App. 4.

S E C R E T. Copy No....

118th INFANTRY BRIGADE ORDER No. 66.

Ref. France Sheet 57D, 1/40000. 15/11/16

1. The 118th Infantry Brigade Group will move tomorrow November 16th, in accordance with Table A overleaf.

2. Billeting Parties (except those of 13th Gloucesters and 132 Field Ambulance) will report to a/Staff Captain outside ORVILLE CHURCH at 12-30 p.m. tomorrow.

3. On arrival in billets Units will send to Brigade Headqrs. 2 runners each over and above those already with the Brigade. O.C. 13th Gloucester Regt., 234 Field Co.R.E., 132nd and 134th Field Ambulances and No. 4 Co. A.S.C. will send their runners provided with rations for 24 hours.

4. 1st Line Transport and Baggage waggons will marhh in rear of their own Units.

5. A halt will be made at mid-day and the men provided with a hot meal.

6. Units not in possession of the above Reference map will report to Brigade Headquarters (21 Rue MONLAGNAC, WARLOY) at 9-15 p.m. today.

7. Reports of arrival in billets to be sent to Brigade Headquarters.

8. The average pace of the march will not exceed 2 miles per hour.

9. Steel helmets will not be worn.

10. Billeting parties of all troops going to AMPLIER & ORVILLE Area will meet their Units at Cross roads, H/10.a.2.8.

11. Acknowledge.

[signature] Captain.
for Brigade Major, 118th Inf. Bde.

Issued at 7-30 p.m.

Copies to :-

1/6 Cheshire R.	234 Co. R.E	39th Division.
4/5 Black Watch.	No. 4 Co.A.S.C.	G.O.C.
1/1 Cambs.Regt.	Signals.	Staff Captain.
1/1 Herts. Regt.	132 & 134 Field Ambulance.	War Diary.
118th M.G.Coy		File.
118th T.M.Bty.	13th Gloucesters	

TABLE A

Units in order of march	Moves to	Route	Starting point	Time of passing Starting point.	Remarks
13th Gloucester R.	LONGUEVILLETTE	Most convenient	U.24.c.2.8. Road Junction.	10-30 a.m.	To march independently
132nd Field Ambulance	BRETEL	do	do.	10-40 a.m.	do.
118th Inf. Bde. H.Q.	AMPLIER & ORVILLE Area.		do.	10-50 a.m.	
4/5 Black Watch	do.	VADENCOURT - TOUTENCOURT - RAI CHEVAL-MARIEU - SARTO.	do.		Troops will halt 10 minutes before clock hour, and March will be resumed at clock hour.
1/1 Cambs. Regt.	do.	do.	do.		
1/1 Herts. Regt.	do.	do.	do.		
1/6 Cheshire R.	do	do	do		
118th M.G.Coy	do.	do	do.		
118th T.M.Bty.	do.	do.	do.		
2[illegible] Field Co. R.E.	do.	do.	do.		
154 Field Ambulance	do.	do.	do.		
No. 4 Coy. A.S.C.	do.	do.	do.		

Nov. App. 3a.

A.D.M.S.
No. B.10
Date 7.11.16
39th DIVISION

SECRET.

Copy No. 4

Report on Medical Arrangements
in connection with
Operations on November 13th. 1916.

Reference
Map Sheet 57 D SE 1/20,000

1. The 39th. Division had as its objective the HANSA LINE from R.14.c.2.1. to R.13.b.4.6., the MILL at R.13.a.2.7. and the crossing Q.18.b.85.40.
   The attack was delivered at dawn in a thick mist, all our objectives being gained with brilliant dash, and severe losses inflicted on the enemy, some 1350 prisoners being captured.

Regimental Aid Posts.

2. Those were established as follows:-

RIGHT SECTOR.		LEFT SECTOR.	
HERTS	R.19.d.7.6.	BLACK WATCH..	R.19.c.9.1.
CAMBS)		16th.SHERWOODS..	
CHESHIRES)...	R.25.b.2.8.		SPEYSIDE.

LOCATION OF FIELD AMBULANCES

3. 132nd. Field Ambulance.
   A.D.S. LANCASHIRE DUMP (H.Q.).......Q.35.d.1.6.
   A.D.S. PAISLEY AVENUE ....Q.30.c.7.3.
   ROSS CASTLE ....Q.30.b.3.0.
   JOHNSONS POST ....R.25.c.1.3.

   133rd. Field Ambulance. (Corps Collecting Station)
   EAST CLAIRFAYE (H.Q.) ....0.29.b.8.8.

   134th. Field Ambulance.(Divisional Collecting Station for walking cases)
   CABSTAND ....W.10.c.4.3.

BEARERS

4. The Bearer Division of No.132 Field Ambulance re-inforced by all available bearers of Nos.133 and 134 Field Ambulances, carried out the evacuation from the front line. Before the attack, all bearers were in position in the various Aid Posts and Advanced Posts mentioned above. Able assistance was rendered by 50 Reserve Regimental Bearers who were stationed at PAISLEY AVENUE A.D.S. Another party of 50 Regimental Bearers gave most valuable aid at the A.D.S. COOKERS (63rd.R.N.Division) there being no occasion to use them at the former place.

EVACUATION

5. (a) Collection of wounded. Wounded were collected by the Regimental and R.A.M.C. bearers and brought to the R.A.Posts mentioned above. Evacuation from there began at once and proceeded with great speed. A large number of unwounded German Prisoners were utilised as Stretcher Bearers, and all bearers worked with such energy and effect that the fighting line was comparatively clear by 3pm. It was reported quite clear by 7-30 pm.
   On leaving the Regimental Aid Posts, cases were conducted to point R.25.b.2.9. where stretcher cases were placed on trolleys and conveyed to the Advanced Dressing Stations. Walking cases for the most part followed the same route. Those stretcher cases for LANCASHIRE DUMP were met at the SOUTHERN CAUSEWAY by Motor Ambulances.

(b) PAISLEY AVENUE A.D.S. Here wounded began to arrive at 6-15 am. Lying and sitting cases were treated and given A.T.S. also refreshments, smokes etc. and sent directly to C.C.S. by Motor Ambulance parked at SOUTHERN CAUSEWAY. Only those walking cases requiring immediate attention were treated, the remainder being passed on to LANCASHIRE DUMP where they were picked up in Motor Buses and taken to the CABSTAND.

During the morning the influx of cases at the A.D.S. was considerable; all were dealt with promptly and at no time was there any congestion. In the afternoon cases arrived at intervals.

(c) LANCASHIRE DUMP A.D.S. Lying wounded began to arrive at 8 am. Lying and sitting cases were disposed of as atPAISLEY AVENUE and the loading of walking cases into Motor Buses was expeditiously carried out under direction of CAPT. PORTER. There was no congestion at this post at any time and sufficient cars were always ready to meet demands.

The supply of Motor Ambulances for PAISLEY AVENUE and the SOUTHERN CAUSEWAY was regulated here and on several occasions batches of cars were dispatched to relieve the congestion at the A.D.S. COOKERS (63rd. R.N. Division)

(d) CABSTAND.(Collecting Station for walking cases) Here the first cases arrived at 8-30am. In addition to those of our own Division, a large number of cases from the Divisions operating on our flanks were treated at this post. The evacuation from the CABSTAND was carried out by means of Motor Buses and Char-a-bancs to the Corps Collecting Station at EAST CLAIRFAYE (No.133 Field Ambulance).

6. A Tent Sub-division of No.134 Field Ambulance was held in readiness to move forward and open a new Advanced Dressing Station, should circumstances have required it. As it was not utilised, the Officers in charge were placed at the COOKERS to help there.

7. The following were dealt with:-

From Zero hour to 6 pm. 13/11/16.

BRITISH	(Officers	24
	(O.R.	596
GERMAN PRISONERS	(Officers	1.
	(O.R.	104.

From 6 pm.13/11/16 to 5 pm. 14/11/16.

BRITISH	(Officers	3
	(O.R.	99
GERMAN PRISONERS	(Officers	2.
	(O.R.	25.

TOTAL.

BRITISH	(Officers	27
	(O.R.	695
GERMAN PRISONERS.	(Officers	3
	(O.R.	129

GRAND TOTAL............. 854

8. From an early hour throughout the day, I visited the A.D. Stations, Main Dressing Stations and Corps Collecting Station alternately, superintending the various operations of each Unit and transport movements of wounded convoys. All worked satisfactorily and without a hitch from Zero hour to Sundown.

The Battlefield was cleared of all wounded by 3-40 pm. and the Advanced Dressing Stations and Main Dressing Stations were cleared before nightfall. These satisfactory conditions once again testify to the ability, zeal, and devotion of the Officers and Men in the various units under my command, who, like their Combatant comrades, have cheerfully and stoically undergone some particularly hard work and exposure during the lengthy period that the Division has been in the line.

In the near future I will bring to your notice those deserving of reward for continuous and distinguished service during these operations.

G. W. Brazier-Creagh

Colonel.
A.D.M.S. 39th.Division

17-11-16.

Copies to:- G.
A.Q.
39 Div.R.A.
116 Inf.Bde.
117 " "
118 " "
132 Fld.Amb.
133 " "
134 " "
82 San.Sect.
D.D.M.S.IInd.Corps
A.D.M.S.War Diary, File etc.

Urgent. Nov. App 1. F.A. 2/240.

A.D.M.S.
39 Div.

Cases evacuated to C.C.S. up to 9 P.M.:—

	Lying.	Sitting.
(a) PAISLEY AVENUE		
Officers	5.	—.
O.R.	80.	5.
Prisoners	8.	—.
(b) LANCASHIRE DUMP		
Officers	7.	2.
O.R.	39.	59.
Prisoners.	14.	11.
	153.	77.

9-30 P.M.
13/11/16.

[illegible]
Lt Col.
O.C. 132 Fld. Amb.

3

A.D.M.S.
39th Division.

Answers returned herewith please

132nd FIELD AMBULANCE
5 DEC 1916

for J Morris Capt R.A.M.C. T.
O.C. 132nd FIELD AMBULANCE.

NN. App. 1. b. F.A. 2/12/62.

A.D.M.S.
3 Div.

Beg to report that in connection with recent Operations on the 13/11/16 the preparations were made —
Evacuation from the Front Line, as soon as possible, commenced & were carried out with great speed by the bearers, assisted by the [illegible] bearers. Posts at [illegible] AVENUE A.D.S. and [illegible] [illegible] of the [illegible] [illegible] were made —
In this portion [illegible] [illegible] were all [illegible] cleared [illegible] by [illegible] P.M. the whole [illegible] was cleared —
Evacuation from the A.D.Stations at [illegible] AVENUE & [illegible] [illegible] proceeded steadily all through the day —
By [illegible] 9 P.M. on the day of Operations 163 Stretcher cases & 77 [illegible] cases had been evacuated to [illegible] [illegible] Many other walking cases had been transported to the CAB STAND, [illegible] [illegible] [illegible] hundred cases —
From 9 P.M. onwards the remaining cases were evacuated to C.C.S. and

(2)

(Contd)

the total cases dealt with, from beginning of operations to 6 A.M. on 14/11/16 were —

Lying.	Sitting —
208 —	83 —

This result was due to the whole hearted work of all ranks wherever employed —
The cases received ample refreshments.
I have several names to bring to your notice which will be forwarded in due course —

H. Whitley [illegible]
Lt. Col.
O.C. 132 Fld Amb.

14/11/16 —

Urgent.

No. Aff. L.a. F.A. 2/246.

A.D.M.S.
39 Div.

(1) Attached reports for your information :—

(2) Cases evacuated to C.C.S. since zero hour :—

	Lying.	Sitting.
Officers	15	4
O.R.	143	62
Prisoners	37	11

All is quiet at present.

7.30 A.M.
14/11/16.

A. [illegible] Lt Col.
O.C. 132 F. Amb.

FA 2/323.

A.D.M.S.
39th Division.

Herewith War Diary with Duplicate copy, and Appendices, for November please.

J Morris Capt R.A.M.C.T.
for O.C. 132nd FIELD AMBULANCE.

132nd FIELD AMBULANCE
5 DEC 1916

2

OC 132 Field Ambulance

Your War Diary is returned for compliance with instructions laid down in F.S. Regulations Part II Chapter XVI para 140 (4). Amend and return quickly

B Arrolum[?]
Capt RAMC
for COLONEL.
A. D. M. S.
39TH DIVISION.

A. D. M. S.
No. 6/934
5 DEC 1916
39TH DIVISION.

Nov. App 3

SECRET. Copy No. 1....

R.A.M.C. Operation Order No.15

by

Colonel G.W. Brazier-Creagh, C.M.G., A.D.M.S. 39th.Div.

Ref.Map
1/40,000 57D.
1/20,000 57D SE.

No.6/627. 14-11-16.

The 19th.Division will take over the 39th.Divisional front by 6am. 15th.November, 1916.
On relief, the 39th.Division will be withdrawn to K.area.
In connection with the above, the following reliefs will take place.

1. No. 132 Field Ambulance will hand over the A.D.S. at LANCASHIRE DUMP and the medical evacuation lines through PAISLEY AVENUE, and all subsidiary posts, including the Head-quarters site at Q.33.b.9.5., to a Field Ambulance of the 19th. Division.

2. No.134 Field Ambulance will hand over the CABSTAND to a Field Ambulance of the 19th. Division.

3. No.133 Field Ambulance will hand over the EAST CLAIRFAYE to a Field Ambulance of the 11th. Division.

4. Relief to be completed by 12 noon on Nov.15.
On relief, No.133 Fld.Amb. will move to BEAUVAL and will be temporarily attached to and will march under the orders of the G.O.C. 116th. Infantry Brigade Group.
No.132 and 134 Fld.Ambs. will move on relief to WARLOY and will be temporarily attached to and march under the orders of the G.O.C. 118th. Infantry Brigade Group.
Duplicate lists of non expendable stores and equipment handed and taken over, will be signed by units concerned and forwarded to this office.

5. After noon on the 16th.inst. Rest Station sick of the 39th. Division will be sent to VADENCOURT. In moving from the forward area, 39th.Divisional Rest Station sick and evacuations will be carried out by Field Ambulance cars.

6. Report completion of moves.

7. Acknowledge.

B A Odlum
Capt.
for A.D.M.S. 39th.Div.

Copies to:-
1. No.132 F.Amb.
2. " 133 " "
3. " 134 " "
4. " 82 San.Sect.
5. G.
6. A.Q.
7. Div.R.A.
8. " R.E.
9. 116 Inf.Bde.
10. 117 " "
11. 118 " "
12. 13 Gloster Regt.
13. ADMS. 19th.Div.
14. ADMS. 11th.Div.
15. ADMS. 63rd(RN)Div.
16. DDMS. IInd.Corps.
17-19. Office records.

Nos. 5-16 For information.

Nw. Apx. 2. 6/572 11.11.16.

39th DIVISION

SECRET. Copy No 1....

ADDITIONAL MEDICAL ARRANGEMENTS
in connection with
39th.Divisional Order No.63 dated 25-10-16.

11-11-16

The following instructions are issued:-

1. These arrangements will be completed before Zero hour on Z. day.

2. Distribution of Officers and Personnel.
   (a) No.132 Field Ambulance:-
   LANCASHIRE DUMP - O.C.132 Fld.Amb., Lieut C.H.L. RIXON R.A.M.C. reinforced by Capts. J.H. PORTER and C.H. LILLEY.
   A.D.S. PAISLEY AVENUE.- Capts. MORRIS, PERCEVAL and Lieut. COYLE. R.A.M.C.
   BEARERS RIGHT SECTOR. - Capt. MEECH. R.A.M.C.
   BEARERS LEFT SECTOR. - Capt. S. MILLER. R.A.M.C.
   Regimental Stretcher Bearers will be available as follows:-
   A.D.S. PAISLEY AVENUE.....1 Officer, 50 O.R.
   LANCASHIRE DUMP ....1 Officer, 50 O.R.

   (b) No.133 Field Ambulance:- The following officers will be available for duty at Headquarters EAST CLAIRFAYE:- O.C.133 Fld.Amb., Capts. ROBERTSON, MACARTHUR and Lieuts. ROBINSON and BADO. R.A.M.C.

   (c) No.134 Field Ambulance.
   CABSTAND.(Headquarters):- O.C.134 Fld.Amb., Capt. TAYLOR, Lieut Mc.NEILL, and two officers to be detailed by D.D.M.S. IInd. Corps.
   Lieut.HARRIS R.A.M.C. will be placed in charge of the Tent Sub-division in readiness to move forward and open out as soon as the situation permits.

3. Transport of wounded.
   (a) The 39th.Divisional Motor Ambulances will be pooled and under the control of O.C.No.20 M.A.C. for removal of lying cases.
   (b) Ten Motor Busses or Char-a-bancs together with the pooled G.S. and Horse Ambulance Wagons, [of Nº 132+134 F.A.] 39th.Div. will be placed at the disposal of O.C.134 Fld.Amb. for the transfer of walking cases.

4. Casualties.
   Casualties of both officers and other ranks at the front must be filled immediately and early notification sent to this office.

5. Trolley Lines.
   Any damage to the trolley lines must be reported without delay, to enable this office to communicate with the C.R.E. who will cause the necessary repairs to be effected.

6. Reports.
   Officers in charge of Advanced Posts should send in brief reports on occurrences, without delay, to this office, under cover of O.C.132 Fld.Amb., who will ensure that they are forwarded at once.

B A Odd[illegible]
Capt.
for A.D.M.S. 39th.Div.

Copies to:-No.1 132 F.Amb. 4.G. 7.118 I.Bde.
2 133 " 5.A.Q. 8.117 " "
3 134 " 6.No.20 M.A.C. 9.116 " "
10 & 11.A.D.M.S.39th.Div. War Diary etc.

SECRET

O.C 132 Field Ambulance

Amendment to my 6/572 d/- 11/11/16
With reference to para 2 Sub-section "C"
Lieut. McNEILL is posted to the
Tent Sub-Division under command
of Lieut. HARRIS. Ramc

J H Porter Capt
for

COLONEL,
A. D. M. S.
39th DIVISION.

A.D.M.S. 6/572 12-11-16 39th DIVISION

Copies to No 132 Fld. Amb
133 " "
134 " "
OC 70 M A C.

Issued at. 12 15 pm

SECRET No 6/223.

Ref. 39th Divisional Medical arrangements Order No 63 d/25.10.16.
1st para. second line should read:-

CENTRE .... HERTS R.A.P. R(25.T.8.8 approx)

Please amend and acknowledge.

12.11.16.

J H Porter
Capt
for A.D.M.S. 39 Div.

SECRET. No. 6/223

39th Divisional Medical Arrangements
Order No. 63 dated 25/10/16.
para. second line should read:-
CENTRE.......... HERTS. R.A.P. R(25. b. 8. 8. approx)
please amend and acknowledge.

28. 10. 16

B A Odlum
Capt. D.A.D.M.S
39 DIV.

O.C. 132 Fld Amb

With reference to para 7 of attached medical arrangement d/25/10/16. I have placed 42 Bearers at Paisley Av. provisionally. As there will also be reinforcements from Regimental Bearers at the same place it is left to you to distribute the Ramc Bearers, in consultation with O.C. Bearer Division, where considered desirable in order to avoid congestion at Paisley Av.

J H Porter Capt
for COLONEL
A. D. M. S.
39th DIVISION.

SECRET. MEDICAL ARRANGEMENTS Copy No. 12

in connection with

39th. Divisional Order No. 63 dated 22-10-16

Ref. 1/20,000 Map
Sheet 57D. S.E.

Regimental Aid Posts.	1.	Right Flank ....THIEPVAL (R.25.d.8.8.) Centre ....HERTS R.A.P. (R.28.b.8.2. Approx) Left Flank .......R.A.P. (to be selected)
Field Ambulance Posts.	2.	ROSS CASTLE ....Q.30.b.3.0. JOHNSON'S POST.....R.25.c.1.3.
Advanced Dressing Stations.	3.	PAISLEY AVENUE A.D.S. ....Q.30.c.7.3. LANCASHIRE DUMP A.D.S. ......Q.35.d.1.6.
Collecting Station. (for walking cases)	4.	CABSTAND ....W.10.c.4.3. Headquarters No.134 Field Ambulance.
Corps Collecting Station.	5.	EAST CLAIRFAYE.....O.29.b.8.8. Headquarters No.133 Field Ambulance.

Evacuation. 6. (a) Right Flank. Lying cases will be carried to R.A.P. THIEPVAL, then conducted down the THIEPVAL-AUTHUILLE-AVELUY ROAD to CYCLIST'S POST where Ford Cars will convey them to LANCASHIRE DUMP.
Walking cases will follow the same route.

(b) Centre. From the R.A.P. (R.28.b.8.2.approx) wounded will be conducted along the valley skirting THIEPVAL WOOD on the EAST to A.D.S. PAISLEY AVENUE, where lying and sitting cases will be redressed if necessary, fed, and passed to cars at SOUTH CAUSEWAY by trolley. From here they will be taken direct to C.C.S. Walking wounded will pass through to the CABSTAND.

(c) Left Flank. From R.A.P. wounded will be conveyed along the Northern border of THIEPVAL WOOD to ELGIN and SANDY AVENUES. They will then proceed by these trenches to ROSS CASTLE and PAISLEY AVENUE. From the latter they will be evacuated as in (b).
The large dug-out on the western side of SANDY AVENUE (about Q.30.d.1.9.) might, if necessary, be utilised.
When the line has advanced a suitable distance the German Dressing Station about Q.24.b.central may if circumstances permit, be used as an R.A.P.
Walking Cases- are to be evacuated to CABSTAND from A.D.Stations by means of Motor Lorries and Char-a-bancs under control of O.C. No.134 Fld. Ambulance. Thence to C.C.S. PUCHEVILLERS.

Distribution of Personnel. 7. No.132 Field Ambulance reinforced by personnel from Nos.133 and 134 Field Ambulances will carry out the evacuation; Headquarters being at LANCASHIRE DUMP.

Personnel will be distributed by O.C. No.132 Fld. Ambulance as follows:-

to each R.A.P. ....12 O.R.
THIEPVAL ....1 Officer, 40 O.R.
ROSS CASTLE................5 O.R.
CYCLIST'S POST.............3 O.R.
PAISLEY AVENUE A.D.S.......3 Officers, 72 O.R.
LANCASHIRE DUMP A.D.S......3 Officers, 20 O.R.

Arrangements will be made to reinforce R.A.M.C. Bearers by Regimental Bearers from Battalions in reserve. These will report two hours before zero to Oi/c A.D.S. PAISLEY AVENUE where they will be held in readiness.

Motor Ambulances. 8. The 39th. Divisional Motor Ambulances and those of No.20 M.A.C. will be pooled and under the control of the O.C. No.20 M.A.C. Spare cars may also assist in the evacuation of walking cases from A.D.Stations.

Disposal of Kit and Valuables. 9. Special attention is directed to D.O. No. 20/2 dated 10/5/16 and G.R.O. 1350.

Refreshments. 10. Adequate arrangements will be made at LANCASHIRE DUMP, PAISLEY AVENUE and the CABSTAND for the feeding of wounded.

Prisoners. 11. Arrangements for the Medical examination of German Prisoners at the War Collecting Station (Q.35.d.4.8.) will be made by O.C. No.132 Field Ambulance.

General Instructions 12. O.s C. Medical Units, Osi/c A.D.Stations and Unit M.Os. will keep the A.D.M.S. informed of any occurrence of an important nature affecting the Medical Services. The Officers i/c A.D.Stations and Units may do so directly in order to avoid delay in rectifying matters.

13. Acknowledge.

25-10-16.

J H Porter Capt
for A.D.M.S. 39th.Div.

Copies to:- 1.G.
2.A.Q.
3.Div.R.A.
4.Div.R.E.
5.116 Inf.Bde.
6.117 " "
7.118 " "
8.13 Glosters.
9.D.D.M.S. 11 Corps
10.A.D.M.S. 19th.Div.
11.A.D.M.S. 63rd.Div.
12.No.132 Fld.Amb.
13.No.133 " "
14.No.134 " "
15.82nd San.Sect.
16.20 M.A.C.
17.
18. } A.D.M.S. 39th.Div.
19. } War Diary;

SECRET

Vol 10

140/92

39th Div

War Diary

132nd Field Ambulance

December 1916

Dec 1916

Instructions regarding War Diaries and Intelligence Summaries are contained in F. S. Regs., Part II. and the Staff Manual respectively. Title pages will be prepared in manuscript.

ORIGINAL

WAR DIARY
or
~~INTELLIGENCE SUMMARY.~~
(Erase heading not required.)

132 FLD. AMB.

DECEMBER 1916.

(1)

Map Reference Sheet 27.

Army Form C. 2118.

Place	Date	Hour	Summary of Events and Information	Remarks and references to Appendices
WATOU	1/XII/16		Construction of Horse Standings held up for want of material — unobtainable —	JHB.
	2/XII/16	9 AM – 12 noon	Pathway to latrines partially re-constructed and extended, and field oven erected.	JHB
	3/XII/16	9 AM – 12 noon	Area around Cook House + Q M Stores filled with broken bricks and Rubble.	JHB
	4/XII/16	11 AM	Visit of Inspection by A.D.M.S. 39th Div, and a lecture by him to junior officers.	JHB
	5/XII/16		Meat Store taken down + entirely reconstructed.	
		3 PM	Visit to R E yard to enquire about materials to complete Horse Standings. These materials were not available.	JHB
			Award of seven MILITARY MEDALS to 132 Fld. Amb. (App I)	App I. D.R.O.
	6/XII/16	3 PM.	Horses have had to be removed from Artillery Standings – lent temporarily by	JHB

T2134. Wt. W708–776. 500000. 4/15. Sir J. C. & S.

Instructions regarding War Diaries and Intelligence Summaries are contained in F. S. Regs., Part II. and the Staff Manual respectively. Title pages will be prepared in manuscript.

WAR DIARY
or
~~INTELLIGENCE SUMMARY~~
(Erase heading not required.)

132 FLD. AMB

December 1916 –

Army Form C. 2118.

(2)

Map Reference – Sheet 27 –

Place	Date	Hour	Summary of Events and Information	Remarks and references to Appendices
WATOU	6/XII/16		OC VIII Corps Troops – as they are required for Artillery coming in tomorrow 7/XII/16, and put on mud standings near new standings under construction.	[initials]
"	8/12/16	11 AM.	DDMS VIII Corps visited the FD. Amb. and inspected the various pieces of new work that had been done on the site, and discussed points in connection with P.U.O. –	
"	"	8.30 PM.	A wire was received stating that No: 3989 Pte L.M. HEWITT of the 1st Cambs. Regt. admitted on 5/12/16 had been diagnosed diphtheria, and that swabs were to be at once arranged for, to be taken from the contacts: this was carried out during the course of the night –	[initials]
"	9.12.16	1 PM.	Lieut. W. PATEY RAMC M.O. i/c 179 Brigade R.F.A. admitted to Hpl suffering from pyrexia: in accordance with instructions received later Capt. T.P. CHARLES RAMC was detailed to proceed and take over temporary charge of the 179 Brigade R.F.A. and he left at 4.30 P.M – Preliminary orders were received as to the move of the unit to PROVEN to relieve 130 FLD AMB on 13/12/16 –	[initials]

Instructions regarding War Diaries and Intelligence Summaries are contained in F. S. Regs., Part II. and the Staff Manual respectively. Title pages will be prepared in manuscript.

WAR DIARY
or
~~INTELLIGENCE SUMMARY.~~
(Erase heading not required.)

132 FLD AMB. (3)

December 1916 –

Map Reference – Sheet 27 –

Army Form C. 2118.

Place	Date	Hour	Summary of Events and Information	Remarks and references to Appendices
WATOU	9/12/16	2 P.M.	I proceeded to PROVEN and was shown Fld. Amb. site and D.R. Station there by O.C. 130 Fld. Amb –	A.H.
"	10/12/16	10 P.M.	ADMS. 39 Div Operation Order No: 18 received: unit is to proceed to PROVEN on morning of 13/12/16, and advance party to proceed on 11/12/16 and commence taking over – During the afternoon Lieut. J. STEEL RAMC (S.R.) proceeded to HAZEBROUCK for the 2nd Army Course of instruction in Sanitation –	A.H.
"	11/12/16	9 A.M.	Capt. J. MORRIS RAMC (TF) + Lieut A.A. PORTER RAMC proceeded to PROVEN to commence to take over the D.R.S. + Fld. Amb. sites, and arrange for the arrival of the remainder of the advance party: O.C. 130 Fld. Amb. telegraphed asking for this party not to be sent until 12/12/16, so they were kept back – Sufficient equipment was packed up ready to go over with them to equip new sites, and necessary indents prepared to feed the large number of additional patients who will be in our charge in the D.R.S. on 13/12/16 –	A.H.

Instructions regarding War Diaries and Intelligence Summaries are contained in F. S. Regs., Part II. and the Staff Manual respectively. Title pages will be prepared in manuscript.

132 FLD AMB.

WAR DIARY
or
INTELLIGENCE SUMMARY.

December 1916. (Erase heading not required.)

(4)

Army Form C. 2118.

Map Reference. Sheet 27.

Place	Date	Hour	Summary of Events and Information	Remarks and references to Appendices
WATOU	12/12/16	8AM	Two tent subdivisions proceeded to PROVEN and equipped the Fld. Amb. + D.R.S. sites as the outgoing unit removed their equipment. The remainder of the equipment at WATOU was packed up as far as possible, ready to move.	Alh
"	13/12/16	9AM	All cases transferred to D.R.S. or C.C.S. between 9 + 10 AM: unit moved off at 10 AM + arrived at new site at PROVEN F.7.b.3.3. at 11.30 A.M. The WATOU site was handed over to the 129 Fld. Amb. After dinners the wagons were unloaded + the Fld Amb site equipped by "A" Section, + the D.R.S. by "B" + "C" Sections.	Alh
PROVEN.	14/12/16	9AM	Equipment of new sites continued. 400 additional blankets were received from Ordnance. Construction work carried on, manufacture of wire beds to equip some of the wards.	Alh
"	15/12/16	9AM	Provision made for a dry canteen in the men's dining room.	Alh
"	16/12/16	11AM	DDMS VIII Corps visited + went round the Fld Amb + D.R.S. he	

T2134. Wt. W708–776. 500000. 4/15. Sir J. C. & S.

Instructions regarding War Diaries and Intelligence Summaries are contained in F. S. Regs., Part II. and the Staff Manual respectively. Title pages will be prepared in manuscript.

132 FLD AMB

WAR DIARY
or
~~INTELLIGENCE SUMMARY.~~

(Erase heading not required.)

(5)

Army Form C. 2118.

December 1916 –

Map Reference. Sheet 27 –

Place	Date	Hour	Summary of Events and Information	Remarks and references to Appendices
PROVEN.	16.12.16	11 AM	also discussed the subject of "Trench Foot" – At 5 PM. I visited the ADMS. 39 Div in connection with a case of "Trench feet" – Lieut. J. STEEL RAMC returned from 2nd Army Course of Sanitation –	AH
〃	17.12.16	1 PM	Lieut. W. PATEY. RAMC returned to the Fld Amb from 46 CCS and left later for 134 Fld Amb in accordance with instructions received from ADMS. 39 Div –	AH
〃	〃	6 PM.	Lecture to officers on "Medical Organisation" – During the day pathways at the Eastern end of DRS were double trench boarded, & wired in –	AH
〃	18.12.16	7.45 AM	Lieut. A.H. PORTER. RAMC proceeded to 2nd Army Course of Sanitation –	
		10.30 AM	I visited the camps of the 39th Divisional Train and 177 Tunnelling Company RE; further trench boarding & wiring in of paths provided at DRS, and equipment of Nissen hut with wire beds completed –	AH
〃	19.12.16	6 PM.	Saw a sore throat with Capt. Millar RAMC. SR. & decided to send a swab to No. 1 Mobile Laboratory – Further work done on DRS etc –	AH

T2134. Wt. W768–776. 500000. 4/15. Sir J. C. & S.

Instructions regarding War Diaries and Intelligence Summaries are contained in F. S. Regs., Part II. and the Staff Manual respectively. Title pages will be prepared in manuscript.

WAR DIARY
or
~~INTELLIGENCE SUMMARY.~~
(Erase heading not required.)

132 FLD AMB
December 1916 –

(6)

Army Form C. 2118.

Map Reference – Sheet 27 –

Place	Date	Hour	Summary of Events and Information	Remarks and references to Appendices
PROVEN	20/12/16	3 PM	Report on swab sent overnight to No 1 Mobile Laboratory is negative – Pathway North of Dining rooms in D.R.S. relaid with double row of trench boards and wired in –	A.H.
"	21/12/16	10 PM	Instructions received over phone that the water cart which is to proceed to Senior Officers Training School is to be complete with inventory + spare parts – Lt & QM T. FLINT obtained latest provisional inventory + equipped cart with all available spare parts –	A.H.
"	22/12/16	7.45 AM	Inspected water cart prior to leaving: the cart is in good order –	
		11 AM	A.D.M.S. 39 Div. visited + inspected the Fld. Amb. + D.R.S. he directed special attention to the question of ventilation – During the afternoon all officers who could be spared went to a meeting of the 2nd Army Medical Society at HAZEBROUCK – During the past two days much additional pathing has been laid in the D.R.S. + wiring in of same to keep people on the boards – also provision of fire buckets, night urinal stands, + beds for Nissen hut wards –	A.H.

T2134. Wt. W708–776. 500000. 4/15. Sir J. C. & S.

Instructions regarding War Diaries and Intelligence Summaries are contained in F. S. Regs., Part II. and the Staff Manual respectively. Title pages will be prepared in manuscript.

WAR DIARY
or
~~INTELLIGENCE SUMMARY~~.
(Erase heading not required.)

Army Form C. 2118.

132 FLD. AMB.
December 1916.

(7)

Map Reference. Sheet 27.

Place	Date	Hour	Summary of Events and Information	Remarks and references to Appendices
PROVEN	23/12/16	4 PM	Lieut A.H. PORTER RAMC rejoined from the 2nd Army Course of Instruction in Sanitation.	AH
"	24/12/16	2.30 PM	Attended conference at the office of the ADMS. 39 Div at 2.30 PM.	AH
"	25/12/16	Noon	Dinners for patients were served, and patients visited by the DADMS. representing the ADMS. 39 Division who was unable to be present: a good dinner had been provided for the patients + personnel, the latter dining at 2.15 PM. The DMS visited the Fld. Amb + DRS. at 2.45 PM. + visited most of the wards: he also went into the dining room + said a few words to the personnel. he also inspected the new Nissen hut wards: before leaving he expressed his satisfaction with what he had seen. From 6 PM to 8.30 PM. a concert was held for the patients + personnel.	AH
"	26/12/16	10 AM.	Much additional pathway wired in + relaid in D.R.S: and the conversion of the men's dining room was commenced, with a different arrangement of tables which will seat many more: good	

T2134. Wt. W708-776. 500000. 4/15. Sir J. C. & S.

Army Form C. 2118.

WAR DIARY
or
~~INTELLIGENCE SUMMARY.~~
(Erase heading not required.)

Instructions regarding War Diaries and Intelligence Summaries are contained in F. S. Regs., Part II. and the Staff Manual respectively. Title pages will be prepared in manuscript.

132 FLD AMB
December 1916 –

(5)

Map Reference. Sheet 27 –

Place	Date	Hour	Summary of Events and Information	Remarks and references to Appendices
PROVEN	26.12.16		progress made in all directions – At 5 P.M. a Conference of Medical Officers of the Fld. Amb. + units in the neighbourhood was held, at which Sanitary Diaries, Ventilation + Overheating, and disposal of Infectious Cases were discussed –	A.H.
"	27.12.16	11 A.M.	Visited camp of Lancashire Hussars Yeomanry – Arrangements for ironing Khaki clothing of patients in D.R.S. bath room were completed, stove having been removed from drying room to bath room for this purpose: other work done today includes:– provision of night urinal stands outside huts, completion of a cement stand for putting night urinal pails upon during the day, commencement of a new drain past the patients' Ablution Shed, wiring continued along billet + bath house and general clearing up of ground behind Nissen huts –	A.H.
"	28.12.16	11 A.M.	D.D.M.S. VIII Corps and A.D.M.S. 39 Div. inspected Fld: Amb: + Divisional Rest Station – Drain past patients' Ablution Shed completed; wiring in of duck boards past ablution shed, billet + bath house completed –	A.H. –

Instructions regarding War Diaries and Intelligence Summaries are contained in F. S. Regs., Part II. and the Staff Manual respectively. Title pages will be prepared in manuscript.*

WAR DIARY
or
~~INTELLIGENCE~~ SUMMARY.
(Erase heading not required.)

Army Form C. 2118.

132 FLD AMB
December 1916.

(9)

Map Reference:- Sheet 27.

Place	Date	Hour	Summary of Events and Information	Remarks and references to Appendices
PROVEN	29/12/16	11.30 AM	Party proceeded to 46 C.C.S. to assist in loading Ambulance Train. Trench boards round cookhouse taken up and cleaned & relaid, & path leading to cookhouse wired in. Soyer Stove placed outside dining room for immersion of cups knives & forks etc after use in boiling water.	AHL
"	30/12/16	10 AM	Further work on trench boards & wiring round cookhouse, Medical Inspection Room, and entrance to men's dining room: improvements carried out in urinals, troughs being widened.	AHL
"	31/12/16	11 AM	Church parade in the patients dining room. Stoves in wards B & C refixed to secure additional safety & new chimney pipes clear of woodwork: retarring of men's dining room commenced	
			Admissions for the month: Officers 7. O.R. 466. Cases ~~evacuated~~ admitted to D.R.S. 446.	AHL

A. Whittington. Lt Col.

2/1/17.

T2134. Wt. W708-776. 500000. 4/15. Sir J. C. & S.

App: I –

Extract from Divisional Routine Order No 482 dated 4-12-16:-

"Under authority delegated by the General Officer Commanding-in-Chief, the General Officer Commanding 2nd Corps has awarded the following decorations to the undermentioned N.C.O and men for gallantry and devotion to duty:—

Military Medal

132nd Field Ambulance

65792	Sergeant.	A. G. REEVE
65880	Private.	E. STEVENS
72040	"	A. L. WEBB
65920	"	J. ABRAHAM
65772	"	H. C. NEALE
82054	"	B. KING
55621	"	T. H. HOBSON

132nd FIELD AMBULANCE
2 JAN. 1917

A Whittingham Lt Col
R.A.M.C.
O.C. 132ND FIELD AMBULANCE.

DUPLICATE

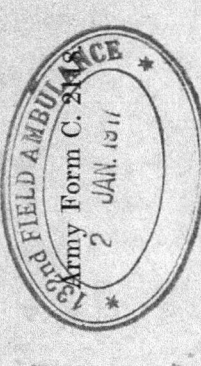

WAR DIARY
or
INTELLIGENCE SUMMARY.
(Erase heading not required.)

Instructions regarding War Diaries and Intelligence Summaries are contained in F. S. Regs., Part II. and the Staff Manual respectively. Title pages will be prepared in manuscript.

132 FLD. AMB. DECEMBER 1916.

(1) Map Reference Sheet 27.

Place	Date	Hour	Summary of Events and Information	Remarks and references to Appendices
WATOU	1/XII/16		Construction of Horse Standings held up for want of material — unobtainable —	JHB
	2/XII/16	9 AM 12 noon	Pathway to latrines partially re-constructed and extended, and field oven erected.	JHB
	3/XII/16	9 AM 12 noon	Area around Cook House & QM Stores filled with broken bricks and rubble	JHB
	4/XII/16	11 AM	Visit of Inspection by ADMS. 39th Div, and a lecture by him to junior officers.	JHB
	5/XII/16		Meat Store taken down & entirely reconstructed.	
		3 PM	Visit to RE yard to enquire about materials to complete Horse Standings. These materials were not available.	JHB
			Award of seven MILITARY MEDALS to 132 Fld. Amb. (App I)	App I DRO
	6/XII/16	3 PM.	Horses have had to be removed from Artillery Standings — lent temporarily by	JHB

T2134. Wt. W708—776. 500000. 4/15. Sir J. C. & S.

32nd FIELD AMBULANCE

Instructions regarding War Diaries and Intelligence Summaries are contained in F. S. Regs., Part II. and the Staff Manual respectively. Title pages will be prepared in manuscript.

132 FLD AMB

December 1916 –

WAR DIARY
or
INTELLIGENCE SUMMARY.
(Erase heading not required.)

(2)

Map Reference – Sheet 27 –

Army Form C. 2118.

Place	Date	Hour	Summary of Events and Information	Remarks and references to Appendices
WATOU	6/XII/16		OC VIII Corps Troops – as they are required for Artillery coming in tomorrow 7/XII/16, and put in mud standings near new Standings under Construction	[illegible]
"	7/12/16	11 AM	DDMS VIII Corps visited the FLD AMB and inspected the various pieces of new work that had been done on the site and discussed points in connection with P.U.O. –	
"	"	8.30 PM	A wire was received stating that No 3919 Pte L M HEWITT of the [illegible] Canadian Regt admitted on 5/12/16 had been diagnosed diphtheria, and that swabs were to be at once arranged for, to be taken from the contacts. this was carried out during the course of the night –	[illegible]
"	9.12.16	PM	Lieut W. PATEY RAMC MO i/c 179 Brigade RFA admitted to Hospl suffering from pyrexia: in accordance with instructions received Capt T P CHARLES RAMC was detailed to proceed and take over temporary charge of the 179 Brigade RFA and he left at 4.30 PM – Preliminary orders were received as to the move of the unit to PROVEN to relieve 130 FLD AMB on 12/12/16 –	[illegible]

T2131. Wt. W708–776. 500000. 4/15. Sir J. C. & S.

Instructions regarding War Diaries and Intelligence Summaries are contained in F. S. Regs., Part II. and the Staff Manual respectively. Title pages will be prepared in manuscript.

132 FLD AMB

WAR DIARY
or
INTELLIGENCE SUMMARY.
(Erase heading not required.)

(3)

Army Form C. 2118.

December 1916

Map Reference. Sheet 27.

Place	Date	Hour	Summary of Events and Information	Remarks and references to Appendices
WATOU	9/12/16	2PM	Proceeded to PROVEN and was shown the Fd Amb site and DRStation there by O.C. 130 Fd Amb.	AH
"	10/12/16	10PM	ADMS 38 Div Operation Order No 18 received unit is to proceed to PROVEN on morning of 13/12/16, an advance party to proceed on 11/12/16 and commence taking over during the afternoon. Lieut. J. STEEL RAMC (TF) proceeded to HAZEBROUCK for the 2nd Army course of instruction in Sanitation.	AH
"	11/12/16	9AM	Capt J. MORRIS RAMC (TF) & Lieut AA PORTER RAMC proceeded to PROVEN to commence to take over the DRS & Fd Amb site, and arrange for the arrival of the remainder of the advance party. O.C. 130 Fd Amb telegraphed asking for this party not to be sent until 12/12/16, as they were full up. Sufficient equipment was packed up ready to go on with them to equip new site, and necessary stores prepared to feed the large number of additional patients who will be in our charge in the DRS on 13/12/16.	AH

T2134. Wt. W708–776. 500000. 4/15. Sir J. C. & S.

132nd FIELD AMBULANCE

Instructions regarding War Diaries and Intelligence Summaries are contained in F. S. Regs., Part II. and the Staff Manual respectively. Title pages will be prepared in manuscript.

132 FLD AMB. — December 1916.

WAR DIARY
or
INTELLIGENCE SUMMARY.
(Erase heading not required.)

(4)

Army Form C. 2118.

Map Reference: Sheet 27.

Place	Date	Hour	Summary of Events and Information	Remarks and references to Appendices
WATOU	12/12/16	9AM	Two tent subdivisions proceeded to PROVEN and re-equipped the Fd Amb. & DRS sites as the outgoing unit removed their equipment. The remainder of the equipment at WATOU was packed up as far as possible, ready to move.	AH
"	13/12/16	9AM	All cases transferred to DRS or CCS between 9 & 10 AM. Unit moved off at 10 AM & arrived at new site at PROVEN E.1.b.3.3 at 11.30 AM. The WATOU site was handed over to the 129 Fd Amb. After dinner the wagons were unloaded & the Fd Amb site equipped by A section, & the DRS by B & C sections.	AH
PROVEN	14/12/16	9AM	Equipment of new site continued. 400 additional blankets were received from Ordnance. Construction work carried on, manufacture of wire beds to equip some of the wards.	AH
"	15/12/16	9AM	Provision made for a dry canteen in the men's dining room.	AH
"	16/12/16	9AM	DDMS VIII Corps visited & went round the Fd Amb & DRS. He	

T2134. Wt. W708–776. 500000. 4/15. Sir J. C. & S.

Army Form C. 2118.

WAR DIARY
or
INTELLIGENCE SUMMARY.
(*Erase heading not required.*)

Instructions regarding War Diaries and Intelligence Summaries are contained in F. S. Regs., Part II. and the Staff Manual respectively. Title pages will be prepared in manuscript.

132 FLD AMB (5)

December 1916 – Map Reference Sheet 27 –

Place	Date	Hour	Summary of Events and Information	Remarks and references to Appendices
PROVEN	16th	11 AM	also discussed the subject of "Trench Feet" – At 5 PM visited the ADMS 38th Div in connection with a case of "Trench feet" – Lieut J STEEL RAMC returned from 2nd Army Course of Sanitation.	AH
"	17th	1 PM	Lieut H PATEY RAMC returned to the Fd Amb from 46 CCS and left later for 134 Fd Amb in accordance with instructions received from ADMS 38 D I –	AH
"	"	5 PM	Lecture to officers on "Medical Organisation" – During the day pathways at the Eastern end of DRS were double lined borders, turned in –	AH
"	18th	7.45 AM	Lieut A H PORTER RAMC proceeded to 2nd Army Course of Sanitation. Visited the camps of the 38th Divisional Train and 177 Tunnelling Company RE. paths [illegible] brick bordering [illegible] of paths provided at DRS, and equipment of Nissen hut with [illegible] completed –	AH
"	19th	6 PM	Saw a bad throat with Capt Millar RAMC SR & decided to send a swab to No 1 Mobile Laboratory – Further work done on DRS paths –	AH

T2134. Wt. W708–776. 500000. 4/15. Sir J. C. & S.

Instructions regarding War Diaries and Intelligence Summaries are contained in F. S. Regs., Part II. and the Staff Manual respectively. Title pages will be prepared in manuscript.

132 FLD AMB
December 1916

WAR DIARY
or
INTELLIGENCE SUMMARY.
(Erase heading not required.)

(6)

Map Reference Sheet 27.

Army Form C. 2118.

Place	Date	Hour	Summary of Events and Information	Remarks and references to Appendices
PROVEN	20/12/16	3 PM	Report on meat sent overnight to No 1 Mobile Laboratory is negative. Pathway North of Dining rooms in DRS relaid with double row of trench boards and wired in.	AH
"	21/12/16	10 AM	Instruction received over phone that the water cart which is to proceed to [illegible] Officers Training School is to be complete with [illegible] & spare parts. Staff Sgt T FLINT obtained latest [illegible] & equipped cart with all available spare parts.	AH
"	22/12/16	7.45 AM	Inspected water cart prior to leaving. The cart is in good order.	
		11 AM	ADMS 3rd Div. visited & inspected the RD Aid Post & DRS. He directed special attention to the question of ventilation. During the afternoon all three water carts to be proved went to be [illegible] to the 2nd Army Medical [illegible] at HAZEBROUCK. During the past few days much additional pathing has been laid in the DRS & [illegible] to keep people on the boards. Also provision of fire buckets [illegible] wood [illegible] & [illegible] for [illegible] hut wards.	AH

T2134. Wt. W708–776. 500000. 4/15. Sir J. C. & S.

Instructions regarding War Diaries and Intelligence Summaries are contained in F. S. Regs., Part II. and the Staff Manual respectively. Title pages will be prepared in manuscript.

WAR DIARY
or
INTELLIGENCE SUMMARY.
(Erase heading not required.)

Army Form C. 2118.

Place	Date	Hour	Summary of Events and Information	Remarks and references to Appendices

T2134. Wt. W708-776. 500000. 4/15. Sir J. C. & S.

Instructions regarding War Diaries and Intelligence Summaries are contained in F. S. Regs., Part II. and the Staff Manual respectively. Title pages will be prepared in manuscript.

WAR DIARY
or
INTELLIGENCE SUMMARY.
(Erase heading not required.)

Army Form C. 2118.

132 FLD AMB
December 1916 –

(5)

Map Reference Sheet 27 –

Place	Date	Hour	Summary of Events and Information	Remarks and references to Appendices
PROVEN	26/12/16		progress made in all directions – At 5PM a Conference of Medical Officers of the Fd Amb & units in the neighbourhood was held, at which Sanitation, Diarrhoea, Ventilation, Overheating, and disposal of Infectious Cases were discussed –	AH.
"	27/12/16	11AM	Visited camp of Lancashire Hussars Yeomanry – Arrangements for removing Khaki clothing of patients in DRS bath room were completed, this having been removed from drying room to bath room for this purpose. [illegible] [illegible] – [illegible]	AH.
	28/12/16	11AM	D.D.M.S. VIII Corps, inspected Fdn Amb & Divisional Rest Station. Drain past patients' Ablution Shed completed; [illegible] duck boards for [illegible] bath [illegible] been completed –	AH.

Instructions regarding War Diaries and Intelligence Summaries are contained in F. S. Regs., Part II. and the Staff Manual respectively. Title pages will be prepared in manuscript.

132 FLD AMB

December 1916

WAR DIARY
or
INTELLIGENCE SUMMARY.
(Erase heading not required.)

(9)

[illegible] – Sheet 27

Army Form C. 2118.

Place	Date	Hour	Summary of Events and Information	Remarks and references to Appendices
PROVEN	[illegible]	[illegible]	[illegible]	
			[illegible]	
			[illegible]	
			[illegible]	
			[illegible]	[initials]
	[illegible]	[illegible]	[illegible]	
			[illegible]	
			[illegible]	[initials]
	[illegible]	[illegible]	[illegible]	
			[illegible]	
			[illegible]	
			[illegible]	
			[illegible]	
			for the month [illegible]	[initials]

[signature]
Lt Col.
R.A.M.C.
O.C. 132nd FIELD AMBULANCE.

£4/7/-

T2134. Wt. W708–776. 500000. 4/15. Sir J. C. & S.

App: I

Extract from Divisional Routine Order No 482 dated 4-12-16:-

"Under authority delegated by the General Officer Commanding-in-Chief the General Officer Commanding 2nd Corps has awarded the following decorations to the undermentioned N.C.O and men for gallantry and devotion to duty:-

Military Medal

132nd Field Ambulance

65792	Sergeant	A. G. REEVE
65880	Private	E. STEVENS
72040	"	A. L. WEBB
65920	"	J. ABRAHAM
65772	"	H. C. NEALE
82054	"	B. KING
55621	"	T. H. HOBSON

132nd FIELD AMBULANCE
2 JAN. 1917

A Whittle Johns
Lt Col
R.A.M.C.
O.C. 132ND FIELD AMBULANCE.

39
Original

SECRET

XXI

39

CONFIDENTIAL

WAR DIARY
of
132nd FIELD AMBULANCE
from 1/1/17 to 31/1/17
(Volume II)

Original –

Instructions regarding War Diaries and Intelligence Summaries are contained in F. S. Regs., Part II. and the Staff Manual respectively. Title Pages will be prepared in manuscript.

WAR DIARY
or
~~INTELLIGENCE SUMMARY~~

JANUARY 1917 – (Erase heading not required.) Map Reference = Sheet 27. ①

Army Form C. 2118.

132nd FIELD AMBULANCE 2 JAN. 1917

Place	Date	Hour	Summary of Events and Information	Remarks and references to Appendices
PROVEN	1/1/17	10.15AM	Daily inspection of Fld. Amb. and D.R. Station. New work in hand is construction of pathway to Q.M. Stores & wiring in of same, retarring of roof of men's dining hall: the tables are now complete in the men's dining room, and 120 men can now be seated for meals.	AHL.
"	"	5.30PM.	Lieut. C.H.L. RIXON. RAMC. proceeded to 17 Notts & Derby Regt for temporary duty.	
"	2/1/17	10.15AM	Daily inspection performed – weather bright & clear.	
	"	5.PM.	Held conference of Medical Officers. Work done during the day: – completion of retarring of men's dining room which is now in good order, and is now in use for meals, and also is very comfortable for the men to sit in after dark, being well lighted: dry goods canteen running very satisfactorily.	AHL
"	3/1/17	10.15AM	Daily inspection. At 11.45AM. the A.A & Q.M.G. 39 Div. visited and went round the D.R.S. and Fld Amb. At 2.30 P.M. attended court of enquiry at Divisional Headquarters re articles of farriers equipment which were lost. Work done during the day on flooring of men's dining room, digging & plotting ground alongside men's dining hall & planting same with bulbs, tarring of latrine buckets.	AHL.

2449 Wt. W14957/M90 750,000 1/16 J.B.C. & A. Forms/C.2118/12.

Army Form C. 2118.

Instructions regarding War Diaries and Intelligence Summaries are contained in F. S. Regs., Part II. and the Staff Manual respectively. Title Pages will be prepared in manuscript.

WAR DIARY
or
~~INTELLIGENCE~~ SUMMARY
(Erase heading not required.)

January 1917. (2) Map Reference - Sheet 27.

FIELD AMBULANCE 5

Place	Date	Hour	Summary of Events and Information	Remarks and references to Appendices
PROVEN	4/1/17	10.15AM	The Major General Commanding the Division, accompanied by the A.D.M.S. visited and inspected the Field Ambulance and Divisional Rest Station, remaining for one hour & a half: he expressed his satisfaction with what he had seen before leaving. During the day the flooring of the men's Dining Hall was almost completed, much more bedding & planting of bulbs was done, & repair of stoves in various parts of the D.R.S. Swab sent to No 1 Mobile Laboratory from a case of sore throat.	RLh.
"	5/1/17	10.15AM	Daily inspection. Swab sent to No: 1 Mobile Laboratory overnight (Pte LEIGH) reported negative at 12.15 P.M. One case of ? Scarlet fever evacuated from D.R.S. to C.C.S., necessary notification & measures of isolation & disinfection carried out. At 2.15 P.M. visited "F" Camp to see Captain S. MILLER. RAMC. who had charge of this case for part of his time in D.R.S. On return rendered full report on case to A.D.M.S. Work done during the day:- bedding & planting of bulbs, tarring of QM Stores commenced, whitewashing of guard room, & separate latrine etc put up for patients isolated in connection with above case. All Officers who could be spared attended 2nd Army Medical Society meeting at BAILLEUL during the afternoon.	RLh.
"	6/1/17	10.15AM	Daily Inspection. No: 65867 Pte. H. EVERALL mentioned in Despatch from Commander-in-Chief dated 13/11/16, published in Supplement to the London Gazette dated 4/1/17.	

2449 Wt. W14957/M90 750,000 1/16 J.B.C. & A. Forms/C.2118/12.

Instructions regarding War Diaries and Intelligence Summaries are contained in F. S. Regs., Part II. and the Staff Manual respectively. Title Pages will be prepared in manuscript.

WAR DIARY
or
~~INTELLIGENCE SUMMARY~~
(Erase heading not required.)

Army Form C. 2118.

January 1917 – (3) Map Reference:- Sheet 27 –

Place	Date	Hour	Summary of Events and Information	Remarks and references to Appendices
PROVEN	6/1/17		Work done during the day included tarring of Q.M. Stores, further bedding around wards, repair of trench boards & wiring –	A.H.
"	7/1/17	11 AM	Visited D.R.S. at HILHOEK L 20 b.6.4. Sunday –	A.H.
"	8/1/17	10.15 AM	Daily inspection – Work done included completion of tarring of Q.M. Stores, and digging up of large beds behind huts A.B.C.D. and latrine tarred – At 2.30 P.M. lecture given to Officers & N.C.Os on the water cart – Wet weather – At 6 P.M. Captain SINCLAIR MILLER M.C. R.A.M.C. (S.R.) returned from temporary duty at the Reinforcement Camp –	A.H.
"	9/1/17	10 AM	Daily inspection – at 11.15 AM visited L'EBBE FARM at F 29. d. 5. 9. Cold & wet weather – Work done included further digging up of ground, repair of trench boards & boundary wire, tarring of new latrine in Reft. site – Conference of Medical Officers held at 5 P.M., subject discussed being "Sanitation & Care of Soldiers' feet", the discussion being opened by Capt. J. MORRIS. R.A.M.C. (T.F.) – From 6.30 P.M. to 8.30 P.M. a Concert was given in the Dining Hall for patients and personnel –	A.H.

2449 Wt. W14957/M90 750,000 1/16 J.B.C. & A. Forms/C.2118/12.

Army Form C. 2118.

WAR DIARY
or
~~INTELLIGENCE~~ SUMMARY
(Erase heading not required.)

Instructions regarding War Diaries and Intelligence Summaries are contained in F. S. Regs., Part II. and the Staff Manual respectively. Title Pages will be prepared in manuscript.

January 1917 – (4) Map Reference :– Sheet 27

132nd FIELD AMBULANCE 13 JAN 1917

Place	Date	Hour	Summary of Events and Information	Remarks and references to Appendices
PROVEN	10.1.17	10.15 AM	Daily Inspection – weather cold & wet – work done during the day consisted of repairing of walls of clothing store, rewiring & mending of trench boards, whitewashing of latrines in Fd Amb: site & further digging of beds in D.R.S –	Alh
	11.1.17	10.15 AM	Daily inspection – weather cold, rain and sleet – work of yesterday continued today – At 3 P.M. attended Conference of ADMS. a good deal of snow fell in the latter part of the day –	Alh
	12.1.17	10.15 AM	Daily inspection – weather wet & cold – At 1.30 PM all Officers who could be spared attended the meeting of the 2nd Army Medical Society at BAILLEUL – work done during the day consisted of preparation of the ground for the erection of new huts, repairing plaster walls of wards and trench boards –	Alh

2449 Wt. W14957/M90 750,000 1/16 J.B.C. & A. Forms/C.2118/12.

Instructions regarding War Diaries and Intelligence Summaries are contained in F. S. Regs., Part II. and the Staff Manual respectively. Title Pages will be prepared in manuscript.

WAR DIARY
or
~~INTELLIGENCE SUMMARY~~
(Erase heading not required.)

Army Form C. 2118.

(5)

January 1917 – Map Reference: Sheet 27 –

Place	Date	Hour	Summary of Events and Information	Remarks and references to Appendices
PROVEN	13.1.17	10.15 AM	Very cold & wintry weather – Daily inspection – Remainder of day spent in preparation & packing up as far as possible for move of unit on 14/1/17 –	A.L.H.
"	14.1.17	9.30 AM	Unit marched to HILLHOEK, arriving there at 12.30 P.M., and took over the D.R.S. at L 20.b.6.6: a cold fine morning following snow – D.R.S. site at PROVEN was handed over to 129 Fld. Amb. – Remainder of day spent in unpacking and getting new D.R.S. site equipped –	A.L.H.
HILLHOEK	15.1.17	10 AM	Daily Inspection – bright cold morning after sharp frost – Work on site commenced:– lathing of Nissen Hut, whitewashing of Cook house, relaying & repair of trench boards, and reorganisation of bath house arrangements: boiler out of action, assistance obtained from 227 Field Coy R.E. with a view to getting necessary repairs done – Water tanks scrubbed out –	A.L.H.

Army Form C. 2118.

Instructions regarding War Diaries and Intelligence Summaries are contained in F. S. Regs., Part II. and the Staff Manual respectively. Title Pages will be prepared in manuscript.

WAR DIARY
or
~~INTELLIGENCE SUMMARY~~
(Erase heading not required.)

(6)

January 1917 — Map Reference :- Sheet 27 —

Place	Date	Hour	Summary of Events and Information	Remarks and references to Appendices
HILLHOEK	16.1.17	10.15 AM	Cold weather, hard frost during the night, and some snow has fallen. Daily inspection — Reconstruction of bathing arrangements continued, & repair of Soyer's Stove for Bath house completed: White washing of cook house completed, rearrangement of Soyer Stove at Cookhouse to take chimneys of same out through the back — Tarring of Nissen huts continued & cleaning & repair of trench boards —	A.H.
HILLHOEK	17.1.17	10.15 AM	A considerable amount of snow has fallen during the night and continues to fall: daily inspection — work done during the day was:— Canvas screening placed round ablution place of patients & personnel, work on Bath house & provision of a room at same for ironing of patients clothes commenced: building of Field Oven in Cookhouse commenced to provide additional roasting accomodation which is much needed; repair of stove piping in many huts —	A.H.
"		5 PM	Conference held —	
"	18.1.17	9 AM	Thawing, rain & snow falling alternately — At 10.30 AM the A.D.M.S visited and inspected the D.R.S leaving again at 11.30 AM.	

2449 Wt. W14957/M90 750,000 1/16 J.B.C. & A. Forms/C.2118/12.

Army Form C. 2118.

WAR DIARY
or
~~INTELLIGENCE SUMMARY~~
(Erase heading not required.)

Instructions regarding War Diaries and Intelligence Summaries are contained in F. S. Regs., Part II. and the Staff Manual respectively. Title Pages will be prepared in manuscript.

January 1917 — (7) — Map Reference:- Sheet 27 -

Place	Date	Hour	Summary of Events and Information	Remarks and references to Appendices
HILLHOEK	18.1.17		Work continued during the day on the following:- installment of boiler & shower bath in bath house, building of field oven in cookhouse, wiring of pathways & trench boards, lining of Nissen huts, & provision of tin lined bread store in QM. Store - At 4.40 P.M. Lieut A.H. PORTER RAMC proceeded to 134 Fd. Ambulance for temporary duty -	AH.
"	19.1.17	9 AM.	Some frost during the night, today thaw continues: daily inspection - In the afternoon all officers who could be spared attended the meeting of the 2nd Army Medical Society at REMY SIDING - Lieut C.H.L. RIXON RAMC took over temporary medical charge of the 16th Notts & Derby Regt. during the morning - Work done during the day included:- whitewashing the interior of wards commenced, lining of Nissen Huts continued, building of field oven & closing in of Cookhouse continued, work on bath house plant progressing well, provision of shelter for Sawyer Stove at bath house, & night urinal stands outside wards commenced -	AH.

2449 Wt. W14957/M90 750,000 1/16 J.B.C. & A. Forms/C.2118/12.

Instructions regarding War Diaries and Intelligence Summaries are contained in F. S. Regs., Part II. and the Staff Manual respectively. Title Pages will be prepared in manuscript.

WAR DIARY
or
~~INTELLIGENCE SUMMARY~~
(Erase heading not required.)

Army Form C. 2118.

(8)

January 1917 – Map Reference:– Sheet 27 –

Place	Date	Hour	Summary of Events and Information	Remarks and references to Appendices
HILLHOEK	20.1.17	10 AM.	Hard frost – Captain D. F. KENNARD RAMC reported his arrival and is taken on the strength of the unit – Daily inspection, new work is progressing well – work continued during the day on bath house, Kitchen, tarring of huts, whitewashing of wards, and road into D.R.S –	ADL
"	21.1.17	9 A.M.	Sunday – Church parade held at 9 A.M – Hard frost continues – Daily inspection at 10.15 A.M –	ADL
"	22.1.17	10.15 AM	Hard weather still continues – Daily inspection – At 11.30 AM the D.D.M.S. VIII Corps visited and went round the D.R.S – Work done during the day included, continuation of road making into D.R.S, tarring of Nissen huts, whitewashing of wards, tin lined bread store in Q.M. Store completed, further work on new oven in Cookhouse, construction of new barber's shop commenced: Conversion of part of large barn into reception room to free one Nissen hut for reception of further patients & increase accommodation in D.R.S –	ADL

2449 Wt. W14957/M90 750,000 1/16 J.B.C. & A. Forms/C.2118/12.

Army Form C. 2118.

WAR DIARY
or
~~INTELLIGENCE SUMMARY~~
(Erase heading not required.)

Instructions regarding War Diaries and Intelligence Summaries are contained in F. S. Regs., Part II. and the Staff Manual respectively. Title Pages will be prepared in manuscript.

January 1917 — (9) Map Reference :— Sheet 27 —

Place	Date	Hour	Summary of Events and Information	Remarks and references to Appendices
HILLHOEK	23.1.17	10 AM	An exceedingly hard frost during the night followed by beautifully clear bright morning — Daily inspection: found work progressing well — Work done during the day consisted of following — whitewashing of interior of wards continued, instalment of boiler in wash house continued, new reception room completed, new field oven in cookhouse completed, erection of a new barber's shop continued —	AL.h.
HILLHOEK	24.1.17	10 AM	Hard frost continues — Daily inspection — work continued on lathing of Nissen huts, & whitewashing of wards, barber's shop, boiler in wash house and roadway into D.R.S. & wagon lines — At 5 pm. Conference of medical officers held when the duties of a Regimental Medical Officer were discussed —	AL.h.
"	25.1.17	10 AM	Hard frost still continues — Daily inspection — work continued on all items mentioned in yesterday's report — At 4.15 PM. Capt: J.P. CHARLES RAMC proceeded to take over medical charge of the 39th Divl Train and is struck off the strength of the 132 Fd. Amb. from today's date —	AL.h.

2449 Wt. W14957/M90 750,000 1/16 J.B.C. & A. Forms/C.2118/12.

Instructions regarding War Diaries and Intelligence Summaries are contained in F. S. Regs., Part II. and the Staff Manual respectively. Title pages will be prepared in manuscript.

WAR DIARY
or
~~INTELLIGENCE SUMMARY~~.
(Erase heading not required.)

(10)

Army Form C. 2118.

132nd FIELD AMBULANCE 26.1.17

January 1917 — Map Reference: — Sheet 27 —

Place	Date	Hour	Summary of Events and Information	Remarks and references to Appendices
HILLHOEK	26.1.17	10 AM.	Hard frost with bitterly cold wind continues — Daily inspection, much progress made with work in hand: boiler in wash house, tarring + whitewashing of huts, and building of barber's shop —	A.L.
"	27.1.17	10 AM.	Bitterly cold weather continues — Daily inspection — Barber's shop completed, stoves placed in Dining Hall, QM. Stores, and butcher's shop, whitewashing + tarring of huts continued — At 6 PM. orders were received for twice daily inspection of all small box respirators — All were at once inspected + found in good order —	A.L.
"	28.1.17	10 AM.	Hard frost still continues — Daily Inspection — Sunday, parade service held at 9 AM — Inspection of all box respirators carried out twice during the day, and found satisfactory —	A.L.
"	29.1.17	10 AM.	Bitterly cold weather + hard frost continues — Daily inspection found all work proceeding satisfactorily — Work done during the day consisted of following — Boiler in wash house now completed, whitewashing +	

T2134. Wt. W708—776. 500000. 4/15. Sir J. C. & S.

Instructions regarding War Diaries and Intelligence Summaries are contained in F. S. Regs., Part II. and the Staff Manual respectively. Title pages will be prepared in manuscript.

WAR DIARY
or
~~INTELLIGENCE SUMMARY.~~
(Erase heading not required.)

Army Form C. 2118.

(11)

– January 1917 –

Map Reference :– Sheet 27 –

Place	Date	Hour	Summary of Events and Information	Remarks and references to Appendices
HILLHOEK	29.1.17		tarring of wards + huts continued, also inside of barbers shop – Repair + wiring of trench boards – Box respirators inspected twice during the day + found in good condition – Practice parade + lecture on Gas defence given to Bearer Division – At 4.30 P.M. orders were received for an officer to proceed to take over medical charge of the 39th Divl Reinforcement Camp + 39th Divl School: Captain D. F. KENNARD RAMC left to take over these duties at 6.30 PM –	AH
"	30.1.17	10 AM	Cold weather continues, snow is also falling slightly – Work on improvements continued – ADMS visited the D.R.S. at 3pm and inspected it, and new work which has been carried out – Captain J. MORRIS RAMC T.F. awarded the Military Cross (London Gazette Jan 26th 1917) –	AH
"	31.1.17	10 AM	Some snow during the night, less cold – Daily inspection: new field oven in kitchen + new boiler in wash house working very satisfactorily – Work continued on tarring + whitewashing of huts + wards – New drying stove placed in bath house for drying of patients uniforms – New barbers shop is now in use –	A

T.2134. Wt. W708–776. 500000. 4/15. Sir J. C. & S.

Instructions regarding War Diaries and Intelligence Summaries are contained in F. S. Regs., Part II. and the Staff Manual respectively. Title pages will be prepared in manuscript.

WAR DIARY
or
~~INTELLIGENCE~~ SUMMARY.
(Erase heading not required.)

Army Form C. 2118.

132nd FIELD AMBULANCE 31.1.17

(12)

January 1917. Map reference:- Sheet 27 -

Place	Date	Hour	Summary of Events and Information	Remarks and references to Appendices
HILLHOEK	31.1.17		Conference of medical officers was held at 5 PM. when the subject discussed was "Indenting for supplies of all kinds".	
			Total admissions for the month:-	
			Officers. O.R.	
			To Field Ambulance. 3. 143.	
			To 39th Divl Rest Station. - 742 -	

132nd FIELD AMBULANCE 1/2/17.

A Whittlejohns - Lt Col R.A.M.C. - O.C. 132nd FIELD AMBULANCE.

T2134. Wt. W708-776. 500000. 4/15. Sir J. C. & S.

39

Vol 12

CONFIDENTIAL

War Diary of 132nd Field Ambulance

from Feb: 1st: 1917 to Feb: 28th: 1917

(Volume II.)

140/997

39th Div

121/4

ORIGINAL –

Instructions regarding War Diaries and Intelligence Summaries are contained in F. S. Regs., Part II. and the Staff Manual respectively. Title Pages will be prepared in manuscript.

WAR DIARY
or
~~INTELLIGENCE SUMMARY~~
(Erase heading not required.)

Army Form C. 2118.

(1)

February 1917 – Map Reference — Sheet 27 –

Place	Date	Hour	Summary of Events and Information	Remarks and references to Appendices
HILLHOEK	1/2/17	10 AM	Frosty weather continues, bright clear day – Daily inspection – Work done during the day:– Lettering & whitewashing of wards & huts, repair of stove pipes & protecting buildings at their exits, repair of boundary wire & trench boards – Provision of improved latrine seating also taken in hand –	AH.
"	2.2.17	10 AM	Extremely hard frost during the night followed by bright clear day – Work done during the day:— lettering & whitewashing of wards & huts, repair of boiler in bath house taken in hand, and new latrine seats continued –	AH.
"	3.2.17	10 AM	Weather remains same – Daily inspection, new work progressing satisfactorily – Repair of boiler in bath house completed & good progress made in other new work during the day –	AH.
"	4.2.17	10 AM	Frost continues – Daily Inspection – Sunday parade service held at 11 A.M. – Work in hand continued – In the afternoon a football match was played with DADOS's XI –	AH.

2449 Wt. W14957/M90 750,000 1/16 J.B.C. & A. Forms/C.2118/12.

Army Form C. 2118.

WAR DIARY
or
~~INTELLIGENCE SUMMARY~~
(Erase heading not required.)

(2)

Instructions regarding War Diaries and Intelligence Summaries are contained in F. S. Regs., Part II. and the Staff Manual respectively. Title Pages will be prepared in manuscript.

February - 1917 -

Map Reference :- Sheet 27 -

Place	Date	Hour	Summary of Events and Information	Remarks and references to Appendices
HILLHOEK	5.2.17	10AM	More snow has fallen during the night, and hard frost still continues - At 2 P.M. presided at a Medical Board at L'EBBE FARM on P.B. men - Work continued during the day on tarring of huts, repair of trench boards & boundary wire, and new latrines -	Alh.
"	6.2.17	10 AM	Very severe frost during the night - Daily inspection - Tarring of huts continued, also new latrines: erection of wind screen round horse lines latter in hand -	Alh.
"	7.2.17	10AM	Severe frost continues - Daily inspection - Tarring and whitewashing of huts & wards continued, screen to protect horse lines from the wind completed, patients' new latrine seating completed -	Alh.
"	8.2.17	10AM	Severe weather continues, very hard frost during the night - Daily inspection; orderly room transferred to another building, obtained from	

2449 Wt. W14957/M90 750,000 1/16 J.B.C. & A. Forms/C.2118/12.

Army Form C. 2118.

③

WAR DIARY
or
~~INTELLIGENCE SUMMARY~~
(Erase heading not required.)

Instructions regarding War Diaries and Intelligence Summaries are contained in F. S. Regs., Part II. and the Staff Manual respectively. Title Pages will be prepared in manuscript.

February 1917 — Map Reference:- Sheet 27 —

Place	Date	Hour	Summary of Events and Information	Remarks and references to Appendices
HILLHOEK	8.2.17	Noon	former, setting free a Nissen hut, which has been equipped and provides fourteen additional beds for the D.R.S. — Work in hand continued —	AH
"	9.2.17	10AM.	Severe weather continues — Daily inspection — New latrines for personnel in course of construction, and improvement of walls of forage store taken in hand. Whitewashing of wards + other repairs continued — All horses + mules passed through the dip during the afternoon —	AH
"	10.2.17	10AM.	Weather remains the same, there having been a very severe frost during the night — Daily inspection — At 2PM. Court of Inquiry was held on the circumstances under which the water cart was smashed + proceedings forwarded to HeadQuarters —	AH
"	11.2.17	11AM.	Weather is very much milder, + there are indications of a thaw — Sunday Parade Service was held at 10.15AM — Captain SINCLAIR MILLER RAMC proceeded to take over temporary command of 133 Fd. Amb —	AH

2449 Wt. W14957/M90 750,000 1/16 J.B.C. & A. Forms/C.2118/12.

132nd FIELD AMBULANCE 12/2/17

Instructions regarding War Diaries and Intelligence Summaries are contained in F. S. Regs., Part II. and the Staff Manual respectively. Title pages will be prepared in manuscript.

WAR DIARY
or
~~INTELLIGENCE SUMMARY.~~
(Erase heading not required.)

(4)

Army Form C. 2118.

February 1917 — Map Reference :— Sheet 27 —

Place	Date	Hour	Summary of Events and Information	Remarks and references to Appendices
HILLHOEK	12.2.17	10.15 A.M.	Slight frost in the night; this morning there is a slight thaw — Daily inspection — Work in hand is as follows :— Whitewashing, flattening of dining hall, construction of new permanent latrine for personnel is now well on, repair of trench boards etc —	A.H.
"	13.2.17	10.15 A.M.	Weather is bo[?] cold — Daily inspection — At 4 P.M. A.D.M.S. 39 Div. visited the D.R.S.	A.H.
"	14.2.17	10.15 A.M.	Another hard frost during the night, weather is very bright + cold again — Visited WORMHOUDT + BOLLEZEELE + saw D.R.S. Fd Amb + C.R.S. for Officers at former place, + collecting Post at latter — Work completed includes rebuilding of incinerator, + completion of new latrines —	A.H.
"	15.2.17	10.15 A.M.	Hard frost followed by a very fine morning : at 10.15 A.M. Lieut. A.H. PORTER + party left to take over the collecting post at BOLLEZEELE (A 24. c. 3. 4.) — Captain SINCLAIR MILLER R.A.M.C. rejoined at 4 P.M. —	A.H.
"	16.2.17	10.15 A.M.	Cold weather continues — Daily inspection — Day spent in preparing for move — D.D.M.S. VIII Corps visited the D.R.S. about noon —	A.H.

2353 Wt. W2544/1454 700,000 5/15 D. D. & L. A.D.S.S./Forms/C. 2118.

132nd FIELD AMBULANCE 17/2/17

Instructions regarding War Diaries and Intelligence Summaries are contained in F. S. Regs., Part II. and the Staff Manual respectively. Title pages will be prepared in manuscript.

Army Form C. 2118.

WAR DIARY
or
~~INTELLIGENCE SUMMARY.~~
(Erase heading not required.)

February 1917 — (5) — Map Reference:– Sheet 27 –

Place	Date	Hour	Summary of Events and Information	Remarks and references to Appendices
HILLHOEK	17.2.17	9 A.M.	Unit proceeded from HILLHOEK to WORMHOUDT, the latter place being reached at 2.30 P.M.: D.R.S. + Fld Amb. Site at C.16.b.5.3 and the Corps Rest Station for Officers at C11.C.0.2 were taken over from 2/1 West Lancs Fld Amb.: remainder of day spent in equipping new sites – Weather conditions have completely changed, there being a pronounced thaw + temperature mild –	A.H.
WORMHOUDT	18.2.17	9 A.M.	Mild weather continues: equipment of new sites continued – Good progress made.	A.H.
"	19.2.17	9 A.M.	Weather mild – At 2 P.M. proceeded to BOLLEZEELE to inspect the Collecting Post, and found the A.D.M.S. inspecting same –	A.H.
"	20.2.17	10 A.M.	Wet weather – Daily inspection – Arrangements working satisfactorily – At 3.30 P.M. Captain J. D. MACKINNON, RAMC (T.C.) and Lieut. W. M. CHRISTIE RAMC (T.C.) reported their arrival and are taken on the strength of the Field Ambulance from this date –	
"	21.2.17	10 A.M.	The A.D.M.S. visited the Fld Amb. site ~~and~~ D.R.S. and Corps Officers Rest Station – At 2 P.M. orders were received re forthcoming move to STEENVOORDE –	A.H.

2353 Wt. W2544/1454 700,000 5/15 D. D. & L. A.D.S.S./Forms/C. 2118.

Instructions regarding War Diaries and Intelligence Summaries are contained in F. S. Regs., Part II. and the Staff Manual respectively. Title pages will be prepared in manuscript.

WAR DIARY
or
~~INTELLIGENCE SUMMARY.~~
(*Erase heading not required.*)

Army Form C. 2118.

February. 1917 — (6) — Ref Reference Sheet 27 + 28

Place	Date	Hour	Summary of Events and Information	Remarks and references to Appendices
WORMHOUDT	22.2.17	10 AM	Visited Fld Amb. site at STEENVOORDE (Q1.b.4.6) – At 2 PM party of one officer + 23 O.R. left to take over baths laundries etc from 23rd Division at POPERINGHE, YPRES, and WINNIPEG Camp H 19.b.2.4 –	AH
"	23.2.17	10 AM	Damp misty weather – visited A.D.M.S. 39 Div re forthcoming move – At 12 noon party of 4 NCOs + 8 men proceeded to the Fld Amb. at VLAMERTINGHE MILL (H8.a.9.9.) (Sheet 28) for employment in Foot Preparation Rooms, and an advance party left for STEENVOORDE (Q1.b.4.6) also – "B" Section equipment packed for transit tomorrow –	AH.
"	24.2.17	7.30 AM	Captain SINCLAIR MILLER and party proceeded to STEENVOORDE and took over the Fd. Amb. site at Q1.b.4.6 – Party at BOLLEZEELE Collecting Post under Lieut. A.H. PORTER RAMC rejoined HeadQuarters at Party from 70 Fld Amb ~~took~~ over the Corps Rest Station for Officers during the day at WORMHOUDT –	AH.

132nd FIELD AMBULANCE 25/2/17

Instructions regarding War Diaries and Intelligence Summaries are contained in F. S. Regs., Part II. and the Staff Manual respectively. Title pages will be prepared in manuscript.

WAR DIARY
or
~~INTELLIGENCE SUMMARY.~~
(Erase heading not required.)

February 1917 –

(7) Pref Reference:– Sheet 27

Army Form C. 2118.

Place	Date	Hour	Summary of Events and Information	Remarks and references to Appendices
WORMHOUDT.	25.2.17	9.30 AM	Proceeded to POPERINGHE to visit Divisional Baths & Laundry to which taking over party proceeded on 22/2/17 – At 2:30 P.M. Lieut A.H. PORTER RAMC proceeded to take over medical charge of the 16th Rifle Brigade and is struck off the strength of the unit from todays date – Lieut: J. ANDERSON. RAMC on relief by Lieut. A.H. PORTER reported his arrival and is taken on the strength of the unit from todays date –	AH.
"	26.2.17	10 AM	Bright sunshine – Packing of wagons for move of remainder of unit to STEENVOORDE –	AH.
"	27.2.17	9 AM.	Headquarters of unit marched to STEENVOORDE, Q1.b.4.6, and arrived there at 11.30 AM – WORMHOUDT site handed over to advance party from 70th Fld. Amb. –	
STEENVOORDE	28.2.17		Dull weather – Equipment of site completed – Patients dealt with during the month – Admissions – Fld. Amb: Officers 7. O.R. 281. DRS. O.R. 563 –	AH.

A H Littlejohns Lt Col – R.A.M.C.

O.C. 132nd FIELD AMBULANCE.

132nd FIELD AMBULANCE 1/3/17.

2353 Wt. W2544/1454 700,000 5/15 D. D. & L. A.D.S.S./Forms/C. 2118.

39 ORIGINAL

Vol 13

CONFIDENTIAL

War Diary
of
132nd Field Ambulance

March 1st 1917 to March 31st 1917

(Volume II)

39th Div
140/042
pm
Mar 1917

ORIGINAL

Instructions regarding War Diaries and Intelligence Summaries are contained in F. S. Regs., Part II. and the Staff Manual respectively. Title Pages will be prepared in manuscript.

WAR DIARY
or
~~INTELLIGENCE SUMMARY~~
(Erase heading not required.)

Army Form C. 2118.

March 1917 — (1) Map Reference: — Sheet 27

Place	Date	Hour	Summary of Events and Information	Remarks and references to Appendices
STEENVOORDE	1.3.17	10 A.M.	Dull cold weather — Daily inspection — At noon the A.D.M.S. inspected the site and informed me that my unit would also take over the 2nd Army Rest Station at MONT DES CATS (R 19. b. 7. 5½) from the NORTH MIDLAND C.C.S. — At 2.30 P.M. visited the Army Rest Station and was shown over it by the Commanding Officer — Returned to Headquarters of unit at 6.30 P.M. + reported results of visit to A.D.M.S. in writing —	A.H.
"	2.3.17	Noon	Visited A.D.M.S. at Headquarters for interview in connection with requirements at Army Rest Station — During the day a considerable advance party proceeded to MONT DES CATS to learn routine + commence taking over —	A.H.
"	3.3.17	7 A.M.	Remainder of ~~advance~~ taking over party proceeded to MONT DES CATS: Captain J.D. MACKINNON + Lieut. W. CHRISTIE also proceeded: Captain SINCLAIR MILLER having rejoined head-quarters also proceeded to the Army Rest Station: at 2 P.M. I visited it and found taking over well in hand, + staff ready to take full charge on 4th inst —	A.H.

2449 Wt. W14957/M90 750,000 1/16 J.B.C. & A. Forms/C.2118/12.

Army Form C. 2118.

WAR DIARY
or
~~INTELLIGENCE~~ SUMMARY

(2)

Instructions regarding War Diaries and Intelligence Summaries are contained in F. S. Regs., Part II. and the Staff Manual respectively. Title Pages will be prepared in manuscript.

March 1917 –

(Erase heading not required.)

Map Reference:– Sheet 27.

Place	Date	Hour	Summary of Events and Information	Remarks and references to Appendices
STEENVOORDE	4·3·17	9 A.M.	Headquarters of unit transferred to MONT DES CATS, R 19.b.7.5½, where the Second Army Rest Station in the CONVENT DES TRAPPISTES was taken over from the NORTH MIDLAND CCS – Lieut & Qmr R. COX RAMC reported for duty at 12 NOON and is taken on the strength of the Field Ambulance from today's date – Ten officers and 243 O.R taken over as patients in the Army Rest Station, of which equipment as required proceeded during the day –	AAh
MONT DES CATS	5·3·17	10 A.M.	Snowing – a fair amount of snow has fallen during the night – Indents for Ordnance Stores required to equip the Army Rest Station submitted for approval – Lt & Qm J. FLINT. RAMC proceeded to the 38 Div for duty –	AAh
"	6·3·17	10 A.M.	Milder weather – Daily inspection – A.D.M.S. 39 Div: visited the Fd: Amb: at STEENVOORDE and the Army Rest Station during the afternoon –	AAh
"	7·3·17	10 A.M.	Very cold East wind – Daily inspection –	AAh
"	8·3·17	10 A.M.	Considerable fall of snow during the night – The accomodation at	

2449 Wt. W14957/M90 750,000 1/16 J.B.C. & A. Forms/C.2118/12.

Instructions regarding War Diaries and Intelligence Summaries are contained in F. S. Regs., Part II. and the Staff Manual respectively. Title Pages will be prepared in manuscript.

WAR DIARY
or
~~INTELLIGENCE SUMMARY~~
(Erase heading not required.)

Army Form C. 2118.

132nd FIELD AMBULANCE * 1 APR 1917 *

March 1917 – (3) Map Reference :– Sheet 27.

Place	Date	Hour	Summary of Events and Information	Remarks and references to Appendices
MONT DES CATS.	8.3.17		STEENVOORDE has been reorganised and now has 95 beds available: fire buckets have now been provided for all wards & billets, the ground at the back of the Fld Amb. levelled up with a view to future use: materials were drawn from the R.E. Park yesterday and good progress made in the construction of a meat store, whilst increased Pack Store accommodation needed will be provided by utilising the cellar underneath the house for this purpose – Lieut. C.H.L. RIXON. RAMC rejoined the Fld. Amb. and is taken on the strength of the unit from todays date –	A.H.
"	9.3.17	9 A.M.	Brilliant sunshine, snow & ice are still lying about – Considerable improvement in the general appearance of the A.R.S. site at MONT DES CATS: Ordnance indents from Ordnance & British Red Cross Society are awaited – Outside Kitchen has had good cover erected over it –	A.H.
"	10.3.17	9 A.M.	Snowing; a considerable amount of snow has fallen during the night –	A.H.
"	11.3.17	9 A.M	Mild weather, snow has all melted – DADMS visited the A.R.S. during the afternoon –	A.H.

2449 Wt. W14957/M90 750,000 1/16 J.B.C. & A. Forms/C.2118/12.

Instructions regarding War Diaries and Intelligence Summaries are contained in F. S. Regs., Part II. and the Staff Manual respectively. Title Pages will be prepared in manuscript.

WAR DIARY
or
~~INTELLIGENCE SUMMARY~~
(Erase heading not required.)

March 1917 –

(4)

Map Reference :— Sheet 27.

Army Form C. 2118.

Place	Date	Hour	Summary of Events and Information	Remarks and references to Appendices
MONT DES CATS.	12.3.17	9AM.	Mild weather – Visited STEENVOORDE during the afternoon and found everything in good order at the Rest Amb Site in charge of Captain J. MORRIS. RAMC (TF) – A capital meat store has now been completed near the Kitchen –	AH
"	13.3.17	10AM.	Mild weather continues – Daily inspection – Arrangements are working satisfactorily, but equipment of all sorts on indent is still awaited, which will improve the arrangements when received – The Officers ward has been rendered more comfortable by the provision of new chairs, crockery, bedspreads etc received from the British Red Cross Society –	AH
"	14.3.17	10AM.	Mild weather, cloudy – At STEENVOORDE, additional shelves have been completed in the Dispensary, whilst good progress has been made in the construction of a larger Pack Store – In the Officers Hpl at MONT DES CATS a cooking range is being placed in the Kitchen which will enable the food for the Officers to be cooked next door to their mess room, instead of it having to be carried a considerable distance from the main Kitchen –	AH

Army Form C. 2118.

Instructions regarding War Diaries and Intelligence Summaries are contained in F. S. Regs., Part II. and the Staff Manual respectively. Title Pages will be prepared in manuscript.

WAR DIARY
or
~~INTELLIGENCE~~ SUMMARY
(Erase heading not required.)

March 1917 – (6.) Map Reference:– Sheet 27 –

Place	Date	Hour	Summary of Events and Information	Remarks and references to Appendices
MONT DES CATS	15.3.17	10AM.	Mild weather continues – Work on improvements at STEENVOORDE continued, also at MONT DES CATS – Divisional Routine Order No: 682 of 14/3/17 contains the following:– HIS MAJESTY the KING of ITALY has awarded the following decoration to the undermentioned man:– BRONZE MEDAL for MILITARY VALOUR No: 65867 Pte. H. EVERALL. 132nd Field Ambulance –	AH.
"	16.3.17	10AM.	Slight frost during the night: fine morning: at 10.45 A.M. the DDMS visited the 2nd Army Rest Station & inspected same – New cooking range in the Officers' Hospital is now completed –	AH.
"	17.3.17	10AM.	Bright sunshine – Lt R.N. WALKER RAMC reported at 4 P.M. for temporary duty –	AH.
"	18.3.17	10AM.	Bright weather continues – Capt. GATCHELL RAMC reported for temporary duty in charge at STEENVOORDE –	AH.
"	20.3.17	10AM.	Stormy weather with some snow – Good progress has now been made with the new Pack Store at STEENVOORDE, which is now almost complete – At MONT DES CATS, a lot of progress has been made in the outside Kitchen & butcher's shop –	AH.

2449 Wt. W14957/M90 750,000 1/16 J.B.C. & A. Forms/C.2118/12.

Army Form C. 2118.

Instructions regarding War Diaries and Intelligence Summaries are contained in F. S. Regs., Part II. and the Staff Manual respectively. Title Pages will be prepared in manuscript.

WAR DIARY
or
INTELLIGENCE SUMMARY
(Erase heading not required.)

(6)

March 1917 — Map Reference :— Sheet 27 —

Place	Date	Hour	Summary of Events and Information	Remarks and references to Appendices
MONT DES CATS	21.3.17	10 A.M.	Snow has fallen & covered the ground, but is melting in the sunshine. At 2.30 P.M. attended a conference at the office of the A.D.M.S; afterwards proceeding to STEENVOORDE, where everything was in good order. The new pack store there has been completed & is good, a new drier range constructed whilst a field oven is also being built.	AHL
"	22.3.17	10 A.M.	More snow has fallen. Daily inspection. Outside kitchen is now almost complete; Latrines have now been covered in also: Isolation tent much improved.	AHL
"	23.3.17	10 A.M.	More snow & some frost during the night. Visited STEENVOORDE at 5 P.M. and found everything in good order. The D.D.M.S. X Corps had visited the site during the morning.	AHL
"	24.3.17	10 A.M.	Frost during the night. Daily inspection.	AHL
"	25.3.17	10 A.M.	Bright morning, a good deal warmer. VIDINAGE apparatus arrived at 10.15 A.M. to empty septic tanks at A.R.S. Work carried on all day & not completed. D.A.D.M.S. 2nd Army visited the A.R.S. at 4.30 P.M.	AHL

2449 Wt. W14957/M90 750,000 1/16 J.B.C. & A. Forms/C.2118/12.

Army Form C. 2118.

Instructions regarding War Diaries and Intelligence Summaries are contained in F. S. Regs., Part II. and the Staff Manual respectively. Title Pages will be prepared in manuscript.

WAR DIARY
or
INTELLIGENCE SUMMARY

(Erase heading not required.)

March 1917 — Map Reference — Sheet 27 —

Place	Date	Hour	Summary of Events and Information	Remarks and references to Appendices
MONT DES CATS	26.3.17	10 AM.	Raining, cold high wind – Emptying of septic tanks completed –	AH.
"	27.3.17	10 AM	Some more snow, very cold wind – Good progress made with the alteration of latrines to make them fly proof – Repainting of Transport wagons of unit is being completed as fast as possible, as paint is received –	
"	28.3.17	10 AM	Bright sunshine; warmer – Work in hand progressing well –	AH.
"	29.3.17	10 AM	Raining – Daily inspection – Good progress in the latrines construction, also provision of bath room for officers – Lieut. R.N. WALKER RAMC returned to 134 Fd. Amb. – Good progress made in repainting of wagons –	AH.
"	30.3.17	10 AM	Bright sunshine, warmer – Ordnance Stores required for the Army Rest Station began to arrive today – Other work progressing –	AH.
"	31.3.17	10 AM	Fine morning – Daily inspection – At 4 PM the Divisional Commander visited MONT DES CATS and inspected the 2nd Army Rest Station, and before leaving expressed his pleasure at all he had seen –	

2449 Wt. W14957/M90 750,000 1/16 J.B.C. & A. Forms/C.2118/12.

Instructions regarding War Diaries and Intelligence Summaries are contained in F. S. Regs., Part II. and the Staff Manual respectively. Title Pages will be prepared in manuscript.

WAR DIARY
or
INTELLIGENCE SUMMARY

(Erase heading not required.)

March 1917.

(8)

Army Form C. 2118.

Map Reference — Sheet 27.

Place	Date	Hour	Summary of Events and Information	Remarks and references to Appendices
MONT DES CATS	31.3.17		Cases dealt with during the month were as follows:—	
			(1) STEENVOORDE. Officers 20.	
			Other Ranks 375.	
			(2) MONT DES CATS. Officers 49.	
			Other Ranks 1442.	AW

A Whittingham
Lt Col
R.A.M.C.
O.C. 132nd FIELD AMBULANCE.

2449 Wt. W14957/M90 750,000 1/16 J.B.C. & A. Forms/C.2118/12.

ORIGINAL.

Vol 14

Confidential

War Diary

— of —

132nd Field Ambulance R.A.M.C

from April 1st 1917 to April 30th 1917

(Volume II.)

April 1917

ORIGINAL

Army Form C. 2118.

Instructions regarding War Diaries and Intelligence Summaries are contained in F. S. Regs., Part II. and the Staff Manual respectively. Title Pages will be prepared in manuscript.

WAR DIARY
or
INTELLIGENCE SUMMARY

(Erase heading not required.)

April 1917 — (1) — Map Reference — Sheet 27

132nd FIELD AMBULANCE * 1 MAY. 1917 *

Place	Date	Hour	Summary of Events and Information	Remarks and references to Appendices
MONT DES CATS	1.4.17	10 A.M.	Fine morning, bright but cold — Showers of hail & snow during the course of the day — At 12.30 P.M. I visited STEENVOORDE and found the Fld. Amb. site in good order — At 5 P.M. the D.M.S. Second Army visited the Army Rest Station and inspected it —	A.H.
"	2.4.17	11 A.M.	A good deal of snow has fallen during the night, and there is a cold wind blowing — Daily inspection — Good progress being made with all work in hand, also in repainting of wagons —	A.H.
"	3.4.17	10 A.M.	Much snow has fallen during the night, there being several inches on the ground this morning, but most of this has melted during the day. Capt: GATCHELL RAMC left during the evening to proceed to the 11th Royal Sussex Regt in accordance with instructions received from ADMS.	A.H.
"	4.4.17	11 A.M.	Milder, but some sleet mixed with rain falling — Visited STEENVOORDE & found all in good order — Good progress in repainting of wagons —	A.H.

2449 Wt. W14957/M90 750,000 1/16 J.B.C. & A. Forms/C.2118/12.

Instructions regarding War Diaries and Intelligence Summaries are contained in F. S. Regs., Part II. and the Staff Manual respectively. Title Pages will be prepared in manuscript.

WAR DIARY
or
~~INTELLIGENCE SUMMARY~~
(Erase heading not required.)

Army Form C. 2118.

(2)

April 1917 –

Map Reference :– Sheet 27

Place	Date	Hour	Summary of Events and Information	Remarks and references to Appendices
MONT DES CATS	5.4.17.	9 AM.	Bright sunshiny morning – Daily inspection – Fly proof latrines are now nearly completed, whilst the outside Kitchen has been improved by replastering the field ovens + instalment of six additional Soyer Stoves – New incinerator at STEEN VOORDE is reported completed by the Officer in charge there – and all transport wagons repainted except two horse ambulance wagons –	AHL.
"	6.4.17.	9 A.M.	Bright sunshiny morning – Daily inspection – Latrines here now been converted completely + are flyproof + of excellent type – At 10.45 A.M. Capt. J. D. MACKINNON reported his departure for duty with the 47th Division + is struck off the strength of the unit from todays date –	AHL.
"	7.4.17.	10 A.M.	Some snow through the night, followed by bright cold morning – Daily inspection, everything in good order – A concert was given in the evening from 6 P.M. to 8.15 P.M. –	AHL.
"	8.4.17.	10 A.M.	Fine weather all day – The D.D.M.S. VIII Corps and Consulting Physician to the Second Army visited the Army Rest Station during the afternoon –	AHL.

Instructions regarding War Diaries and Intelligence Summaries are contained in F. S. Regs., Part II. and the Staff Manual respectively. Title Pages will be prepared in manuscript.

WAR DIARY
or
~~INTELLIGENCE~~ SUMMARY
(Erase heading not required.)

Army Form C. 2118.

(3)

April 1917 — Map Reference — Sheet 27 —

Place	Date	Hour	Summary of Events and Information	Remarks and references to Appendices
MONT DES CATS	9.4.17	10 AM	Cold morning — some rain sleet + snow — Captain CHL. RIXON. RAMC. left in the evening to take over medical charge of the 16th Rifle Brigade — and is struck off the strength from this date —	A.h.
"	10.4.17	10 AM	More snow — Captain BOLT RAMC. reported his arrival for duty, + is taken off the strength from todays date: he proceeded forthwith to take over temporary medical charge of three batteries at WATOU —	A.h.
"	11.4.17	10 AM	Weather still cold + some snow showers —	A.h.
"	12.4.17	10 AM	No change in the weather conditions — Conference held at 3.30 PM at which X Corps scheme was discussed —	A.h.
"	13.4.17	10 AM	Orders received to hold unit in readiness to move at 48 hours notice — Visited STEENVOORDE + met the A.D.M.S who was inspecting the Fld Amb. site there, + expressed his satisfaction at improvements effected there —	A.h.
"	14.4.17	10 AM	Bright cold morning — All transport has now been repainted and the the construction of new dining hall for patients at STEENVOORDE is now almost completed — Having been notified at 3.30 P.M. that	

Instructions regarding War Diaries and Intelligence Summaries are contained in F. S. Regs., Part II. and the Staff Manual respectively. Title Pages will be prepared in manuscript.

WAR DIARY
or
~~INTELLIGENCE SUMMARY~~

(Erase heading not required.)

April 1917. (4) Map Reference:– Sheet 27.

Army Form C. 2118.

Place	Date	Hour	Summary of Events and Information	Remarks and references to Appendices
MONT DES CATS	14.4.17.	3.30PM	The unit will lathe over the D.R.S. at PROVEN (F7.b.5.5) on 16th inst. I visited PROVEN & made arrangements re despatch of an Advance Party on the 15th. Advance party from 69th Fd Amb. arrived at MONT DES CATS during the day.	A.L.
MONT DES CATS	15.4.17.	6AM.	Dull wet day. Remainder of 69th Fd. Ambs personnel arrived at MONT DES CATS to take over Second Army Rest Station. Advance party proceeded to PROVEN to take over Divisional Rest Station at F7.b.5.5.	A.L.
MONT DES CATS	16.4.17	6AM	69th ~~Fd Amb~~ took over the Second Army Rest Station, & personnel of 132nd Field Ambulance proceeded during the morning to PROVEN. The Fd. Amb. Site at STEENVOORDE was handed over to 69th ~~Fd Amb~~ at 8AM, and on relief unit marched at 9AM. to PROVEN which was reached at Noon. D.R.S. at F7.b.5.5 taken over from 129th Fd. Amb at 8.30 AM. by our Advance party. All 39 Division patients transferred to PROVEN.	A.L.
PROVEN.	17.4.17	10AM.	Wet day. Equipment of D.R.S. proceeding. At 3.30 PM. attended Conference of DDMS. The ADMS visited PROVEN after this meeting.	A.L.

Army Form C. 2118.

WAR DIARY
or
INTELLIGENCE SUMMARY

(6)

(Erase heading not required.)

Instructions regarding War Diaries and Intelligence Summaries are contained in F. S. Regs., Part II. and the Staff Manual respectively. Title Pages will be prepared in manuscript.

April 1917. MAP Reference - Sheet 27

Place	Date	Hour	Summary of Events and Information	Remarks and references to Appendices
PROVEN.	18-IV-17	5. P.M.	Very cold morning - ground covered with snow. Capt W. M. CHRISTIE RAMC detailed by A.D.M.S. 39th Div to act as Sanitary Officer of PROVEN. Instructions received from A.D.M.S 39th Div to increase D.R.S. accomodation to 200 beds, and Field Ambulance Hospital accomodation to 100 beds. Partial reconstruction of Cook house at Horselines commenced. Work of fitting seats - fly proof - to top of latrine pails continued.	JHH
"	19-IV-17	6 P.M.	Very cold morning with sleet & rain. Necessary accomodation in D.R.S and Field Ambulance obtained by putting personel from 2 D.R.S. wards into billets in the village, and removing Sgts Mess from Marquee to billet in the village, and the erection of 3 bell tents & one Operating tent. Considerable progress made with reconstruction of Cookhouse at A.S.C. billet and construction of Dressing room in the D.R.S. Indent for Blankets, Soyer stoves and Palliasses for extra accomodation sent in to A.D.M.S for approval.	JHH
"	20-IV-17	6 P.M.	Cold morning but dry. Fair amount of sunshine during the day. Visit of inspection by A.D.M.S. at NOON. Dressing Room completed, and ready for use tomorrow morning. Clothing Inspection of Personel. Indented for 40 Bedsteads iron, as instructed by A.D.M.S. this morning for use in large NISSEN hut.	JHH

2449 Wt. W14957/M90 750,000 1/16 J.B.C. & A. Forms/C.2118/12.

Instructions regarding War Diaries and Intelligence Summaries are contained in F. S. Regs., Part II. and the Staff Manual respectively. Title Pages will be prepared in manuscript.

WAR DIARY
or
INTELLIGENCE SUMMARY

(Erase heading not required.)

April 1917. (6) MAP Reference – Sheet 27.

Army Form C. 2118.

132nd F[ield Amb]ULANCE 1 MAY. 1917

Place	Date	Hour	Summary of Events and Information	Remarks and references to Appendices
PROVEN.	21-IV-17	6. P.M.	Weather cold, but dry – very little sunshine. At noon, visited by Consulting Physician 2nd Army. Cookhouse at A.S.C. billet completed, and put into use this afternoon. All patients interrogated (ADMS's letter D31 dated 19-IV-17) with reference to supply & efficiency of clothing during winter months. Result in affirmative. Held kit inspection this afternoon.	JHB.
"	23-IV-17	6 P.M.	Milder – very fine day, sunshine throughout. About 6 A.M. Gas Attack by the enemy. several cases of "slightly gassed" among 1st L.H.Y. about F 13 a. No cases have been reported in PROVEN. Tent pitching practice this morning.	JHB.
"	24-IV-17	5. P.M.	Fine sunshine all day, but wind very cold again. None of the eight gassed cases, – all of 1st LHY. – were admitted to Hospital – All progressing very satisfactorily – Resting in their billets. Tent pitching practice again today.	JHB
"	26-IV-17	6. P.M.	Dull day, very little sunshine, again very cold. Gassed cases better, and fit for duty tomorrow. Work of making latrine seats to fit top of latrine pails, stopped during the last 3 days for lack of material	JHB
"	27-IV-17	5. P.M.	Much milder. Sunshine nearly all day. It now appears that the gas which caused slight casualties on the 23 as above was liberated by the Enemy at NIEVPORT.	JHB
"	28-IV-17	6 P.M.	First warm Spring day. Bright sunshine throughout	

Instructions regarding War Diaries and Intelligence Summaries are contained in F. S. Regs., Part II. and the Staff Manual respectively. Title Pages will be prepared in manuscript.

WAR DIARY
or
INTELLIGENCE SUMMARY
(Erase heading not required.)

Army Form C. 2118.

April 1917 (7) — Map Reference — Sheet 27

Place	Date	Hour	Summary of Events and Information	Remarks and references to Appendices
PREVEN	[illegible]		Fine weather. Daily inspection — Cases dealt with during the month were as follows :—	
			Admissions —	
			A. 132nd Field Ambulance. Sick. Officers 4. O.R. 348 –	
			Officers / Other Ranks.	
			B. 2nd Army Rest Station – { Sick. 6 635 –	
			Wounded. 1 12 –	
			C. 39th Divisional Rest Station – { Sick Nil. 338 –	
			Wounded. Nil. 4 –	
			Totals. Officers. 11. Other Ranks. 1337 –	
			R. Whittyjohns – Lt Col – R.A.M.C. O.C. 132nd FIELD AMBULANCE.	

SECRET.

ORIGINAL.

Vol 15

140/2/61

Confidential

War Diary

of

132nd Field Ambulance

From May 1st 1917 to May 31st 1917

(Volume 2)

May 1917

ORIGINAL –

Instructions regarding War Diaries and Intelligence Summaries are contained in F. S. Regs., Part II. and the Staff Manual respectively. Title Pages will be prepared in manuscript.

WAR DIARY
or
INTELLIGENCE SUMMARY
(Erase heading not required.)

Army Form C. 2118.

MAY 1917 –

(1) Vol

Map Reference — Sheet 27

Place	Date	Hour	Summary of Events and Information	Remarks and references to Appendices
PROVEN	1/5/17	11 AM	Beautiful weather sunshine & clear sky – Daily inspection – Lieut G.E. DOWNS RAMC (T.C) reported his arrival at 3.30 PM and is taken on the strength of the unit from to-days date –	A.L.
"	2/5/17	10 AM	Fine weather continues – Daily inspection – Lieut E.P. CARMODY RAMC (T.C) reported his arrival during the afternoon & is taken on the strength of the Field Ambulance from this date –	A.L.
"	3/5/17	11 AM	Fine weather continues – Daily inspection – ADMS's approval obtained for the holding of a Sports meeting on the 9th inst, weather and other circumstances permitting – At 11 PM signal of "gas alert" received all patients & personnel roused at once, & helmets & box respirators placed in the alert position: message received at 12.15 AM false alarm –	A.L.
"	4/5/17	10 AM	Fine weather continues – Daily inspection – All Officers who could be spared attended the meeting of the Second Army Medical Society during the afternoon –	A.L.
"	5/5/17	10 AM	Fine weather continues – Daily inspection – Lecture to new Officers on Medical Organisation at 6 PM –	A.L.

2449 Wt. W14957/M90 750,000 1/16 J.B.C. & A. Forms/C.2118/12.

Instructions regarding War Diaries and Intelligence Summaries are contained in F. S. Regs., Part II. and the Staff Manual respectively. Title Pages will be prepared in manuscript.

WAR DIARY
or
INTELLIGENCE SUMMARY
(Erase heading not required.)

Army Form C. 2118.

MAY 1917 ② Map Reference — Sheet 27

Place	Date	Hour	Summary of Events and Information	Remarks and references to Appendices
PROVEN.	6/5/17.	9.30 AM.	High wind blowing, much dust, but fine weather — Sunday parade service — Daily inspection — warning message re GAS received 10 P.M.; all precautions taken —	A.H.
"	7/5/17	10 A.M.	Fine weather continues — visited STEENVOORDE at 11 AM —	A.H.
"	8/5/17	10 A.M.	Weather dull + cool — daily inspection — attended Conference at office of A.D.M.S. at 3 P.M., returning to headquarters of unit at 6 P.M. —	A.H.
"	9/5/17	9.30 A.M.	Beautiful day — Daily inspection — Sports meeting held during the afternoon the A.D.M.S. arrived at 2 P.M. and officiated as Chief Judge; the other judges in the inter-Field Ambulance transport competition being the A.D.V.S. + O.C. Divl Train: the unit was awarded 1st for the G.S + water cart turn outs, 2nd for the riding pony, and 3rd for the ambulance wagon turn out — Of the open flat events the quarter mile fell to the unit, the 100 yds to 4 M.A.C., and the ½ mile + mile to 46 C.C.S — There was a large attendance at a very good afternoon sport, which included the D.D.M.S. VIII Corps —	A.H.
"	10.5.17	9.30 A.M.	Beautiful weather continues — daily inspection — Captain W. M. CHRISTIE R.A.M.C. admitted to hospital — attended Conference of D.D.M.S. VIII Corps at 3.30 P.M. —	A.H.
"	11.5.17	9.30 A.M.	Fine + very hot weather continues — daily inspection — All officers who	

2449 Wt. W14957/M90 750,000 1/16 J.B.C. & A. Forms/C.2118/12.

Army Form C. 2118.

Instructions regarding War Diaries and Intelligence Summaries are contained in F. S. Regs., Part II. and the Staff Manual respectively. Title Pages will be prepared in manuscript.

WAR DIARY
or
~~INTELLIGENCE SUMMARY~~
(Erase heading not required.)

May. 1917. (3) Map Reference:— Sheet 27.

Place	Date	Hour	Summary of Events and Information	Remarks and references to Appendices
PROVEN.	11.5.17		Could be spared attend meeting of Second Army Medical Society at 3 PM.	AL
〃	12.5.17	9 A.M.	Lieut. G.E. DOWNS. RAMC. attended 2nd Div. Artillery Course. Very hot & dry weather continues. Conference held at 5.30 PM at which all points raised at recent conferences of ADMS & DDMS were discussed.	AL
〃	13.5.17	9 AM	Hot dry weather continues. Sunday parade service held at 9.30 AM.	AL
〃	14.5.17	10 AM	Weather hot & close, some rain during the night. Daily inspection.	AL
〃	15.5.17	10 AM	Weather cooler. Slight fall of rain. Cookhouse whitewashed in & out.	AL
〃	16.5.17	10 AM	Cold day. Daily inspection. Visited ADMS in the afternoon. Heavy rain fell towards evening.	AL
〃	17.5.17	10 AM	Heavy rain throughout the night, which continues this morning. Very much needed. Daily inspection. Lecture given to new Officers on Correspondence & Field Messages, reading of squared maps, diaries, and traffic regulation.	AL

2449 Wt. W14957/M90 750,000 1/16 J.B.C. & A. Forms/C.2118/12.

Army Form C. 2118.

WAR DIARY
or
~~INTELLIGENCE SUMMARY~~
(Erase heading not required.)

Instructions regarding War Diaries and Intelligence Summaries are contained in F. S. Regs., Part II. and the Staff Manual respectively. Title Pages will be prepared in manuscript.

MAY 1917.

(4)

Map Reference — Sheet 27.

Place	Date	Hour	Summary of Events and Information	Remarks and references to Appendices
PROVEN.	18.5.17	10AM	Beautiful weather – Interviewed several candidates for temporary Commissions in the Infantry. During the afternoon all Officers who could be spared attended the meeting of the Second Army Medical Society.	AHL
	19.5.17	10AM	Dullish weather. Daily inspection, arrangements working satisfactorily. Flowers & vegetables in the D.R.S. doing very well.	AHL
	20.5.17	9.30AM	Beautiful weather. Sunday – parade service.	AHL
	21.5.17	10AM	Fine weather continues – Lieut. J. STEEL RAMC (S.R.) proceeded to take over medical charge of the 13th R. SUSSEX. Left at 1.45 PM. At 4PM Captain J. MORRIS RAMC (T.F.) left for WORMHOUDT to take over temporary command of a Section of 134 Field Ambulance.	AHL
	22.5.17	10AM	Raining hard. Daily inspection – Good progress has been made in staining tents with logwood. At 2.45 PM the A.D.M.S. visited and inspected the D.R.S.	AHL
	23.5.17	10AM	Fine weather. Instruction to newly joined Officers on R.O. A.F. returns, and how supplies of every kind are indented for & obtained.	AHL

2449 Wt. W14957/M90 750,000 1/16 J.B.C. & A. Forms/C.2118/12.

Instructions regarding War Diaries and Intelligence Summaries are contained in F. S. Regs., Part II. and the Staff Manual respectively. Title Pages will be prepared in manuscript.

MAY 1917.

WAR DIARY
or
~~INTELLIGENCE SUMMARY~~
(Erase heading not required.)

(5)

Map Reference – Sheet 27.

Army Form C. 2118.

Place	Date	Hour	Summary of Events and Information	Remarks and references to Appendices
PROVEN.	24.5.17	9.30AM	Heavy rain during the night: beautiful fresh morning. – Daily inspection. – Lieut. J STEEL RAMC (S.R.) rejoined from temporary medical charge of the 13th R. SUSSEX Regt. – Instruction to new Officers on water testing apparatus, and Fld. Amb. panniers. –	A.H.
"	25.5.17	9.30AM	Beautiful weather. – Daily inspection. – Repainting of transport wagons being carried out. –	A.H.
"	26.5.17	9.30AM	Fine weather continues. – Daily inspection. – Two men from 187 Labour Coy are attached for training in first aid & water duties respectively. – Open air concert for patients held in the evening. –	A.H.
"	27.5.17	9.30AM	Fine weather. – Very hot. – Sunday, parade service held. – Daily inspection. –	A.H.
"	28.5.17	2.40AM	"WIND DANGEROUS" message received. – All patients & personnel aroused, box respirators etc in the Alert Position. – Message proved to be a false alarm. – Fine weather continues. – Daily inspection. – Instruction to new Officers on duties of Regimental Medical Officer. – Captain W.M. CHRISTIE RAMC. rejoined from hospital on discharge. –	A.H.
"	29.5.17	9.30AM	Dull & cool morning. – Daily inspection. – Further instruction to Officers on duties of R.M.O. – Captain J. MORRIS RAMC (T.F.) rejoined from temporary duty with 134 Fld. Amb. –	A.H.

2449 Wt. W14957/M90 750,000 1/16 J.B.C. & A. Forms/C.2118/12.

Army Form C. 2118.

Instructions regarding War Diaries and Intelligence Summaries are contained in F. S. Regs., Part II. and the Staff Manual respectively. Title Pages will be prepared in manuscript.

WAR DIARY
or
~~INTELLIGENCE SUMMARY~~

(Erase heading not required.)

May 1917 — (6) Map Reference — Sheet 27

Place	Date	Hour	Summary of Events and Information	Remarks and references to Appendices
PROVEN.	30.5.17	9.30 AM	Dull cool morning — Daily inspection — The following are Extracts from the London Gazette:— (1) London Gazette 28/5/17 — Award of the Bronze Medal for Military Valour (Italian) to No: 66867 Pte. H. EVERALL. RAMC — (2) London Gazette, 29/5/17 — Mentioned in Despatches — No: 38943. Sgt. Major B. G. SHARPE. RAMC —	Akh
"	31.5.17	9.30 AM	Fine weather — Daily inspection — Everything in good order — Cases dealt with during the month were as follows —	
			Officers — Other Ranks	
			Sick 8 — 840 —	
			Wounded — — 5 —	Akh

A Whittlepshire (?) Lt Col. —
O.C. 132nd FIELD AMBULANCE. R.A.M.C.

ORIGINAL.

Vol 16

140/2230

Confidential

War Diary

— of —

132nd Field Ambulance

From June 1st 1917 to June 30th 1917

(Volume II.)

6

June 1917

B.E.F.

SUMMARY OF MEDICAL WAR DIARIES of 132nd F.A. 39th Div.

18th Corps. 5th ARMY.

Western Front Operations - June 1917.

Officer Commanding - Lt.Col. A. Littlejohns.

SUMMARISEB UNDER THE FOLLOWING HEADING :-

Phase "D" - Battle of Messines. June 1917.

132nd F.A. 39th Div. 18th Corps. 5th ARMY. Western Front
June 1917.

O.C. = Lt.Col. A. Littlejohns.

PHASE "D". - Battle of Messines. June 1917.

Headquarters at Proven D.R.S.

June 10th. Transfer. To 5th ARMY.

19th. Medical Arrangements. D.R.S. site dismantled.

21st. Moves. To Herzeele.

Ops. R.A.M.C. Work on site of C.R.S. at D.9.d.8.8.

27th. Moves. Detachment. 1 & 47 to 133rd F.A.

30th. Casualties. Total for month.

Admitted to 132nd F.A.	6 & 270 sick.	0 & 1 W.
" " D.R.S.	0 & 275 "	0 & 17 W.

B.E.F.

SUMMARY OF MEDICAL WAR DIARIES of 132nd F.A. 39th Div.

18th Corps. 5th ARMY.

Western Front Operations - June 1917.

Officer Commanding - Lt.Col. A. Littlejohns.

SUMMARISED UNDER THE FOLLOWING HEADING :-

Phase "D" - Battle of Messines. June 1917.

132nd F.A. 39th Div. 18th Corps. 5th ARMY. Western Front June 1917.

O.C. = Lt.Col. A. Littlejohns.

PHASE "D". - Battle of Messines. June 1917.

Headquarters at Proven D.R.S.

June 10th.	Transfer. To 5th ARMY.
19th.	Medical Arrangements. D.R.S. site dismantled.
21st.	Moves. To Herzeele.
	Ops. R.A.M.C. Work on site of C.R.S. at D.9.d.8.8.
27th.	Moves. Detachment. 1 & 47 to 133rd F.A.
30th.	Casualties. Total for month.

Admitted to 132nd F.A.	6 & 270 sick.	0 & 1 W.
" " D.R.S.	0 & 275 "	0 & 17 W.

Secret. ORIGINAL.

Instructions regarding War Diaries and Intelligence Summaries are contained in F. S. Regs., Part II. and the Staff Manual respectively. Title Pages will be prepared in manuscript.

WAR DIARY
or
~~INTELLIGENCE SUMMARY~~
(Erase heading not required.)

Army Form C. 2118.

June. 1917.

(1)

Map Reference:- Sheet 27

Place	Date	Hour	Summary of Events and Information	Remarks and references to Appendices
PROVEN	1.6.17	9.30 AM	Beautiful weather - Daily inspection - Lieut E P CARMODY RAMC left at 9.30 AM to report to O.C 134 Field Ambulance for a course of instruction at DUHALLON A.D.S. in forward area work -	AH
"	2.6.17	9.30 AM	Fine weather continues - Daily inspection - Lt + Qm. R. COX. RAMC rejoined the Field Ambulance during the afternoon from MONT DES CATS.	AH
"	3.6.17	9.30 AM	Fine weather, with nice cool breeze - Sunday; parade service held at 9.30 AM - Daily inspection -	AH
"	4.6.17	9.30 AM	Fine weather continues - The A.D.M.S. visited the Field Ambulance to inspect two men as to temporary unfitness for Front line work -	AH
"	5.6.17	9.30 AM	Extremely hot weather continues - Orders received at 6 PM. for Lieut. J. STEEL RAMC (SR) to proceed to take over ~~temporary~~ medical charge of the 1/6 Cheshire Regt tomorrow morning -	AH

2449 Wt. W14957/M90 750,000 1/16 J.B.C. & A. Forms/C.2118/12.

Instructions regarding War Diaries and Intelligence Summaries are contained in F. S. Regs., Part II. and the Staff Manual respectively. Title Pages will be prepared in manuscript.

WAR DIARY
or
INTELLIGENCE SUMMARY
(Erase heading not required.)

Army Form C. 2118.

JUNE. 1917.

(2)

Map Reference – Sheet 27

Place	Date	Hour	Summary of Events and Information	Remarks and references to Appendices
PROVEN.	6.6.17.	2 A.M.	"Wind dangerous" received from Town Major – All patients & personnel roused, & gas appliances in Alert position – Hot, fine weather continues – Lieut. J. STEEL. RAMC (SR) left at 10.15 AM to take over temporary medical charge of 1/6 Cheshire Regt. – Daily inspection: everything in good order: Mark V Water Tank received to replace one being returned to Base for repairs – A little rain fell during the evening –	A.H.
"	7.6.17	9.30 AM.	Very hot weather. Daily inspection – The A.D.M.S. visited the unit at about 6 P.M. – Heavy shower of rain during the evening –	A.H.
"	8.6.17	7.30 AM.	Captain W.M. CHRISTIE. RAMC. proceeded to 133 Fld. Amb. for temporary duty – Very hot weather continues – Captain W.M. CHRISTIE. RAMC returned from 133 Fld Amb. at noon, and Lieut. E.P. DOWNS. RAMC left for a course of instruction in forward area work at ESSEX FARM ADS at 2.15 PM –	A.H.
"	9.6.17	9.30 AM.	Fine weather, a little cooler – In the afternoon the 39th Divisional Field Ambulance Sports were held, and a very successful meeting ensued: the 132nd Field Ambulance secured the A.D.M.S. Championship Shield –	A.H.
"	10.6.17	9.30 AM.	Nice cool morning – at 12.45 PM Captain J. MORRIS. M.C. left for WORMHOUDT, in accordance with instructions received from the A.D.M.S., to take over charge of a section of 134 Field Ambulance –	A.H.

2449 Wt. W14957/M90 750,000 1/16 J.B.C. & A. Forms/C.2118/12.

132nd FIELD AMBULANCE 11/6/17.

Instructions regarding War Diaries and Intelligence Summaries are contained in F. S. Regs., Part II. and the Staff Manual respectively. Title Pages will be prepared in manuscript.

WAR DIARY
or
INTELLIGENCE SUMMARY
(Erase heading not required.)

June - 1917 - (3) Map Reference - Sheet 27 -

Army Form C. 2118.

Place	Date	Hour	Summary of Events and Information	Remarks and references to Appendices
PROVEN -	11.6.17	9.30 AM	Nice cool morning: rain has fallen through the night & continues at intervals - At 10 AM a Medical Board assembled to examine men attached to 29th Divl Train -	ARL.
"	12.6.17	9.30 AM	Fine weather - very hot - Daily inspection - Visited farm at D18 b 2½ 8 at 3 PM with a view to its suitability for a Rest Station - Party of twelve (Tent subdivision) personnel detailed for temporary duty at 12 CCS at 5.30 PM -	ARL.
"	13.6.17	9.30 AM	Very hot weather - Small holding party sent to farm at D18 b 2½ 8 - At 1.30 PM orders received to supply working party at Railhead: this party was employed until 10.45 PM - At 6 PM orders were received to commence dismantling immediately all huts not urgently required in the D.R.S., site of which is required for another purpose - Good progress made in this work -	ARL.
"	14.6.17	9 AM	Hot dry weather continues - Four Nissen huts and one mud hut dismantled patients being placed in the dining halls for accommodation - Lieut E.P. CARMODY RAMC took over medical charge of the 12th Herts Rgt.	ARL.

2449 Wt. W14957/M90 750,000 1/16 J.B.C. & A. Forms/C.2118/12.

Army Form C. 2118.

Instructions regarding War Diaries and Intelligence Summaries are contained in F. S. Regs., Part II. and the Staff Manual respectively. Title Pages will be prepared in manuscript.

WAR DIARY
or
INTELLIGENCE SUMMARY
(Erase heading not required.)

June 1917. (2) Map Reference – Sheet 27.

Place	Date	Hour	Summary of Events and Information	Remarks and references to Appendices
PROVEN.	15.6.17	9AM	Hot dry weather continues. Lieut W. C. JOHNSTON RAMC of 133 Fd. Amb. reports his arrival for temporary duty. Dismantling of DRS continued. Conference of Officers, subject dealt with being treatment etc as laid down in circular memorandum of D.M.S. Fifth Army. Holding party withdrawn from farm at D18.b.2½.8.	AKh.
	16.6.17	9AM.	Hot dry weather continues. One private clerk sent to office of DDMS XVIII Corps for a course of instruction.	AKh.
	17.6.17	9AM.	Very hot weather continues. DRS site dismantling continued.	AKh.
	18.6.17	9AM.	Very hot oppressive weather continues. Thunderstorm in the afternoon.	AKh.
	19.6.17	9AM.	Rain through the night, weather dull & cooler. DRS site is being dismantled as soon as accommodation is no longer required. Accompanied DDMS XVIII Corps to HERZEELE at 4PM to see site selected for Corps Rest Station. Orders received to move two Sections to HERZEELE and all DRS huttage etc tomorrow, remaining Section to follow after PROVEN site has been cleared.	AKh.

2449 Wt. W14957/M90 750,000 1/16 J.B.C. & A. Forms/C.2118/12.

Instructions regarding War Diaries and Intelligence Summaries are contained in F. S. Regs., Part II. and the Staff Manual respectively. Title Pages will be prepared in manuscript.

WAR DIARY
or
INTELLIGENCE SUMMARY
(Erase heading not required.)

Army Form C. 2118.

(6)

June 1917.

Map Reference :- Sheet 27.

Place	Date	Hour	Summary of Events and Information	Remarks and references to Appendices
PROVEN.	20/6/17	9 A.M.	Heavy rain during the night. Ten lorries arrived to transport hutting equipment etc. to HERZEELE. "A" + "B" Sections moved to HERZEELE to commence the erection of the Corps Rest Station. Headquarters moved to HERZEELE at 8 P.M. "C" Section remained at PROVEN under command of Captain SINCLAIR MILLER M.C.	AH.
HERZEELE	21/6/17	9 A.M.	Work on site of Corps Rest Station at Dg.a.8.8. commenced. Further material transported from old C.R.S. site during the day. Weather inclined to be showery. Indent for requirements in shape of tents, equipment etc. of Corps Rest Station submitted to D.D.M.S. XVIII Corps.	AH.
"	22/6/17	9 A.M.	Very wet weather interfering with work on new site. Further progress in erection of large Nissen hut.	AH.
"	23/6/17	9 A.M.	Fine weather again. Work on new site continued, large Hpl Nissen hut completed, and good progress made on two small ones; extension of kitchen commenced. "C" Section rejoined Headquarters of the Field Ambulance at 12 Noon. D.D.M.S. XVIII Corps visited the C.R.S. at 3.15 P.M. Lieut. J. DONALDSON, RAMC, is taken on the strength of the Field Ambulance from 20/6/17, & Lieut. E. P. CARMODY is struck off the strength	AH.

2449 Wt. W14957/M90 750,000 1/16 J.B.C. & A. Forms/C.2118/12.

132nd FIELD AMBULANCE 27/6/17.

Instructions regarding War Diaries and Intelligence Summaries are contained in F. S. Regs., Part II. and the Staff Manual respectively. Title pages will be prepared in manuscript.

WAR DIARY
or
INTELLIGENCE SUMMARY.
(Erase heading not required.)

June 1917. (6) Map Reference:- Sheet 27.

Army Form C. 2118.

Place	Date	Hour	Summary of Events and Information	Remarks and references to Appendices
HERZEELE	23.6.17		from today's date on posting as M.O. i/c 14th Hants Regt.	
"	24.6.17	9 AM.	Fine weather - Work continued on Nissen huts. At 1 P.M. boring party of R.E.s arrived & commenced work on two wells. Tents arrived at 1 P.M., incomplete in many respects. D.D.M.S. XVIII Corps visited site at 6 P.M. Two small Nissen huts completed.	
"	25.6.17	9 AM.	Fine weather continues - Work on erection of marquees has been commenced. Lt QrMr COX RAMC went to draw rest of missing canvas required. Four tents, large Hospital Marquees, completed further work delayed by want of other essential parts of tents. Kitchen extension well in hand. Another small Nissen hut almost completed. Heavy rain fell from 8.30 P.M. onwards.	
"	26.6.17	9 AM.	Heavy rain during the night, but not raining at present. Work on C.R.S. continued. Good progress in erection of tents & extension of Kitchen.	
"	27.6.17	9 AM.	Fine weather. 47 O.R. left for duty with 133rd Field Ambulance, as did Captain W.M. CHRISTIE RAMC also. Work done on the Corps Rest Station to date :- ten large Hpl marquees, one large Nissen hut, and three small	

132nd FIELD AMBULANCE 27/6/17

Instructions regarding War Diaries and Intelligence Summaries are contained in F. S. Regs., Part II. and the Staff Manual respectively. Title pages will be prepared in manuscript.

WAR DIARY
or
~~INTELLIGENCE SUMMARY.~~
(*Erase heading not required.*)

June 1917 — (7) — Map Reference:— Sheet 27 —

Army Form C. 2118.

Place	Date	Hour	Summary of Events and Information	Remarks and references to Appendices
HERZEELE 27.6.17	27.6.17		Nissen huts completed: great extension of Kitchen with flooring of same + fixing of the Soyer Stoves: one Field Oven capable of roasting for 400–500 completed + another partly constructed — Two wells are being sunk — Surface drainage commenced —	A.h.
HERZEELE	28.6.17	9 A.M.	Heavy rain during the night but fine morning: work continued: four large Hpl marquees + 2 Bell tents pitched, work on wells + Kitchen continued — Seven other ranks left for work on the Corps Collecting Station for lightly wounded on the 26th inst + were attached to HQrs of 133 Fld Amb — The DDMS XVIII Corps visited the CCS site about 6.30 P.M. and expressed his satisfaction at the progress which has been made —	A.h.
"	29.6.17	9 A.M.	Heavy rain during the night, but fine this morning: work continued: Extension of Kitchen now practically complete, provision of two large field ovens, the Soyer Stoves installed, cutting up table; a very satisfactory Kitchen — Further tentage erected + good progress made in sinking wells + surface drainage —	A.h.

2353 Wt. W2544/1454 700,000 5/15 D. D. & L. A.D.S.S./Forms/C. 2118.

132nd FIELD AMBULANCE 30/6/17.

Instructions regarding War Diaries and Intelligence Summaries are contained in F. S. Regs., Part II. and the Staff Manual respectively. Title Pages will be prepared in manuscript.

June 1917 –

WAR DIARY
or
INTELLIGENCE SUMMARY

(Erase heading not required.)

(8)

Map Reference :– Sheet 27 –

Army Form C. 2118.

Place	Date	Hour	Summary of Events and Information	Remarks and references to Appendices
HERZEELE	30.6.17	9 AM	Heavy rain through the night which continues this morning – Work continued : construction of large grease trap commenced, in accordance with design of O.C. 42 Sanitary Section who is constructing the boxes in connection with it –	
			Cases dealt with during the month were as follows:–	
			Admissions to 132 Fld. Amb. – Officers: Sick 6. Wounded —. O.R.: Sick 270. Wounded 1.	
			Admissions to 39th DRS – Officers: Sick —. Wounded —. O.R.: Sick 275. Wounded 17.	
			A Whittington – Lt Col. R.A.M.C. O.C. 132nd FIELD AMBULANCE.	

132nd FIELD AMBULANCE 1/7/17.

2449 Wt. W14957/M90 750,000 1/16 J.B.C. & A. Forms/C.2118/12.

Original - Secret -

Confidential

War Diary

of

132nd Field Ambulance

from July 1st 1917 to July 31st 1917

(Volume 2)

B.E.F.

SUMMARY OF MEDICAL WAR DIARIES OF 132nd F.A. 39th Div.

18th Corps. 5th ARMY.

To 2nd Army Area from 8th August.

Western Front Operations - July ~~- August~~ 1917.

Officer Commanding - Lt.Col. A. Littlejohns.

SUMMARISED UNDER THE FOLLOWING HEADINGS:-

Phase "D" 1. - Passchendaele Operations, "July- Nov. 1917."

(a) - Operations commencing 1/7/17.

B.E.F.

132nd F.A. 39th Div. 18th Corps. 5th ARMY. Western Front.

O.C. = Lt.Col. A. Littlejohns. July - Aug.1917.

2nd ARMY AREA from 8th August.

PHASE "D" 1. - Passchendaele Operations, "July - Nov. 1917."

(a) Operations commencing 1/7/17.

H.Q. at Herzelle.

July 3rd.	Medical Arrangements.	C.R.S. opened.
10th.	Casualties.	242 patients under treatment at C.R.S.
11th-20th.	Ops. R.A.M.C.	C.R.S. Routine.
21st.	Moves.	To A.23.c.2.9. on relief by 35th F.A.
25th.	Moves. Detachment.	1 and 1 T.S.D. to 18th Corps W.W.C.P.
31st.		Res. B.S.D. to Duhallow A.D.S.

132nd F.A. 39th Div. 18th Corps. 5th ARMY. Western Front.

O.C. = Lt.Col. A. Littlejohns. July - ~~Aug~~.1917.

2nd ARMY AREA from 8th August.

PHASE "D" 1. - Passchendaele Operations, "July - Nov. 1917."

(a) Operations commencing 1/7/17.

H.Q. at Herzelle.

July 3rd.	Medical Arrangements. C.R.S. opened.
10th.	Casualties. 242 patients under treatment at C.R.S.
11th-20th.	Ops. R.A.M.C. C.R.S. Routine.
21st.	Moves. To A.23.c.2.9. on relief by 35th F.A.
25th.	Moves. Detachment. 1 & 1 T.S.D. to 18th Corps W.W.C.P.
31st.	Res. B.S.D. to Duhallow A.D.S.

132nd FIELD AMBULANCE 1/7/17.

ORIGINAL

Instructions regarding War Diaries and Intelligence Summaries are contained in F. S. Regs., Part II. and the Staff Manual respectively. Title Pages will be prepared in manuscript.

WAR DIARY
or
INTELLIGENCE SUMMARY
(Erase heading not required.)

Army Form C. 2118.

(1)

July. 1917.

Map Reference:— Sheet 27

Place	Date	Hour	Summary of Events and Information	Remarks and references to Appendices
HERZEELE.	1/7/17.	9 A.M.	Fine morning — work on Corps Rest Station continued — D.A.D.M.S. 39 Div: visited the Fd. Ambulance at 12.45 P.M. — Good progress made with surface drainage; and Ablution place commenced —	ALh.
"	2/7/17	9 A.M.	Fine day — work on surface drainage, altering + fixing of trench boards, ablution place + wells continued, + good progress made — Lieut J. DONALDSON. RAMC proceeded to take over medical charge of the 6th B.W.I. at 5 P.M. —	ALh.
"	3/7/17	9 A.M.	Fine weather — work continued — A few patients received in the afternoon — At 10 P.M. wire received from DDMS XVIII Corps to open CRS + be prepared to receive up to 300 cases from 9 A.M. on the 4th inst. — Arrangements as regards rations for these were fixed up by midnight —	ALh.
	4/7/17	9 A.M.	Dull + overcast — incessant rain — work on site continued — Equipped 194 beds — Ablution place practically completed; latrine commenced; DDMS XVIII Corps visited the site and was pleased with the progress made —	ALh.

2449 Wt. W14957/M90 750,000 1/16 J.B.C. & A. Forms/C.2118/12.

132nd FIELD AMBULANCE 5/7/17 -

Instructions regarding War Diaries and Intelligence Summaries are contained in F. S. Regs., Part II. and the Staff Manual respectively. Title Pages will be prepared in manuscript.

Army Form C. 2118.

WAR DIARY
or
INTELLIGENCE SUMMARY

(Erase heading not required.)

July, 1917. (2) Map Reference :— Sheet 27

Place	Date	Hour	Summary of Events and Information	Remarks and references to Appendices
HERZEELE.	5/7/17.	9 A.M.	Dull weather but fine still – Constructional work continued: good progress with new latrine building which will accomodate thirty pails with fly proof seats & self closing lids –	Alh.
"	6/7/17.	9 A.M.	Fine weather continues – Work on CRS continued – Improvisation of pack saddlery got on with – Extension of bath house taken in hand –	Alh.
"	7/7/17.	9 A.M.	Fine weather continues – All work continued and good progress made with new latrine, bath house extensions: Pack Store has been considerably enlarged –	Alh.
"	8/7/17.	9 A.M.	Heavy thunderstorm during the night with very heavy rain, which continued this morning – Work on latrines, pack store & other work in hand continued: Still a great deal to be done – 179 patients in the CRS tonight –	Alh.
"	9/7/17.	9 A.M.	Dull but no rain – Work continued and good progress made on latrines, pack store, bath house extension etc –	Alh.

2449 Wt. W14957/M90 750,000 1/16 J.B.C. & A. Forms/C.2118/12.

Instructions regarding War Diaries and Intelligence Summaries are contained in F. S. Regs., Part II. and the Staff Manual respectively. Title Pages will be prepared in manuscript.

WAR DIARY
or
INTELLIGENCE SUMMARY

(3)

July 1917 — *(Erase heading not required.)* — Map Reference — Sheet 27 —

Army Form C. 2118.

Place	Date	Hour	Summary of Events and Information	Remarks and references to Appendices
HERZEELE.	10/7/17.	9 AM.	Dull but fine – Work on CRS continued – 242 patients under treatment at CRS, in addition to constructional work in hand –	A.H.
"	11/7/17	9 AM.	Bright sunshine – Work continued & much progress made –	A.H.
"	12/7/17	9 AM.	Fine weather continues – Work continued & progress made – 314 patients in the CRS tonight – D.M.S. XVIII Corps visited CRS this evening, & classified some men after inspection –	A.H.
"	13/7/17	9 AM.	Fine weather, very warm – Apparatus for heating bath water was received yesterday – Good progress made with all work in hand –	A.H.
"	14/7/17	9 AM.	Wet morning – A.D.M.S. 39 Div. inspected CRS – Work in hand continued – Lieut. J. N. WORCESTER Medical Corps U.S.A. reported his arrival at 8.30 PM on the 13th inst. and is taken on the strength of the unit from that date – Attended Conference at A.D.M.S.'s Office at 4 PM – 420 patients now in CRS –	A.H.

2449 Wt. W14957/M90 750,000 1/16 J.B.C. & A. Forms/C.2118/12.

132nd FIELD AMBULANCE
15/7/17

Instructions regarding War Diaries and Intelligence Summaries are contained in F. S. Regs., Part II. and the Staff Manual respectively. Title Pages will be prepared in manuscript.

WAR DIARY
or
INTELLIGENCE SUMMARY
(Erase heading not required.)

Army Form C. 2118.

July 1917 — (4) Map Reference — Sheet 27 & 28.

Place	Date	Hour	Summary of Events and Information	Remarks and references to Appendices
HERZEELE	15/7/17	9 AM	Heavy rain in the night, but fine this morning — Constructional work continued — DDMS visited the Corps Rest Station at 5.45 PM. and looked round —	AHL
	16/7/17	9 AM	Slightly overcast but fine — work in hand continued — Good progress is being made with the installation of water heating apparatus —	AHL
	17/7/17	9 AM	Fine but hot — work continued — Visited the ADMS at his Headquarters at 2 PM & following his instructions I visited a site to park the Fld Ambulance at in a few days time —	AHL
	18/7/17	9 AM	Cloudy — work practically completed everywhere now in CRS — Party arrived from No: 35 Fld. Ambulance to take over CRS — Visited new site where unit is to park on being relieved here & met an Officer of Belgian Mission to discuss site — Heavy rain fell in the evening — (Sheet 28).	AHL
	19/7/17	8 AM	Advance party proceeded to A 23. C. 2. 9. to take over site & pitch Canvas — weather cleared to fine during the afternoon —	AHL

2449 Wt. W14957/M90 750,000 1/16 J.B.C. & A. Forms/C.2118/12.

132nd FIELD AMBULANCE 20/7/17.

Army Form C. 2118.

WAR DIARY
or
INTELLIGENCE SUMMARY
(Erase heading not required.)

Instructions regarding War Diaries and Intelligence Summaries are contained in F. S. Regs., Part II. and the Staff Manual respectively. Title Pages will be prepared in manuscript.

July 1917.

Map Reference – Sheet 27. 28.

Place	Date	Hour	Summary of Events and Information	Remarks and references to Appendices
HERZEELE	20/7/17	10 A.M.	C.R.S. handed over to Officer Commanding 35th Fd. Amb. advance party: Fd. Amb. equipment packed ready to march.	A.H.
"	21/7/17	8 A.M.	Unit left HERZEELE and marched to new site at A 23.C.2.9. (Sheet 28) & parked at 1.30 P.M. Canvas erected & necessary arrangements made for cooking, etc: deep narrow trench started.	A.H.
A 23C.2.9.	22/7/17	9 A.M.	Fine weather. Trench completed during the day. Lt G.E. DOWNS RAMC rejoined Headquarters at 4 P.M. Inspection & practice of Box Respirators & P.H. Helmets.	A.H.
"	23/7/17	9 A.M.	Fine weather & hot. Camp in good order. Lieut: J. STEEL RAMC rejoined the unit.	A.H.
"	24/7/17	9 A.M.	Hot & oppressive weather. Captain J. MORRIS. M.C. RAMC (T) rejoined the unit on return from charge of a section of 134 Fd. Amb.	A.H.
"	25/7/17	9 A.M.	Heavy rain. Captain J MORRIS M.C. RAMC (T) with one tent subdivision proceeded to report for duty to O.C. XVIII Corps Walking Wounded Collecting Post at 9.30 A.M. At 2.30 P.M. Captain SINCLAIR MILLER. M.C. RAMC (SR)	

2449 Wt. W14957/M90 750,000 1/16 J.B.C. & A. Forms/C.2118/12.

Army Form C. 2118.

Instructions regarding War Diaries and Intelligence Summaries are contained in F. S. Regs., Part II. and the Staff Manual respectively. Title Pages will be prepared in manuscript.

WAR DIARY
or
~~INTELLIGENCE SUMMARY~~

(Erase heading not required.)

July 1917 - (6) Map Reference: - Sheet 28.

Place	Date	Hour	Summary of Events and Information	Remarks and references to Appendices
A 23. C. 2. 9.	25/7/17.	2.30 PM	1st Lieut. J. N. WORCESTER Medical Corps U.S.A. proceeded, to report for duty, to O.C. 133 Fld. Amb. -	AHL
"	26/7/17.	9 AM	Dull but much cooler after the rain - Lieut. G. E. DOWNS. RAMC proceeded to take over temporary medical charge of the 14th Bn Hants. R.R. at 7 P.M. - Captain H.P. CAITHNESS. RAMC reported his arrival at 11.30 P.M. & is taken on the strength of the unit -	AHL
"	27/7/17	9 A.M.	Dull & cool. Captain H. D. H. WILLIS-BUND RAMC reported his arrival at 5 P.M. & is taken on the strength -	AHL
"	28/7/17	9 AM	Fine & very hot. The party attached to No: 12 C.C.S. rejoined for duty -	AHL
"	29/7/17	9 AM	Violent thunderstorm with very heavy rain -	
"	30/7/17	9 AM	Inclined to rain - A.D.M.S. 39 Div: visited the camp at Noon -	AHL

2449 Wt. W14957/M90 750,000 1/16 J.B.C. & A. Forms/C.2118/12.

132nd FIELD AMBULANCE 30/7/17-

Instructions regarding War Diaries and Intelligence Summaries are contained in F. S. Regs., Part II. and the Staff Manual respectively. Title Pages will be prepared in manuscript.

WAR DIARY
or
~~INTELLIGENCE~~ SUMMARY
(Erase heading not required.)

(7)

Map Reference — Sheet 28 —

Army Form C. 2118.

Place	Date	Hour	Summary of Events and Information	Remarks and references to Appendices
A 23.C.2.9.	30.7.17	2.30 PM	Captain H.J.H. WILLIS-BUND RAMC & Lieut. J. STEEL RAMC (SR) and two bearer subdivisions left for DUHALLOW ADS —	AR.
"	31.7.17	8.15 AM	Captain SINCLAIR MILLER M.C. RAMC (SR) left for DUHALLOW ADS in accordance with instructions received from ADMS — Lieut. A. BROWN. RAMC. reported his arrival at 11.45 AM. and proceeded for duty to the Corps Main Dressing Station — The reserve bearer subdivision left for DUHALLOW ADS. at 4.30 PM; the weather changed to heavy rain at nightfall —	AR.

132nd FIELD AMBULANCE 1/8/17-

A Whittyjohns —
Lt Col.
R.A.M.C.
O.C. 132ND FIELD AMBULANCE.

2449 Wt. W14957/M90 750,000 1/16 J.B.C. & A. Forms/C.2118/12.

Original -

Secret -

Vol 18

140/2004

Confidential

War Diary

— of —

132nd Field Ambulance

from August 1st 1917 to August 31st 1917

(Volume 2)

3

B.E.F.

SUMMARY OF MEDICAL WAR DIARIES OF 132nd F.A. 39th Div.

18th Corps. 5th ARMY.

To 2nd Army Area from 8th August.

Western Front Operations - ~~July~~ - August 1917.

Officer Commanding - Lt.Col. A. Littlejohns.

SUMMARISED UNDER THE FOLLOWING HEADINGS:-

Phase "D" 1. - Passchendaele Operations, "July- Nov. 1917."

(a) - Operations commencing 1/7/17.

Aug. 5th. <u>Moves.</u> 1 & 13 to 48th Division.

All bearers rejoined in evening.

8th. <u>Moves and Transfer</u>. By train to Meteren 2nd ARMY AREA.

5th. <u>Moves.</u> 1 & 13 to 48th Division.

All bearers rejoined in evening.

8th. <u>Moves and Transfer</u>. By train to Meteren 2nd ARMY AREA.

132nd FIELD AMBULANCE 1/8/17.

ORIGINAL

Instructions regarding War Diaries and Intelligence Summaries are contained in F. S. Regs., Part II. and the Staff Manual respectively. Title Pages will be prepared in manuscript.

WAR DIARY
or
~~INTELLIGENCE SUMMARY~~
(Erase heading not required.)

Army Form C. 2118.

August 1917.

(1)

Map Reference:– Sheet 28.

Place	Date	Hour	Summary of Events and Information	Remarks and references to Appendices
A 23 C.2.9.	1/8/17	9 A.M.	Very wet morning, following heavy rain all night. Captain H.D.H. WILLIS-BUND RAMC posted as M.O i/c 1/1st CAMBS. Captain SINCLAIR MILLER M.C. rejoined headquarters at 5.30 P.M.	A.H.
"	2/8/17	9 A.M.	Slight rain continues.	A.H.
"	3/8/17	9 A.M.	Rain continues.	A.H.
"	4/8/17	9 A.M.	Weather improving. Lt: A. BROWN RAMC is posted to the unit and taken on the strength from 31/7/17. Lieut: J. STEEL RAMC (S.R.) has been posted as M.O i/c ~~16 Notts + Derby Rgt~~ 13 R. Sussex Rgt + is struck off the strength from today's date.	A.H.
"	5/8/17	9 A.M.	Weather improving. Lt A. BROWN RAMC + 13 bearers proceeded to the 41st Division for temporary duty. Capt. H.P. CAITHNESS RAMC proceeded to take over medical charge of the 16 Notts + Derby Rgt. Lieut. P.E. CARROLL RAMC reported his arrival + is taken on the strength of the unit: he proceeded to 134 Fd. Amb. for temporary duty. All Bearers rejoined headquarters during the afternoon + evening. Lieut. WORCESTER U.S.A. M.C. rejoined.	A.H.
"	6/8/17	9 A.M.	Weather fine.	A.H.

2449 Wt. W14957/M90 750,000 1/16 J.B.C. & A. Forms/C.2118/12.

Army Form C. 2118.

Instructions regarding War Diaries and Intelligence Summaries are contained in F. S. Regs., Part II. and the Staff Manual respectively. Title Pages will be prepared in manuscript.

WAR DIARY
or
~~INTELLIGENCE~~ SUMMARY
(Erase heading not required.)

August 1917- (2) Map Reference:- Sheet 28.27.

Place	Date	Hour	Summary of Events and Information	Remarks and references to Appendices
A 23.c.2.9.	7/8/17.	9AM.	Fine weather - Orders received re move of unit to EECKE area on the following day - All officers rejoined unit, except Lieut. A. BROWN.	Alh.
"	8/8/17	4AM.	Camp struck: transport proceeded by road + personnel by train to METEREN + occupied Fld: Amb: Site at X15. d.3.7. at noon. Captain A.E.W. IDRIS. RAMC reported his arrival + is taken on the strength - Lieut. E.P. DOWNS. RAMC rejoined from medical charge of 14 Hants.	Alh. Alh.
METEREN	9/8/17	9AM.	Unsettled weather - Captain A. BROWN. RAMC rejoined from 48 Division - Equipment of site proceeding - Lieut: J.L. McELROY. U.S.A M.C. reported his arrival + is taken on the strength - Sixty five patients admitted.	Alh.
"	10/8/17	9AM.	Fair weather - Lieut: J.N. WORCESTER. U.S.A. M.C. proceeded to take over temporary medical charge of the 11th R. SUSSEX. Regt. One hundred + forty nine patients remaining -	Alh.
"	11/8/17	9AM.	Dull + showery weather - Lieut: J.L. McELROY U.S.M.S. left for temporary duty with 134 Fld: Amb - I visited the M.D.S. situated at about M6.d. + saw the arrangements there -	Alh.

2449 Wt. W14957/M90 750,000 1/16 J.B.C. & A. Forms/C.2118/12.

Instructions regarding War Diaries and Intelligence Summaries are contained in F. S. Regs., Part II. and the Staff Manual respectively. Title Pages will be prepared in manuscript.

WAR DIARY
or
~~INTELLIGENCE SUMMARY~~
(Erase heading not required.)

Army Form C. 2118.

(3)

August 1917 -

Map Reference :- Sheet 27.

Place	Date	Hour	Summary of Events and Information	Remarks and references to Appendices
METEREN.	12/8/17	4AM.	Captain SINCLAIR MILLER. M.C. left with party of bearers to proceed to A.D.S. at VOORMEZEELE. A.D.M.S. 39 Div visited the D.R.S. at 11AM. & inspected it -	A.H.
〃	13/8/17	4AM.	Remainder of two bearer subdivisions left for VOORMEZEELE - D.D.M.S. X Corps visited the D.R.S. at 11AM. and inspected it - One Sgt & 8 men left for WESTOUTRE to report to Captain J.H. PORTER RAMC. at 4.30 PM - Patients remaining 199 -	A.H.
〃	14/8/17	9AM.	Weather improving - Daily inspection -	A.H.
〃	15/8/17	9AM.	Unsettled weather - New latrine commenced, additional accommodation being required -	A.H.
〃	16/8/17	9AM.	Unsettled weather - Party returned from WESTOUTRE yesterday evening - New latrine is nearly completed - Captain A.E.W. IDRIS. RAMC having been evacuated to C.C.S. is struck off the strength from today's date -	A.H.
〃	17/8/17	9AM.	Fine morning - Daily inspection -	A.H.

2449 Wt. W14957/M90 750,000 1/16 J.B.C. & A. Forms/C.2118/12.

Instructions regarding War Diaries and Intelligence Summaries are contained in F. S. Regs., Part II. and the Staff Manual respectively. Title Pages will be prepared in manuscript.

WAR DIARY
or
~~INTELLIGENCE SUMMARY~~
(Erase heading not required.)

Army Form C. 2118.

(4).
Map Reference: Sheet 27.

Place	Date	Hour	Summary of Events and Information	Remarks and references to Appendices
METEREN.	19.8.17	9 AM	Weather continues to be fine – Latrine now completed –	AH
"	21.8.17	9 AM.	Fine weather – Captain A.P. CAITHNESS RAMC is posted to the Medical charge of the 16th Bn Notts & Derby Rgt and is struck off the strength from today's date –	AH
"	22.8.17	9 AM.	Fine weather & hot – DDMS X Corps visited the D.R.S. & inspected it. Orders having been received to provide accomodation for four officers, search was made for same & a small house suitable with necessary accomodation has been found – Indents for necessary equipment (B.R.C.S.) passed to ADMS. for approval –	AH
"	23.8.17	9 AM.	Dull inclined to be showery – Attended Conference at the Office of the ADMS at 3 PM –	AH
"	24/8/17	9 AM	Cool & windy – Good progress is being made in the construction of a new bath house – Rest Station for four officers equipped & good progress made in getting it ready for reception of officers tomorrow –	AH

132nd FIELD AMBULANCE 25/8/17.

Instructions regarding War Diaries and Intelligence Summaries are contained in F. S. Regs., Part II. and the Staff Manual respectively. Title Pages will be prepared in manuscript.

WAR DIARY
or
~~INTELLIGENCE SUMMARY~~

(Erase heading not required.)

(5)

Map Reference:– Sheet 27.

Army Form C. 2118.

Place	Date	Hour	Summary of Events and Information	Remarks and references to Appendices
METEREN	25/8/17	9 AM	Fine fresh morning – Daily inspection – Officers' Rest Station is now equipped & ready for reception of patients – One Officer admitted –	A.H.
	26/8/17	9 AM	Dull & overcast weather – Daily inspection – Good progress with the new bath house – An extension of the meat store to twice its previous size has been carried out –	A.H.
	27/8/17	9 AM	Heavy rain during the night; which recurred at midday; the A.D.M.S. visited the D.R.S. at 4.15 P.M: he also inspected the Rest Stn for Officers which has been started, & expressed his satisfaction with it –	A.H.
	28/8/17	9 AM	Very stormy night, high wind blowing – Good progress being made with new bath house – Storm has done much damage to the garden in the D.R.S. –	A.H.
	29/8/17	9 AM	Stormy weather continues – Daily inspection – Captain SINCLAIR MILLER, M.O. & two bearer subdivisions rejoined headquarters at 9 P.M –	A.H.

2449 Wt. W14957/M90 750,000 1/16 J.B.C. & A. Forms/C.2118/12.

132nd FIELD AMBULANCE 31/8/17 -

Instructions regarding War Diaries and Intelligence Summaries are contained in F. S. Regs., Part II. and the Staff Manual respectively. Title Pages will be prepared in manuscript.

WAR DIARY
or
~~INTELLIGENCE SUMMARY~~ (6)
(Erase heading not required.)

Map Reference:- Sheet 27.

Army Form C. 2118.

Place	Date	Hour	Summary of Events and Information	Remarks and references to Appendices
METEREN.	30.8.17	9 A.M.	Stormy weather, but not so much rain — Captain SINCLAIR MILLER M.C. left to take over temporary command of 133 F.D. Ambulance. Good progress has been made with the new bath house, floor of bricks & cement being now complete: cement gutter to conduct water away is not yet hardened —	AH
"	31.8.17	9 A.M.	Heavy showers - Daily inspection - Bath house completed & will be ready for use tomorrow — Patients admitted during the month — Wounded - Sick - ; Officers - 7. 4. ; Other Ranks - 352. 684.	AH

Patients admitted during the month:

	Wounded	Sick
Officers	7	4
Other Ranks	352	684

132nd FIELD AMBULANCE 1/9/17 -

A Whittepheus- Lt Col.
R.A.M.C.
O.C. 132nd FIELD AMBULANCE.

Vol 19

Confidential

War Diary

— of —

132nd Field Ambulance

from September 1st 1917 to September 30th 1917

(Volume 2)

140/24+38

11

Instructions regarding War Diaries and Intelligence Summaries are contained in F. S. Regs., Part II. and the Staff Manual respectively. Title Pages will be prepared in manuscript.

WAR DIARY
or
~~INTELLIGENCE SUMMARY~~
(Erase heading not required.)

Army Form C. 2118.

(1)

Sept: 1917 — Map Reference:- Sheet 27.

Place	Date	Hour	Summary of Events and Information	Remarks and references to Appendices
METEREN	1/9/17	9AM	Weather dull & threatening — New bath house now complete and taken into use today — Captain W.T. BROWN. RAMC reported his arrival during the evening, and is taken on the strength from today's date — Buckets having now been received, the new latrine is taken into use —	Alh.
"	2/9/17	9AM.	Unsettled weather continues — The Officers Rest Station has been equipped for one more bed, the accomodation now being for five Officers & fully occupied — Good progress has been made in the protection of tents with lower walls of sandbags, as a protection against enemy aircraft raids —	Alh.
"	3/9/17	9AM.	Beautiful sunshiny morning — Daily inspection — Good progress being made with new field oven — Lieut P.E. CARROLL RAMC left at 5.15 P.M. to take over temporary medical charge of the 17th Bn. Notts & Derby Rgt — Considerable progress has been made in the sandbag protection of the tentage, which is now approaching completion —	Alh.

2449 Wt. W14957/M90 750,000 1/16 J.B.C. & A. Forms/C.2118/12.

Instructions regarding War Diaries and Intelligence Summaries are contained in F. S. Regs., Part II. and the Staff Manual respectively. Title Pages will be prepared in manuscript.

Army Form C. 2118.

WAR DIARY
or
INTELLIGENCE SUMMARY
(Erase heading not required.)

Sept: 1917 – Map Reference – Sheet 27 – (2)

Place	Date	Hour	Summary of Events and Information	Remarks and references to Appendices
METEREN.	4/9/17	9 A.M.	Beautiful weather – D.D.M.S. X Corps visited the D.R. Station at 12.15 P.M. he also inspected the Officers' Rest Station – 1 N.C.O. + 5 men left for STEENVOORDE at 6 P.M. to establish a Collecting Post at Q16.7.8 –	A.H.
"	5/9/17	9 A.M.	Very fine weather continues – 1st Lieut: S.W. THOMPSON. M.O.R.C. U.S.A. reported his arrival + is taken on the strength of the unit from today's date – Good progress in new field oven, and sandbag protection of canvas – Captain W.T. BROWN. awarded the MILITARY CROSS (D.R.O. No: 1048 of 4/9/17).	A.H.
"	6/9/17	9 A.M.	Fine morning – I visited the STEENVOORDE Collecting Post at 12 noon + saw the Medical Officer i/c 16th Rifle Brigade who is in charge of same – The new field oven is completed: this has been constructed of bricks + corrugated iron, with flues, to admit of heat being circulated all round the oven as well as under: it has in a double oven, + should roast for several hundred – Heavy thunderstorm in the evening –	A.H.

2449 Wt. W14957/M90 750,000 1/16 J.B.C. & A. Forms/C.2118/12.

*Instructions regarding War Diaries and Intelligence Summaries are contained in F. S. Regs., Part II. and the Staff Manual respectively. Title Pages will be prepared in manuscript.

WAR DIARY
or
~~INTELLIGENCE SUMMARY~~
(Erase heading not required.)

September 1917 –

(3)

Army Form C. 2118.

Place	Date	Hour	Summary of Events and Information	Remarks and references to Appendices
METEREN.	7/9/17.	9AM.	Lieut: G.E. DOWNS. RAMC proceeded to take over medical charge of the 12th Bn Royal Sussex Rgt, and Lieut: T.N. WORCESTER MORC U.S.A to take over medical charge of the 1/1 Bn Herts Rgt: they are struck off the strength from today's date –	AH.
〃	8/9/17	9AM.	Weather dull & overcast – The new field oven is roasting well – New dixie trial commenced – 1st Lieut: S.W. THOMPSON. MORC U.S.A. was evacuated to C.C.S, sick & is struck off the strength – Captain W. CROMLEY. MORC USA & 1st Lieut C.S. BOGART. MORC USA arrived at 6 P.M. and are taken on the strength temporarily –	AH.
〃	9/9/17	9AM.	Fine weather – Attended conference at the office of the A.D.M.S. at 10.30 A.M. –	AH.
〃	10/9/17	9AM.	Fine weather continues: Lieut A. BROWN. RAMC left yesterday evening for temporary duty with 134 Field Ambulance, Lieut T.L. McELROY MORC. USA proceeding at the same time for temporary duty with 7 KRRC – At 12 noon held a conference on medical organisation for newly joined officers –	AH.

2449 Wt. W14957/M90 750,000 1/16 J.B.C. & A. Forms/C.2118/12.

Army Form C. 2118.

WAR DIARY
or
~~INTELLIGENCE SUMMARY~~
(Erase heading not required.)

Instructions regarding War Diaries and Intelligence Summaries are contained in F. S. Regs., Part II. and the Staff Manual respectively. Title Pages will be prepared in manuscript.

September 1917 – ④ Map Reference – Sheet 27 –

Place	Date	Hour	Summary of Events and Information	Remarks and references to Appendices
METEREN	11/9/17	9 AM.	Beautiful weather continues – 1st Lt. C.S. BOGART. M.O.R.C. U.S.A. left to report to O.C. 134 Fd: Amb: –	A.H.
"	12/9/17	9 AM	Fine weather continues – The new field oven, constructed recently, is roasting very well – New disinfector has also been constructed of bricks & corrugated iron & is very satisfactory – Captain W.T. BROWN. M.C. RAMC left for 134. Fd: Ambulance to learn the evacuation from the Front Line – Personnel etc withdrawn from STEENVOORDE Collecting Post, which is now closed –	A.H.
"	13/9/17	9 A.M.	Dull & less warm weather – Daily inspection –	A.H.
"	14/9/17	9 AM	Dull weather continues – Captain W.T. BROWN. M.C. RAMC returned to Head Quarters at 12 Noon –	A.H.
"	15/9/17	9 AM	Fine bright morning – Daily inspection –	A.H.
"	16/9/17	9 AM	Fine weather continues – Daily inspection – A thousand blankets were drawn from LOCRE and handed over to 133 Fd: Ambulance –	A.H.
"	17/9/17	9 AM	Rather high wind, but fine – The A.D.M.S. 39 Div: visited the D.R.S. and inspected cases brought forward for his inspection –	A.H.

2449 Wt. W14957/M90 750,000 1/16 J.B.C. & A. Forms/C.2118/12.

Army Form C. 2118.

WAR DIARY
or
~~INTELLIGENCE SUMMARY~~
(Erase heading not required.)

Instructions regarding War Diaries and Intelligence Summaries are contained in F. S. Regs., Part II. and the Staff Manual respectively. Title Pages will be prepared in manuscript.

(5)

September 1917 – Map Reference:– Sheet 27 –

Place	Date	Hour	Summary of Events and Information	Remarks and references to Appendices
METEREN.	17/9/17	12.30 P.M.	The Bearer Division is moving up to be attached to O.C. 134 Field Ambulance for duty at BRASSERIE. (N6.a.1.1. Sheet 28) – Lieut J. L. McELROY. M.O.R.C. U.S.A. rejoined for duty in the afternoon –	ALh.
"	18/9/17	9 A.M.	Dull weather followed by light rain later in the day – Daily inspection –	ALh.
"	19/9/17	9 A.M.	High wind blowing, but fine – Parade Service was held at 11 A.M. – Lieut J. L. McELROY. left for temporary duty with 134 Fd. Ambulance Heavy rain at 10 P.m. –	ALh.
"	20/9/17	9 A.M.	Dull weather – Recent improvements in the site are construction of cupboard for ward utensils, in connection with the Nissen huts, completion of protection of tents by walls of sandbags & earth, which have been covered with sods – The skylight of the dining room of the Officers Rest Station has been provided with adjustable curtains, to screen lights from aerial observation after dark – 58 slightly wounded & sick were transferred from the X Corps M.D.S. for walking wounded during the day –	ALh.

2449 Wt. W14957/M90 750,000 1/16 J.B.C. & A. Forms/C.2118/12.

Army Form C. 2118.

WAR DIARY
or
~~INTELLIGENCE~~ SUMMARY (6)

Instructions regarding War Diaries and Intelligence Summaries are contained in F. S. Regs., Part II. and the Staff Manual respectively. Title Pages will be prepared in manuscript.

September 1917 — *(Erase heading not required.)* — Map Reference — Sheet 27 —

Place	Date	Hour	Summary of Events and Information	Remarks and references to Appendices
METEREN.	21/9/17	9 A.M.	Weather is fine with bright sunshine – Captain SINCLAIR MILLER. M.C. RAMC (S.R) having been posted to the command of 133 Field Ambulance is struck off the strength from 30/8/17 –	AH
"	22/9/17	9 A.M	Weather dull & overcast – Orders received at 7 P.M to take over temporarily the Corps Main Dressing Stn for lightly wounded –	AH
"	23/9/17	7.45 A.M.	One tent-subdivision proceeded to take over the M.D.S. for lightly wounded at LA CLYTTE. An officer of the 41st Division remained in charge of this M.D.S –	AH
"	24/9/17	9 A.M	Fine weather continues – Captain H.P. CAITHNESS. RAMC is taken on the strength, & proceeded to the M.D.S at LA CLYTTE for duty –	AH
	25/9/17	6 P.M.	Fine weather – Daily inspection – Lieut-Col A.S. Littlejohns D.S.O. RAMC has departed temporarily in charge of M.D.S. for lightly wounded at LA CLYTTE.	JH
	26/9/17	5.30 P.M	Bright sunny weather continues. Daily inspection.	JH
	27/9/17	6 P.M.	Weather conditions glorious – Improvements to Dixie trail completed – daily inspection	JH

2449 Wt. W14957/M90 750,000 1/16 J.B.C. & A. Forms/C.2118/12.

Army Form C. 2118.

Instructions regarding War Diaries and Intelligence Summaries are contained in F. S. Regs., Part II. and the Staff Manual respectively. Title Pages will be prepared in manuscript.

WAR DIARY
or
INTELLIGENCE SUMMARY (6)

September 1917 *(Erase heading not required.)* Map. Reference:- Sheet 27.

Place	Date	Hour	Summary of Events and Information	Remarks and references to Appendices
METEREN.	28/9/17	6 P.M.	Lieut Col Littlejohns D.S.O. R.A.M.C. Retired from M.D.S. for lightly wounded at LA CLYTTE having handed over to 21st Division. - Daily inspection.	JM
	29/9/17	5 P.M.	Fine weather still continues. 39th Div has been transferred from X Corps to IX Corps.	JM
	30/9/17	12. midnight	Admitted during September 1917	
			Field Ambulance. Sick: — Wounded: —	
			Officers. Sick: 8. Wounded: 20	
			O Ranks. Sick: 613. Wounded: 822	
			Germans. Sick: –. Wounded: 3	
			39th D.R.S.	
			Officers. Sick: 10. Wounded: 2	JM
			O Ranks. Sick: 637. Wounded: 144	
			Totals. Sick: 1268. Wounded: 991	
			23rd Field Ambulance arrived today to take over, tomorrow, this D.R.S. site. Awaiting orders to move.	

J Morris Capt. R.A.M.C. T.F.
f/ O.C. 132nd FIELD AMBULANCE.

132nd FIELD AMBULANCE 1-X-17.

2449 Wt. W14957/M90 750,000 1/16 J.B.C. & A. Forms/C.2118/12.

Original –

Secret –

Vol 2

War Diary

— of —

132nd Field Ambulance

from October 1st 1917 to October 31st 1917

(Volume 2)

1402 + 99

4

5

Oct. 1917

132nd FIELD AMBULANCE 1/10/17

ORIGINAL

Instructions regarding War Diaries and Intelligence Summaries are contained in F. S. Regs., Part II. and the Staff Manual respectively. Title Pages will be prepared in manuscript.

WAR DIARY
or
INTELLIGENCE SUMMARY
(Erase heading not required.)

SECRET

Army Form C. 2118.

(1)

October 1917 Map Reference Sheet 28.

Place	Date	Hour	Summary of Events and Information	Remarks and references to Appendices
KEERSEBROM CAMP. S.10 D Sheet 28.	1/10/17	8 p.m.	At 12.45 P.M. moved from METEREN D.R.S site at X 15. 2.5 (Sheet 27) to KEERSEBROM CAMP at S 10. D (Sheet 28) with transport of A Section. Remainder of transport left at X 16. D Sheet 27 on account of lack of available accomodation here. Weather gloriously fine. D.R.S site at METEREN handed over to 23rd Field Ambulance. Present site used to be "Prisoners of War Camp", but more recently has been used as a Divisional Rest Station, and has been taken over today from 48th Field Ambulance. It consists of NISSEN & WOODEN Huts - good latrines, Cook house & Incinerator.	JHH
"	2/10/17	5 p.m.	A Field obtained this morning for Horse transport. This afternoon remainder of Transport arrived at 2.30 p.m. Daily inspection. Weather remains gloriously fine. Considerable amount of work done in repairing Road approaching site.	JHH
"	3/10/17	6 p.m.	At 6 P.M. last evening site was visited by A.D.M.S. 39 Div. Change in the weather, much cooler, and some rain during the night. Daily Inspection. Considerable improvement to Road - approach from BAILLEUL, and to duck-board walks.	JHH
"	4/10/17	4 p.m.	Weather broken up. S.W wind, and heavy showers of rain. Daily inspection	JHH
"	5/10/17	6 p.m.	R.E material drawn yesterday for building Meat Store & Butchers Shop - work commenced today. good progress. Sandbagging - against Aerial bombs - of 3 Bell tents completed today. Daily inspection. Strong S.W. wind blowing with heavy showers.	JHH

2449 Wt. W14957/M90 750,000 1/16 J.B.C. & A. Forms/C.2118/12.

Instructions regarding War Diaries and Intelligence Summaries are contained in F. S. Regs., Part II. and the Staff Manual respectively. Title Pages will be prepared in manuscript.

WAR DIARY
or
INTELLIGENCE SUMMARY

(Erase heading not required.)

Army Form C. 2118.

October 1917 (2) Map Reference Sheet 28

Place	Date	Hour	Summary of Events and Information	Remarks and references to Appendices
KEERSEBROM CAMP	6/10/17	6.PM.	Weather wet & gusty. Daily inspection. Erection of Meat Store & Butchers Shop proceeding well. Garden Plots of ground in Compound being dug up.	JHS
"	7/10/17	4.PM.	Very wet weather. Tarring of huts commenced but delayed on account of rain. Daily inspection. Meat Store & Butchers Shop nearing completion. Erection of Kitchen for Officers Mess commenced.	JHS
"	8/10/17	6.PM.	Very wet night. NE wind blowing today which has dried up the ground very quickly. Daily inspection. Meat Store & Butchers Shop, and Kitchen for Officers Mess completed. At 2.30 pm. Received warning to be ready to move in 6 hours.	JHS
"	9/10/17	6.30 P.M.	Cold wet day. Visit by D.D.M.S. IX Corps at 11.30 A.M. Tarring of Cook House & roofs of Dispensary & Latrines completed.	JHS
"	10/10/17	6 PM.	Tarring of huts continued. Daily inspection. Work of tarring huts interrupted by rain during the morning, but pushed forward during fine afternoon. Gardening work proceeding well.	JHS
"	11/10/17	6 PM.	Weather cold & showery - fair amount of sunshine between showers. Daily inspection.	JHS
"	12/10/17	9 PM.	Stormy weather - Daily inspection. At 2 P.M. visited A.D.S. at VOORMEZEELE & arranged for advanced parties to proceed thither on 13/10/17 to commence taking over of evacuation from the line -	JHS

2449 Wt. W14957/M90 750,000 1/16 J.B.C. & A. Forms/C.2118/12.

Instructions regarding War Diaries and Intelligence Summaries are contained in F. S. Regs., Part II. and the Staff Manual respectively. Title Pages will be prepared in manuscript.

WAR DIARY
or
~~INTELLIGENCE~~ SUMMARY
(Erase heading not required.)

(3)

Map Reference: Sheets 28.

Army Form C. 2118.

Place	Date	Hour	Summary of Events and Information	Remarks and references to Appendices
KEERSEBROM CAMP	13/10/17	9 AM	Wet & stormy weather – Captain J. MORRIS. M.C. RAMC (T.F) & Lieut BOGART MORC USA left for VOORMEZEELE with advance party about 80 O.R. –	A.H.
"	14/10/17	9 AM	All arrangements made to complete relief at VOORMEZEELE, but relief was postponed 24 hours – A tent subdivision arrived from 134 Field Ambulance to take over here –	A.H.
"	15/10/17	9 P.M.	Remainder of relieving advance parties left for VOORMEZEELE –	A.H.
"	16/10/17	7:30 AM	Headquarters moved to VOORMEZEELE A.D.S. I31.c.4.7. and took over from 49 Fld. Amb. – Visited LARCH WOOD at 3 P.M – Considerable number of casualties passed through during the day, about 120 wounded & gassed (Shell lachrymatory) –	A.H.
VOORMEZEELE	17/10/17	9:30 AM	A.D.M.S. visited VOORMEZEELE and inspected the A.D.S. – Captain J. MORRIS. M.C is suffering slightly from the effects of gas (Shell lachrymatory) but is remaining at duty at LARCH WOOD (I 29. c.1.9.) – Capt. W. HARMENS RAMC and a bearer subdivision from 134 Fld. Amb. reported for duty at 10.30 P.M –	A.H.

2449 Wt. W14957/M90 750,000 1/16 J.B.C. & A. Forms/C.2118/12.

Instructions regarding War Diaries and Intelligence Summaries are contained in F. S. Regs., Part II. and the Staff Manual respectively. Title Pages will be prepared in manuscript.

WAR DIARY
or
~~INTELLIGENCE SUMMARY~~

(Erase heading not required.)

October 1917 (4) Map Reference Sheet 28 –

Army Form C. 2118.

Place	Date	Hour	Summary of Events and Information	Remarks and references to Appendices
VOORMEZEELE	18/10/17	8 AM	Capt: HARMENS. + 134 Bearer Subdivision left for LARCH WOOD ADP + replaced a party to come down for 24 hours rest – The ADMS 7th Division visited VOORMEZEELE at 11.30 AM. and we visited LARCH WOOD ADS. together at 1 P.M. –	AHL
	19/10/17	12 Noon	Captain WAY. RAMC of 134 Fld. Amb: arrived to relieve Captain HARMENS. RAMC, under orders to take over a temporary medical charge of 1/6 Cheshire Regt. – The latter reported his arrival at 6 P.M. – and Captain FERGUSON of 133 Fld Amb has also relieved –	AHL
	20/10/17	5 AM	Visited LARCH WOOD, CANADA STREET, RELAY POST and the 3 RAPs of units in the line – Left RAP. (J 20.d.8.8) is a small "pill box": cases are carried by hand carriage via Relay POST (J.19.d.8.8) to CANADA STREET (I 30.a.4.2) + from Right RAP. (J 25.b.2.8) to CANADA STREET direct, over trench board tracks which are good most of the way, except between Left RAP + Relay Post where the carry is very difficult + arduous – Support RAP. is located at RELAY POST: these posts are "pill-boxes" also: whilst Right RAP is an iron elephant inside a concrete "pillbox" + is good + roomy –	

Instructions regarding War Diaries and Intelligence Summaries are contained in F. S. Regs., Part II. and the Staff Manual respectively. Title pages will be prepared in manuscript.

WAR DIARY
or
INTELLIGENCE SUMMARY.
(Erase heading not required.)

October 1917 — (5) — Map Reference:– Sheet 28.

Army Form C. 2118.

Place	Date	Hour	Summary of Events and Information	Remarks and references to Appendices
VOORMEZEELE	20/10/17.		From CANADA STREET to LARCH WOODS cases are brought by trolley line or hand carriage if line is broken, which it is every day by heavy hostile shelling, although a repair party is constantly re-mending it. From LARCH WOOD cases are carried to VERBRANDEN POST (I.28.b.4.2.) whence cars take them to VOORMEZEELE A.D.S. (I.31.c.4.7.): from here M.A.C. cars carry them direct to C.C.S. – Returned to HdQrs at 12.30 P.M. – During the evening both cars standing at VERBRANDEN POST were damaged by shell fire & had to be replaced & sent to workshops. – Decided to keep one car at this POST by night instead of two, as few cases can come down during darkness, most of the evacuation being carried out from dawn onwards. – The whole of the evacuation route is heavily shelled from time to time, and is worst in this respect at and between CANADA STREET and LARCH WOOD: it is often necessary to keep cases at both places for a time until conditions improve –	A.H.

2353 Wt. W2544/1454 700,000 5/15 D. D. & L. A.D.S.S./Forms/C. 2118.

Instructions regarding War Diaries and Intelligence Summaries are contained in F. S. Regs., Part II. and the Staff Manual respectively. Title pages will be prepared in manuscript.

WAR DIARY
or
~~INTELLIGENCE SUMMARY.~~
(Erase heading not required.)

Army Form C. 2118.

(6)

October 1917 — Map Reference — Sheet 28 —

Place	Date	Hour	Summary of Events and Information	Remarks and references to Appendices
VOORMEZEELE	21/10/17		Captain FERGUSON RAMC rejoined his unit, 133 Fld Amb, yesterday: ~~Lieut.~~ A. BROWN returned to the unit yesterday — Weather remains fine, slight frost at nights —	ALL
"	22/10/17	7PM.	Rain in the night was followed by a fine day: many lightly wounded passed through the ADS. today, total evacuation being over 100 — Lieut A. BROWN RAMC left with an advance	
		7.30PM.	party to take over a site at H 27. C. 3. 7. and prepare an Entraining Centre —	ALL
"	23/10/17	10AM.	Visited X Corps Entraining Centre at H 27. C. 3. 7: this consists of marquees, in many respects very much part worn, sides, ropes & pegs being in poor condition — There is no equipment of any kind in the place —	ALL
"	24/10/17	7PM.	Relieved in the line by Fld Ambulances of the 7th Division — Proceeded to H 27. C. 3. 7 & established my headquarters there — Captain MORRIS R.C. and party from the line went into camp at LA CLYTTE (N 7. a. 2. 0.) — Bearer Subdivisions from 133 & 134 Fld Ambs & Captain L. WAY RAMC —	

Instructions regarding War Diaries and Intelligence Summaries are contained in F. S. Regs., Part II. and the Staff Manual respectively. Title pages will be prepared in manuscript.

WAR DIARY
or
~~INTELLIGENCE SUMMARY.~~
(Erase heading not required.)

Army Form C. 2118.

(7)

October 1917 – Map Reference:– Sheet 28 –

Place	Date	Hour	Summary of Events and Information	Remarks and references to Appendices
VOORMEZEELE	24/10/17	7 P.M.	rejoined their units – Captains CAITHNESS + CRUMLEY + 1/Lt BOGART proceeded to 11 C.C.S. for temporary duty –	Alh.
H 27. c. 3. 7.	25/10/17	9 A.M.	A wild night has levelled nearly all the marquees to the ground: these were repitched as far as possible during the day, and arrangements made for reception, redressing, feeding + entraining a large number of patients.	Alh.
"	26/10/17	9.30 A.M.	Long loads of wounded commenced to arrive + continued to arrive all day, + were entrained: trains left at 1 P.M. with 493 patients, at 7 P.M. with 460 patients, at 10.15 P.M. with 174 patients: many cases, unfit for the train, were also sent by cars to C.C.S. Heavy rain fell almost all day + rendered conditions very bad – Visited by D.D.M.S. X Corps at about NOON –	Alh.
"	27/10/17	10.15 A.M.	weather improved: train left with 115 cases: and another train was despatched at 7.40 P.M. with 143 cases – Visited by A.D.M.S. at 11 A.M. –	Alh.
"	28/10/17	10 P.M.	Weather continues improved – Cases still arrive slowly and a train left with 127 cases at 8.35 P.M. – Six Clerks sent to	

2353 Wt. W2544/1454 700,000 5/15 D. D. & L. A.D.S.S./Forms/C. 2118.

132nd FIELD AMBULANCE 28/10/17

Instructions regarding War Diaries and Intelligence Summaries are contained in F. S. Regs., Part II. and the Staff Manual respectively. Title pages will be prepared in manuscript.

WAR DIARY
or
~~INTELLIGENCE SUMMARY.~~
(Erase heading not required.)

Army Form C. 2118.

(8)

October 1917 — Map Reference — Sheet 28.

Place	Date	Hour	Summary of Events and Information	Remarks and references to Appendices
H27.C.3.7.	27/10/17	7PM	Central Bureaus at REMY SIDING & GODEWAERSVELDE CCS. grouped. Orders received to take over evacuation of the line from 7th Division at 2PM. Necessary arrangements & detail made.	AH
VOORMEZEELE	28/10/17	12Noon	Headquarters reestablished at I 31.C.4.7: all previous forward posts are in the same sites as we handed over, and same personnel as regards numbers were detailed for them. Captain W.T. BROWN is in charge of LARCH WOOD: he has Lt BOGART with him, whilst Captain CAITHNESS & Lt A.BROWN are at CANADA ST. The Officers on detached duty rejoined my headquarters at 12 NOON. Captain CRUMLEY M.O.R.C. U.S.A. took over temporary charge of the 4/5 Black Watch, under orders received from A.D.M.S. The 7th Division left one Officer at VOORMEZEELE for temporary duty with me, and Lieut CH. BANNERMAN. RAMC. of 133 Fld Amb reported for duty at 6 PM. During the afternoon & evening several severely wounded, by bombs dropped, were admitted & passed to CCS. Weather clear & cold.	AH

2353 Wt. W2544/1454 700,000 5/15 D. D. & L. A.D.S.S./Forms/C. 2118.

132nd FIELD AMBULANCE 30/10/17.

Instructions regarding War Diaries and Intelligence Summaries are contained in F. S. Regs., Part II. and the Staff Manual respectively. Title pages will be prepared in manuscript.

WAR DIARY
or
~~INTELLIGENCE SUMMARY.~~
(Erase heading not required.)

Army Form C. 2118.

(9)

October. 1917 –

Map Reference:– Sheet 28 –

Place	Date	Hour	Summary of Events and Information	Remarks and references to Appendices
VOORMEZEELE	30/10/17.	9 A.M.	Wet weather – Captain J. MORRIS. M.C. RAMC (T.F) was admitted to Hpl and evacuated to the Base on 26/10/17, suffering from gas (Shell) + is struck off the strength –	AH.
"	31/10/17	12.45 P.M.	Fine bright weather – ADMS visited the A.D.S. – At 3 P.M. Captain J. YOUNG. RAMC. reported his arrival + is taken on the strength from today's date –	AH.

132nd FIELD AMBULANCE 31/10/17.

A Whittingham –
Lt Col –
R.A.M.C.
O.C. 132nd FIELD AMBULANCE.

2353 Wt. W2544/1454 700,000 5/15 D. D. & L. A.D.S.S./Forms/C. 2118.

CONFIDENTIAL

WAR DIARY
(ORIGINAL)

132 Field Ambulance

From - NOVEMBER 1st 1917
To - NOVEMBER 30th 1917

VOLUME II

ORIGINAL

Instructions regarding War Diaries and Intelligence Summaries are contained in F. S. Regs., Part II. and the Staff Manual respectively. Title pages will be prepared in manuscript.

WAR DIARY
or
~~INTELLIGENCE SUMMARY.~~
(Erase heading not required.)

Army Form C. 2118.

(1)

November 1917 –

Map Reference: – Sheet 28 –

Place	Date	Hour	Summary of Events and Information	Remarks and references to Appendices
VOORMEZEELE	1/11/17	10AM	Fine bright weather – Captain W.T. BROWN M.C. RAMC has been awarded a bar to the MILITARY CROSS for gallantry in the Field during the period 19–28/9/17 – For gallant work in the Field the MILITARY MEDAL was awarded to:– No: 65893 Sgt. R. DINSDALE, No: 69659 Pte H.T. FRANCIS, No: 65867 Pte H. EVERALL, No 72773 Pte O. HARTWELL –	Alh.
"	2/11/17	9AM	Captain J. YOUNG RAMC relieved Lt. A. BROWN RAMC at CANADA STREET, the latter returning to Headquarters – Dull weather with some rain –	Alh.
"	3/11/17	10AM	Dull weather continues – Orders arrived from the A.D.M.S. for 1/Lt BOGART MORC U.S.A. to take over medical charge of the 11th Bn Royal Sussex Rgt this evening –	Alh.
"	4/11/17	10AM	Dull weather continues – Quiet day –	Alh.
"	5/11/17	5AM	Left my Headquarters and visited LARCH WOOD, CANADA STREET, Relay Post at BODMIN COPSE, and Right & Left RAPs. Found all well equipped and evacuation proceeding smoothly – The duckboard tracks to forward Posts have been much improved, and the carry is less severe for Bearers now than it was – Reached my headquarters on return at 10.15 AM –	Alh.

132nd FIELD AMBULANCE

Instructions regarding War Diaries and Intelligence Summaries are contained in F. S. Regs., Part II. and the Staff Manual respectively. Title pages will be prepared in manuscript.

WAR DIARY
or
~~INTELLIGENCE SUMMARY.~~
(Erase heading not required.)

Army Form C. 2118.

(2)

, November, 1917 –

Map Reference:– Sheet 28.

Place	Date	Hour	Summary of Events and Information	Remarks and references to Appendices
VOORMEZEELE	6/11/17	10 AM.	Wet weather – Casualties passing ~~through~~ few through the day –	AH.
"	7/11/17	10 AM	Rain continues – Captain F.W. McMILLAN RAMC reported his arrival at 3 P.M: later he relieved Captain W.T. BROWN. M.C at LARCH WOOD A.D.S, the latter to return to VOORMEZEELE & take over charge of the unit: I proceeded to Divl H.Q. to take over duties of acting A.D.M.S – Captain W.T. BROWN M.C. returned to H.Q at VOORMEZEELE for duty 10pm	AH. WTB
"	8/11/17	10 Am.	Captain GOMPERTZ RAMC detailed to this Ambulance for temporary duty, and took over charge of LARCH WOOD A.D.S., Captain F.W. McMILLAN RAMC remaining. Weather dull, with rain later. Few casualties passed through today.	WTB.
"	9/11/17.	10 am	Weather showery and dull. Few casualties passing through during the day. In evening went with Lt-Col. LITTLEJOHNS D.S.O. RAMC and saw O's C. 15th & 14th Fd Ambs. with reference to taking over their lines of evacuation. Lieut BOGART M.O.R.C. U.S. returned to 132 Fd Amb. on completion of temporary duty with 11th R. Sussex Bn.	WTB.
"	10/11/17	6. am.	Weather wet. I left H.Q 132nd Fd Amb with Capt GOMPERTZ RAMC and reconnoitred all bearer posts in the sector to be taken over. I found it would be feasible to evacuate all RAP's in new & in present sector, down the Menin-Ypres Road to	

2353 Wt. W2544/1454 700,000 5/15 D. D. & L. A.D.S.S./Forms/C. 2118.

132nd FIELD AMBULANCE

Instructions regarding War Diaries and Intelligence Summaries are contained in F. S. Regs., Part II. and the Staff Manual respectively. Title pages will be prepared in manuscript.

WAR DIARY
or
~~INTELLIGENCE~~ SUMMARY.
(Erase heading not required.)

Army Form C. 2118.

(3)

November

Map References Sheet 28.

Place	Date	Hour	Summary of Events and Information	Remarks and references to Appendices
VOORMEZEELE			HOOGE CRATER. These posts were (a) Left of MENIN-YPRES Road:- Left RAP. [J. 15 d 5.3] TOWER RELAY POST [J14 d 9.4]. (b) Right of MENIN-YPRES Rd:- Centre RAP. [J 20 b 5.5] Right RAP [J.20.d.2.7] These posts evacuated via CLAPHAM JUNCTION [J13 d 9.8], + TUNNEL RELAY [J13 a 6.4], down the MENIN-YPRES Road to HOOGE CRATER [I 18 a 3.7.]. Thence by Ambulance Car to ÉCOLE YPRES [I 9 c 5.2]. BODMIN COPSE Aid Post [J19 d 6.6.] would evacuate to CANADA ST. [I 30 d 4.2], then by bearers to SWITCH Car Stand [I 23 d 6.5]. Thence by Ford Car to WOODCOTE Ho. [I 20 c 45.30]. Bearer Posts at JACKDAW CRATER [J19 b 1.9] to bearer post at TANK VIEW [I 24 b 9.1] to bearer post at OBSERVATORY [I 24 c 9.3] to car stand at SWITCH [I 23 d. 6.5]; thence as before to WOODCOTE Ho. [I 20c. 45.30] These observations I communicated to ADMS 39th Div. on my return to Amb H.Q. at 3 p.m. Lieut BANNERMANN RAMC returned to 133 Fd. Amb. by ADMS order, after return to 132 Fd Amb of Lieut BOGART MORC USA. By order of ADMS. 39th Div Lieut VANCE MORC USA reported to ADMS 39 Div. for return to 7th Div	WTB
WOODCOTE HO.	11/11/17	2 p.m	Weather wet. Took over WOODCOTE HOUSE [I 20 c 4.3] from 14th Fd Amb HQ. Capt. GOMPERTZ RAMC with advd party of 1 NCO. + 20 men took over the line of posts SWITCH [I 23 d 6.5] to JACKDAW CRATER [J19 b 1.9]. Capt McMILLAN RAMC. moved out of LARCH WOOD with 40 OR's + all equipment handing over other stores to 37th Div. Amb. The above moves were completed by 2 p.m. as	

2353 Wt. W2544/1454 700,000 5/15 D. D. & L. A.D.S.S./Forms/C. 2118.

Instructions regarding War Diaries and Intelligence Summaries are contained in F. S. Regs., Part II. and the Staff Manual respectively. Title pages will be prepared in manuscript.

WAR DIARY
or
~~INTELLIGENCE SUMMARY.~~
(Erase heading not required.)

Army Form C. 2118.

(4)

November

Map References. Sheet 28.

Place	Date	Hour	Summary of Events and Information	Remarks and references to Appendices
			per ADMS. orders. Capt GOMPERTZ RAMC Capt McMILLAN RAMC. and 84 OR's moved at 4 pm. to ÉCOLE [I 9 c 5.2] and billeted there night 11th - 12th Nov. Capt CRUMLEY MORC USA. returned to 132 Fd Amb. on completion of temporary duty as M.O. to 4/5th Black Watch. Capt CAITHNESS RAMC returned to H.Q. from CANADA ST and reported sick; Gassed (shell) Laryngitis. Lieut P. CARROLL RAMC. proceeded to report to ADMS 7th Div for duty and was struck off the strength of this unit. A.+D. books opened (DDMS Xth Corps Order).	WRB
WOODCOTE HOUSE	12/11/17	10 am.	Weather wet. Capt GOMPERTZ RAMC + party took over the Ypres - MENIN Road line of posts from 15th Fd Amb. Relief complete by 10 am. Capt GOMPERTZ RAMC making his headquarters as O.C. Bearers at CLAPHAM JUNCTION [J 13 d 9.8]. Central Bureau at GODEWAERSVELDE was closed this day, and N.C.O + 3 clerks returned to this Amb for duty. A large number of cases of Trench Feet were evacuated to-day. Total admissions 183 OR's and 3 officers. Of these 110 were 'Trench Feet' - 80 from 5th Div. + 30 from 39th Div/. Only 12 wounded passed through.	WRB
"	13/11/17	7 a.m.	Weather warm + fine. I left HQ at 7am. + visited CLAPHAM JUNCTION [J 13 d 9.8], CANADA ST (I 30 d 9.2) and SWITCH [I 23 d 6.5]. Evacuation proceeding smoothly. Capt YOUNG. RAMC, reported sick from CANADA ST. and was brought back to H.Q. Lieut A. BROWN RAMC. went to	

2353 Wt. W2544/1454 700,000 5/15 D. D. & L. A.D.S.S./Forms/C. 2118.

132nd FIELD AMBULANCE

Instructions regarding War Diaries and Intelligence Summaries are contained in F. S. Regs., Part II. and the Staff Manual respectively. Title pages will be prepared in manuscript.

WAR DIARY
or
~~INTELLIGENCE SUMMARY.~~
(Erase heading not required.)

Army Form C. 2118.

(5)

November

Map References Sheet 28.

Place	Date	Hour	Summary of Events and Information	Remarks and references to Appendices
			CANADA St to replace Capt YOUNG RAMC. Capt CAITHNESS RAMC was sent to D.R.S (134 Fd Amb) suffering from Gas shell (Laryngitis). Lieut BOGART M.O.R.C. U.S.A. proceeded by ADMS order & took over duties of M.O. 16th Bn Rifle Bde. relieving Capt A.W. DENNIS RAMC. Capt C.D. PILE RAMC reported to this Amb. for temporary duty in relief of Lieut BOGART MORC USA. Very few wounded passed through: total admissions 1 officer + 46 OR's.	WTB
WOODCOTE House	14/11/17	10 am.	Weather dull & humid. Capt J. YOUNG RAMC. was sent to DRS (134 Fd Amb) suffering from N.Y.D. Febrile (? Tuberculosis of lungs). Evacuations 39 incl. 5 officers; 1 officer + 14 OR. wounded. Lt.-Col. LITTLEJOHNS D.S.O. RAMC acting A.D.M.S. visited this Amb. this morning, and discussed methods of evacuation of wounded and the suggested improvements to R.A.P.'s. Lieut. & QM. COX. RAMC. proceeded by order of 2nd Army to England to report to War Office.	WTB WTB
"	15/11/17	10 am.	Weather fine & warm. Capt C.W. McCLANAHAN M.O.R.C. USA. reported to this Amb. by order of ADMS for temporary duty. Admissions 4 officers + 113 OR's., incl. 37 trench feet (34 from 39th Div.). Casualties in this unit 1 killed + 2 wounded.	WTB
"	16/11/17	10 am.	Weather fine. Capt C.D. PILE RAMC proceeded this morning by ADMS orders to take over duties of M.O. 16th Bn. Nott. & Derby Regt. from Capt. LINDEMANN sick. Capt. HARMENS RAMC reported from 134th Fd. Amb. (D.R.S.) to this Amb. H.Q. for temporary duty. Capt McCLANAHAN M.O.R.C. USA was sent to CLAPHAM JUNCTION to relieve Capt PILE RAMC. Lt Col LITTLEJOHNS DSO RAMC a/ADMS reported sick and was admitted to D.R.S. 39th Div.	WTB WTB

2353 Wt. W2544/1454 700,000 5/15 D. D. & L. A.D.S.S./Forms/C. 2118.

132nd FIELD AMBULANCE

Instructions regarding War Diaries and Intelligence Summaries are contained in F.S. Regs., Part II. and the Staff Manual respectively. Title pages will be prepared in manuscript.

WAR DIARY
or
~~INTELLIGENCE SUMMARY.~~
(Erase heading not required.)

(6)

Army Form C. 2118.

November

Map References Sheet 28

Place	Date	Hour	Summary of Events and Information	Remarks and references to Appendices
			Admissions 1 officer (W) and 61 OR's including 1 German prisoner (W).	WTB
WOODCOTE HOUSE	17/11/17	10 am.	Weather fine. Lieut. + QM R. COX RAMC, having gone to England to report to War Office was struck off the strength of this unit from today. Lieut + QM HARROLD RAMC reported his arrival and was taken on strength vice Lieut + QM R COX RAMC. Capt CAITHNESS RAMC and Capt YOUNG RAMC having been evacuated sick today were struck off the strength of this unit. Admissions 45, including 15 wounded.	WTB
"	18/11/17	7.30 am.	Weather fine. Reconnoitred system of evacuation from the line, with DADMS 39th Divn, and lines of suggested improvements gone over. Admissions 98, including 2 Officers wounded + 1 officer sick	WTB
"	19/11/17	10 am.	Weather fine. A quiet day. Admissions 74 including 1 officer sick.	WTB
"	20/11/17	10 am	Weather fine. Admissions 84 including 3 officers wounded.	WTB
"	21/11/17	10 am.	Weather wet. Reported progress of work on billets: about 50 yards of bricked drive for cars to enter + leave the yard; the bricks laid being obtained from YPRES 2 G.S. Wagon loads a day. ADMS visited the Amb. in the afternoon. Capt GOMPERTZ RAMC proceeded on temporary duty as M.O. i/c 16th Bn. Notts + Derby's, by order of ADMS. Lieut BOYER MORC U.S.A. reported here for temporary duty vice Capt GOMPERTZ RAMC. Admissions 45 including 12 wounded	WTB

Instructions regarding War Diaries and Intelligence Summaries are contained in F. S. Regs., Part II. and the Staff Manual respectively. Title pages will be prepared in manuscript.

WAR DIARY
or
INTELLIGENCE SUMMARY.
(Erase heading not required.)

(7)

Army Form C. 2118.

November.

Map References Sheet 28.

Place	Date	Hour	Summary of Events and Information	Remarks and references to Appendices
WOODCOTE HOUSE	22/11/17	10 am.	Weather wet. Received notice from Area Commandant GORSON Area to evacuate ÉCOLE. Refused to do this without IX Corps authority and referred matter to ADMS who confirmed. Admissions 47 including 1 officer sick.	WB
"	23/11/17	10 am	Weather dull. Received reconnoitring visit from Col. SHAW DSO RAMC, O.C. 97th Fd. Amb. reference taking over. Arrangements for taking over considered + discussed, WOODCOTE HOUSE + our horse lines nr. VIERSTRAAT inspected. Admissions 44 including 5 wounded officers.	WB
"	24/11/17	7.30 am.	Visited ZILLEBEKE, CANADA ST, BODMIN COPSE, CLAPHAM Jn., ÉCOLE. with O.C. 97th Fd. Amb. acquainting him with system of evacuation, and with proposed improvements of tracks + of posts. Returned to Amb. H.Q at 1 pm. Capt HARMENS RAMC. proceeded to take over duties of M.O. 1/6th Bn Cheshires vice Capt WAY RAMC. reporting sick. Party of 1 officer + 70 men of 97th Fd. Amb. arrived at ÉCOLE as an advance party to take over line, in accordance with ADMS Operation Order No 36 of 23/11/17. 132 Fd Amb. Bearer reserve at ÉCOLE moved to WOODCOTE HOUSE to save accommodation. Admissions during the day 100 including 3 officers. Weather fine.	WB.
"	25/11/17	10 am.	Advance party of 97th Fd. Amb. relieved 15 squads bearers 132 Fd. Amb. at forward posts. Squads relieved returned to ÉCOLE. Lieut A BROWN RAMC proceeded with advanced party of 14 ORs	

2353 Wt. W2544/1454 700,000 5/15 D. D. & L. A.D.S.S./Forms/C. 2118.

132nd FIELD AMBULANCE

Instructions regarding War Diaries and Intelligence Summaries are contained in F. S. Regs., Part II. and the Staff Manual respectively. Title pages will be prepared in manuscript.

(8)

Army Form C. 2118.

WAR DIARY
or
INTELLIGENCE SUMMARY.
(Erase heading not required.)

November

Map References Sheet 28 + 27

Place	Date	Hour	Summary of Events and Information	Remarks and references to Appendices
WOODCOTE HOUSE.			from Tent Subdivision to STEENVOORDE as advance party to take over and open up Dressing Station, c̄ sites at J 22 a 2.2. (Sheet 27) + Q.1.c 6.8 (Sheet 27) with Ambulance H.Q at latter location + Transport Lines at former. A second party of 2 officers and remainder of 30th Div reavers + a Tent subdivision arrived from 97th Fd Amb. at ECOLE and at WOODCOTE HOUSE to take over remainder of our manned posts on 26th Nov. and open up ADS, at WOODCOTE HO. on our departure 26th Nov. (ADMS Operation Order No 36). Weather fair to wet.	WTB
STEENVOORDE.	26/11/17.	12 Noon.	Lt Col. A.S. LITTLEJOHNS. D.S.O. RAMC. returned to duty from 134 Fld. Amb. Headquarters of unit moved to STEENVOORDE (Q1.b.6.8), on completion of relief by 97 Fld Amb. Bearer parties moved to CHIPPEWA for the night.	Alh.
"	27/11/17	1 P.M.	Bearer parties arrived + went into billets at J22.a.2.2. I visited WATOU in the afternoon + occupied site there with an advance party. Remainder of unit to move there tomorrow — less party remaining to man Collecting Post at STEENVOORDE (Q1.b.6.8) —	Alh.
"	28/11/17	9.30 AM.	Unit moved to WATOU and occupied Field Ambulance Site there: Lt A. BROWN. + 20 NCOs + men remained at STEENVOORDE	

2353 Wt. W2544/1454 700,000 5/15 D. D. & L. A.D.S.S./Forms/C. 2118.

132nd FIELD AMBULANCE

Instructions regarding War Diaries and Intelligence Summaries are contained in F. S. Regs., Part II. and the Staff Manual respectively. Title pages will be prepared in manuscript.

WAR DIARY
or
~~INTELLIGENCE~~ SUMMARY.

(Erase heading not required.)

(9)

Army Form C. 2118.

Map Reference:— Sheet 27 –

Place	Date	Hour	Summary of Events and Information	Remarks and references to Appendices
WATOU E.4.b.6.4.	28/11/17		to Reserve Collecting Post there – The WATOU site has suffered very much through having been occupied by troops other than R.A.M.C. for the past few months; Cookhouse, Stores etc all much knocked about; pack Store & ablution sheds have been used as Stables – The A.D.M.S. paid a visit at 3.30 PM	A.H.
"	29/11/17	10 AM	Fine morning – Site has been equipped – general cleaning up of whole surroundings in progress – Pack Store has been remade	
		4 PM	& is now ready for use again – Captain H.S. GROVES. R.A.M.C. & Lieuts: A.S. FINDLAY & F.E. LARKINS. R.A.M.C. reported their arrival & are taken on the strength from this date –	A.H.
"	30/11/17	9.30 AM	Fine weather continues – Progress made in cleaning up of site & transport –	

132nd FIELD AMBULANCE 1/12/17 –

A Whittington – Lt Col –
R.A.M.C.
O.C. 132ND FIELD AMBULANCE

2353 Wt. W2544/1454 700,000 5/15 D. D. & L. A.D.S.S./Forms/C. 2118.

(Confidential)

War Diary

of

132 Field Ambulance

from December 1st 1917 to December 31st 1917

Volume II.

Original –

(1)

Instructions regarding War Diaries and Intelligence Summaries are contained in F. S. Regs., Part II. and the Staff Manual respectively. Title pages will be prepared in manuscript.

WAR DIARY
or
INTELLIGENCE SUMMARY.
(Erase heading not required.)

December 1917 – Map Reference – Sheet 27.

Army Fo[illegible]2118.

Place	Date	Hour	Summary of Events and Information	Remarks and references to Appendices
WATOU. E.4.b.6.4.	1/12/17	10AM.	Fine cold morning – Daily inspection – Clearing up of site + wagons has made good progress: checking of panniers after coming out of the line – Visited STEENVOORDE Collecting Post (Q.1.b.6.8.) at 11.30 AM + found all in good order: paid the personnel there – At 2 P.M. Kit inspection of personnel held to ascertain condition on coming out of line – D.D.M.S. VIII Corps visited the site at 3.30 P.M. –	A.L.
"	2/12/17	10AM.	Fine morning, cold – Captain H.S. GROVES. RAMC. proceeded to take over temporary medical charge of 14 Bn. Hampshire Regt –	A.L.
"	3/12/17	10AM.	Fine weather, very cold, sharp frost in the night – Daily inspection – I visited the Town Major again with reference to the horse standings.	
		4PM.	Horse standings now vacated + occupied by us – Good progress is being made in refitting + transport is now getting into good order –	A.L.
"	4/12/17	10AM.	Weather continues fine, but cold – I visited STEENVOORDE C.P. in the afternoon –	A.L.
"	5/12/17	10AM.	Weather fine but sharp – Preliminary warning received re move to new area – Captain BROWN. M.C. visited 118 Inf. Brigade during the afternoon	

2353 Wt. W2544/1454 700,000 5/15 D. D. & L. A.D.S.S./Forms/C. 2118.

Army Form [redacted] 2118.

Instructions regarding War Diaries and Intelligence Summaries are contained in F. S. Regs., Part II. and the Staff Manual respectively. Title pages will be prepared in manuscript.

WAR DIARY
or
~~INTELLIGENCE SUMMARY.~~
(Erase heading not required.)

(2)

December 1917 – Map Reference – Sheets 27 – CALAIS 13 a –

Place	Date	Hour	Summary of Events and Information	Remarks and references to Appendices
WATOU	5/12/17	4PM.	but could obtain no details as regards move –	AHL
"	6/12/17	10AM.	Fine weather continues, with hard frost – Lieut. A.S. FINDLAY RAMC. posted to 39 DAC. is struck off the strength of the unit from today's date – Transport packed ready to move off – Captain GOMPERTZ RAMC arrived for temporary duty at 10 P.M –	AHL
"	7/12/17	9AM.	Weather milder – Transport moved off under command of Captain W.T. BROWN. MC at 9.45 AM – Captain GOMPERTZ RAMC left in charge of billeting party to report to 118 Infantry Brigade at 5.45 AM –	AHL
"	8/12/17	10AM.	Unit marched to GODESWAERVELDE and entrained at 1.15 P.M: after a short journey we detrained at LOTTINGHEN at 10PM. and marched into billets at VIEIL MOULIER at 11 PM – Transport joined up here –	AHL
VIEIL MOULIER	9/12/17	10AM.	Unit proceeded by march route to BRUNEMBERT which was reached shortly after noon. Weather unpleasant + wet –	AHL
BRUNEMBERT	10/12/17	10AM.	Beautiful sunshiny morning – Visited all billets + stables + made arrangements for equipment of empty farm house as small Hpl: good progress made + sick from 118 + 117 Infantry Brigades collected + accomodated –	AHL

[redacted]2nd FIELD AMBULANCE 11/12/17.

Instructions regarding War Diaries and Intelligence Summaries are contained in F. S. Regs., Part II. and the Staff Manual respectively. Title pages will be prepared in manuscript.

WAR DIARY
or
~~INTELLIGENCE SUMMARY.~~
(*Erase heading not required.*)

(3)

Map Reference:— CALAIS 13.

Army For[redacted]2118.

Place	Date	Hour	Summary of Events and Information	Remarks and references to Appendices
BRONEMBERT.	11/12/17.	10 A.M.	Frosty bright morning — Site equipped & in full swing — 27 patients remaining under treatment —	A.L.
"	12/12/17	10 A.M.	Beautiful weather continues — The A.D.M.S. visited the unit & inspected hospital & billets of personnel at 12.45 P.M.	A.L.
"	13/12/17	10 A.M.	Weather fine, milder — Daily inspection —	A.L.
"	14/12/17	9.30 A.M.	Weather dull & mild — Inspection of unit in marching order —	A.L.
"	15/12/17	9 A.M.	Weather beautifully fine, bright sunshine — Training hours in the morning devoted to Squad Drill and Box Respirator drill —	A.L.
"	16/12/17	11 A.M.	Fine weather, but very cold S.E. wind — Snow fell in considerable quantities in the afternoon —	A.L.
"	17/12/17	10 A.M.	Country is covered with snow — Squad & Company drill during the morning — Part of personnel bathed during the afternoon —	A.L.
"	18/12/17	10 A.M.	Bright sunshiny morning; very cold; hard frost during the night, which continues this morning; roads icebound —	A.L.
"	19/12/17	11 A.M.	Bright morning — Very sharp frost continues — Attended conference at	

2353 Wt. W2544/1454 700,000 5/15 D. D. & L. A.D.S.S./Forms/C. 2118.

Instructions regarding War Diaries and Intelligence Summaries are contained in F. S. Regs., Part II. and the Staff Manual respectively. Title pages will be prepared in manuscript.

WAR DIARY
or
~~INTELLIGENCE~~ SUMMARY.
(Erase heading not required.)

(4)

Map Reference :- CALAIS 13.

Army For[illegible] 2118.

Place	Date	Hour	Summary of Events and Information	Remarks and references to Appendices
BRUNEMBERT	19/12/17	11 AM	the office of the ADMS - Captain R. GOMPERTZ RAMC posted to the unit & is taken on the strength -	A.H.
"	20/12/17	10 AM	Exceedingly hard frost, with brilliant sunshine - Arrangements made for securing local schoolroom for personnel's dinner on Christmas Day -	A.H.
"	21/12/17	10 AM	Hard frost continuing - Captain C. H. WITTS. RAMC posted to the unit & is taken on the strength from today's date - Daily inspection - Major E.H. ELIOTT-LOCKHART, late Scots Greys, visited the unit and gave advice re horsemastership -	A.H.
"	22/12/17	10 AM	Weather not so cold - Tug of war team reached semi-final of Divisional Championship -	A.H.
"	23/12/17	10 AM	Very hard frost - Brilliant sunshine -	A.H.
"	24/12/17	10 AM	Weather milder & thawing - All arrangements completed for xmas festivities of personnel - Tug of war team defeated in Divl semi-finals -	A.H.
"	25/12/17	10 AM	Bright morning thaw continues - Divine Service at 11 AM - The A.D.M.S. visited the men at dinner between 12.30 & 1 PM; a good dinner	

[redacted] 2nd FIELD AMBULANCE 25/12/17

Instructions regarding War Diaries and Intelligence Summaries are contained in F. S. Regs., Part II. and the Staff Manual respectively. Title pages will be prepared in manuscript.

WAR DIARY
or
INTELLIGENCE SUMMARY.
(Erase heading not required.)

(5)

Army For[redacted]2118.

Map Reference:— Calais 13.

Place	Date	Hour	Summary of Events and Information	Remarks and references to Appendices
BRONEMBERT	25/12/17	1PM	was much enjoyed by all ranks, and the A.D.M.S. gave the men a stirring address which was greatly appreciated by all. The tent subdivision was packed during the afternoon, in accordance with orders received. At night a heavy snow storm descended upon the country	A.L.
"	26/12/17	7.30AM	The Section transport moved off under considerable difficulties on account of heavy fall of snow to join 133 Fd Amb transport & march with it to new area. Captain J. MORRIS, M.C. RAMC T.F. rejoined the unit at 1PM & is taken on the strength, resuming the duties of Second in Command.	A.L.
"	27/12/17	10AM.	Snow continues, there being several inches on the ground. Captain GOMPERTZ. RAMC & 12 other ranks proceeded as advance party to L'EBBE FARM (Sheet 27. F29.d.5.8.) on 28th inst.	A.L.
"	28/12/17	9AM.	Very great difficulty experienced in collecting & clearing cases, owing to state of roads with drift snow, which caused many casualties to traffic of all kinds. Roads became impassable towards night in many places.	A.L.

2353 Wt. W2544/1454 700,000 5/15 D. D. & L. A.D.S.S./Forms/C. 2118.

Instructions regarding War Diaries and Intelligence Summaries are contained in F. S. Regs., Part II. and the Staff Manual respectively. Title pages will be prepared in manuscript.

132nd FIELD AMBULANCE 29/12/17.

WAR DIARY
or
~~INTELLIGENCE SUMMARY.~~
(*Erase heading not required.*)

(6)

Army For[illegible]2118.

Map Reference – Sheet Calais 13 – HAZEBROUCK 5A – Sheet 27 –

Place	Date	Hour	Summary of Events and Information	Remarks and references to Appendices
BRUNEMBERT.	29/12/17 – 9 AM.	7.30 9 AM.	Very cold weather – Drift snow making traffic extremely difficult but got transport of unit away to rendez-vous to proceed under charge of 118 Brigade Transport Officer. Lt + QM HARROLD. RAMC in charge of road party – Collection + clearance of cases got through under considerable difficulties by grit of all concerned – During the night Lt A. BROWN. RAMC. left for duty with 134 Fd. Amb.: it was impossible to convey him farther than LOTTINGHEM STATION, owing to drift	
		3 PM.	snow; he was to entrain there. At 3 PM. news was received that the Maltese cart was on the road 2½ miles East of ESCOEUILLES with broken shafts, as result of horse falling into a snow drift. Limbered wagon + party dispatched to unload + bring in, which was accomplished –	AH.
	30/12/17	9 AM.	Bitter weather continues – Move postponed, owing to no lorries being available –	AH.
	[illegible]	8.30 AM.	Unit marched to AFFRINGUES CHATEAU + went into billets for the night –	AH.

132nd FIELD AMBULANCE 2/1/17.

A Whittingham – Lt Col. R.A.M.C.
O.C. 132nd FIELD AMBULANCE

2353 Wt. W2544/1454 700,000 5/15 D. D. & L. A.D.S.S./Forms/C. 2118.

Original

Confidential

Jan. 1918

5

War Diary

— of —

132nd Field Ambulance

from January 1st 1918 to January 31st 1918

(Volume II)

140/2696

Vol 23
39

Army Form C. 2118.

Instructions regarding War Diaries and Intelligence Summaries are contained in F. S. Regs., Part II. and the Staff Manual respectively. Title pages will be prepared in manuscript.

WAR DIARY
or
INTELLIGENCE SUMMARY.
(Erase heading not required.)

132nd FIELD AMBULANCE

(1)

HAZEBROUCK. 5.A. Sheet 27.

Place	Date	Hour	Summary of Events and Information	Remarks and references to Appendices
AFFRINGUES	1/1/18	2AM.	Unit moved off to entrain at WIZERNES at 7AM & detrained at ST JEAN at 11 AM: Bearer Division proceeded to report to O.C. 133 FLD AMB for duty at DUHALLOW, and remainder to L'EBBE FARM (F29. d. 5.8) where the II Corps' Skin Depôt is established. Aid Post in POPERINGHE was taken over on 31st ult. by Lt. A. BROWN. RAMC. & party of six.	Alh.
L'EBBE FARM	2/1/18	9AM.	Tendency to thaw. Lieut. A.S. FINDLAY. RAMC reported his arrival and is taken on the strength. I visited the ADMS at 12 noon. Transport marched in at 2PM.	Alh.
"	3/1/18	9AM.	Hard frost during the night. Some snow falling this morning. Lieut. A. BROWN. RAMC. left to take over medical charge of the 30 DAC & is struck off the strength from today's date.	Alh.
"	4/1/18	9AM.	Hard frost continues. The ADMS visited this site during the morning.	Alh.
"	5/1/18	9AM.	Thawing. Captain W.T. Brown. MC. has taken over charge of the POPERINGHE Aid Post & M.I.R.	Alh.

2353 Wt. W2544/1454 700,000 5/15 D. D. & L. A.D.S.S./Forms/C. 2118.

Instructions regarding War Diaries and Intelligence Summaries are contained in F. S. Regs., Part II. and the Staff Manual respectively. Title pages will be prepared in manuscript.

WAR DIARY
or
~~INTELLIGENCE~~ SUMMARY.
(*Erase heading not required.*)

Army Form C. 2118.

(2)

Map Reference – Sheet 27.

Place	Date	Hour	Summary of Events and Information	Remarks and references to Appendices
L'EBBE FARM. F29.d.5.8.	6/1/18.	9AM.	Hard frost again in the night – Bright clear morning – Daily inspection – Parts have arrived for construction of new bath house, which is being taken in hand – DDMS. II Corps visited the site at 12.15 PM – Captain H.S. GROVES having been posted to medical charge of the 14 Hants Regt is struck off the strength from the 5th inst, from which date Captain C.D. COYLE. RAMC. is taken on the strength of this unit –	Alh
"	7/1/18	"	Heavy rain during the night: thawing hard – Work of erecting new bath house etc commenced – Orders having been received for Captain C.D. COYLE RAMC. to proceed to 134 Field Ambulance for duty, this Officer is struck off the strength from this date – Freezing again at night –	Alh
"	8/1/18	"	Heavy snow has fallen during the early part of the morning – Condition of ground makes building operations very difficult –	Alh
"	9/1/18	"	Severe frost continues – Heavy snow in the afternoon, followed by rain & thaw at night – Progress is being made in the erection of the new bath house –	Alh

2353 Wt. W2544/1454 700,000 5/15 D. D. & L. A.D.S.S./Forms/C. 2118.

Instructions regarding War Diaries and Intelligence Summaries are contained in F. S. Regs., Part II. and the Staff Manual respectively. Title pages will be prepared in manuscript.

WAR DIARY
or
INTELLIGENCE SUMMARY.
(Erase heading not required.)

(3)

Map Reference:— Sheet 27.

Army Form C. 2118.

132nd FIELD AMBULANCE

Place	Date	Hour	Summary of Events and Information	Remarks and references to Appendices
L'EBBE FARM F29. d.5.8.	10/1/18.	9 AM.	Heavy rain during the night: hard thaw & westerly gale blowing this morning — Progress made with erection of new buildings, and work of making superstructures for carrying petrol tins on Water Carts taken in hand —	ALL
"	11/1/18.	9 AM.	Thaw continues, and rain falling —	ALL
"	12/1/18.	9 AM.	Thaw continues — Thaw restrictions imposed at 11 AM — Progress is being made with new constructional work etc — Daily inspection —	
		2.30 PM	1/Lieuts. W. V. EGAN & M. G. MORALES. M.O.R.C. U.S.A. reported their arrival and are taken on the strength of the unit — The A.D.M.S. visited the site at about 3 P.M. —	ALL
"	13/1/18	9 AM.	Fine morning following further frost during the night — In the afternoon all Officers attended a demonstration, by the O.C. II Corps School of Sanitation, on field sanitation —	ALL
"	14/1/18	9 AM.	Considerable fall of snow during the night — Good progress has been made with new buildings, and watercart superstructures —	ALL
"	15/1/18	9 AM.	Heavy rain during the night, hard thaw this morning — Conditions	

Instructions regarding War Diaries and Intelligence Summaries are contained in F. S. Regs., Part II. and the Staff Manual respectively. Title pages will be prepared in manuscript.

WAR DIARY
or
INTELLIGENCE SUMMARY.
(Erase heading not required.)

Army Form C. 2118.

(4)

132nd FIELD AMBULANCE

Map Reference :— Sheet 27.

Place	Date	Hour	Summary of Events and Information	Remarks and references to Appendices
L'EBBE FARM F.29.d.5.8.	15/1/18	9AM	bad – Lecture at noon to newly joined Officers on Field Ambulance work – Heavy rain + gale of wind at night –	A.H.
"	16/1/18	9AM.	There has been a violent gale during the night, resulting in some damage to one of the large HPL marquees – D.D.M.S. 2nd Corps visited the site at 11 AM – Captain H.T. BROWN. M.C. and personnel at M.I.R. POPERINGHE were relieved yesterday by personnel of the 2/2 NORTUMBRIAN FLD AMB + returned to headquarters –	A.H.
"	17/1/18.	9AM.	Snow is falling again – Captain R.H.C. GOMPERTZ RAMC left to take over temporary medical charge of the 1/1 Herts Regt – Instruction to new Officers continued on:– provision of supplies of Stores of all kinds, medical + surgical equipment of Fld Ambulances, testing of water, + protection from gas by the box respirator + P.H. helmet –	A.H.
"	18/1/18.	9AM	Mild weather continues – 1/Lts EGAN + MORALES. M.O.R.C. U.S.A. + a tent subdivision left for temporary duty at No: 12 C.C.S. –	A.H.
"	19/1/18	9AM.	Conditions drier, bright mild morning – RAMC Instructions in connection with 39th Division Order No: 208 received at 5.30 PM –	A.H.

D. D. & L., London, E.C.
(A8004) Wt. W1771/M2 31 750,000 5/17 Sch. 52 Forms/C2118/14

Army Form C. 2118.

Instructions regarding War Diaries and Intelligence Summaries are contained in F. S. Regs., Part II. and the Staff Manual respectively. Title pages will be prepared in manuscript.

WAR DIARY
or
INTELLIGENCE SUMMARY.
(Erase heading not required.)

(5)

Map Reference — Sheet 27 —

Place	Date	Hour	Summary of Events and Information	Remarks and references to Appendices
L'EBBE FARM F29.d.5.8.	20/1/18.	9AM.	Mild weather continues — Bearer Division rejoined from 133 Field Ambulance at 12.15 PM — Packing of wagons is being proceeded with — Superstructures for water carts are completed & being fitted to the carts — Lt. A.S. FINDLAY RAMC. left to take over medical charge of 1/6 Cheshire Regt at 9.30 PM —	AH
"	21/1/18	9AM.	Dull showery weather — Loading of transport for move to new site — Representative of No: 92 Fld: Amb: arrived to arrange taking over of L'EBBE FARM site —	AH
"	22/1/18	9AM.	The unit left L'EBBE FARM and proceeded to HERZEELE which was reached at 1.15 PM — L'EBBE FARM site handed over to the 92nd Field Ambulance — Unit accommodated in HERZEELE in the Chateau site at D10.c.0.9 —	AH
HERZEELE.	23/1/18	9AM	Beautiful mild day — Lts. EGAN & MORALES. M.O.R.C. U.S.A. and tent subdivision personnel rejoined from 12 CCS —	AH

D. D. & L., London, E.C. (A8004) Wt. W1771/M2 31 750,000 5/17 Sch. 52 Forms/C2118/14

Instructions regarding War Diaries and Intelligence Summaries are contained in F. S. Regs., Part II. and the Staff Manual respectively. Title pages will be prepared in manuscript.

WAR DIARY
or
INTELLIGENCE SUMMARY.
(Erase heading not required.)

Army Form C. 2118.

(6)

Map Reference Sheet 27 AMIENS 17 + Sheets 57c + 62c

132nd FIELD AMBULANCE

Place	Date	Hour	Summary of Events and Information	Remarks and references to Appendices
HERZEELE.	24/1/18	9 AM.	Beautiful mild weather – Advance party left to proceed to new area –	
BRAY-SUR-SOMME	26/1/18	8 P.M.	This unit proceeded from HERZEELE by march route and entrained at PROVEN 25/1/18 at 11.40 P.M. Detrained at MERICOURT L'ABBÉ at 1.30 pm today and proceeded by march route to BRAY-SUR-SOMME.	JM
"	27/1/18	6 P.M.	Opened up accomodation for 24 patients in the Hospice. Visited by A.D.M.S. 39th Div who expressed approval of accomodation.	JM
HAUT ALLAINES	29/1/18	8 P.M.	Moved from BRAY-SUR-SOMME, Transport by march route. personnel by train to HAUT ALLAINES. Very hard frost during the night. Fine sunshiny day.	JM
FINS	30/1/18	7 P.M.	Moved from HAUT ALLAINES by march route to V.18.c (Sheet 57c) preparatory to taking over M.D.S. at this site. Hard frost again during the night, glorious sunshiny day	JM
"	31/1/18	6 P.M.	Very hard frost last night. Thick fog all day. Ready to take over site and patients tomorrow. Admissions to Hospital during the month Officers: 4 sick, 1 wounded. Other Ranks: 153 sick, nil wounded.	JM

132nd FIELD AMBULANCE 31-1-18

J Morris Capt R.A.M.C. T.F.
for O.C. 132nd FIELD AMBULANCE.

D. D. & L., London, E.C. (A8004) Wt. W1771/M2 31 750,000 5/17 Sch. 52 Forms/C2118/14

Original - Secret -

Feb. 1918
4

C O N F I D E N T I A L.

W A R   D I A R Y.

O F

132nd. FIELD AMBULANCE

From:- 1st. FEBRUARY 1918.   To:- 28th. FEBRUARY 1918.

(V O L U M E 2)

9/D 24

Original –
Secret –

Instructions regarding War Diaries and Intelligence Summaries are contained in F. S. Regs., Part II, and the Staff Manual respectively. Title pages will be prepared in manuscript.

(1)

WAR DIARY
or
~~INTELLIGENCE SUMMARY.~~

(*Erase heading not required.*)

Army Form C. 2118.

FINS – NURLU ROAD
Map Reference Sheet 57c

Place	Date	Hour	Summary of Events and Information	Remarks and references to Appendices
FINS-NURLU Road (V 18. c)	1/2/18	8 P.M.	Very hard frost last night – Dull, cold & very misty day – I today took over this site from 27th Field Ambulance, 9th Division. It is a very good site, consisting of Nissen & other huts, and canvas – Map Ref Sheet 57c V. 18. c. Accomodation 6 officers + 450 other Ranks. If necessary the accomodation could be greatly increased.	JH
"	2/2/18	5 P.M.	Hard frost again last night – Bright Sunshine all day. Daily inspection a large number of sick seen daily at sick parade from units situated in the vicinity having no Medical Officer	JH
"	3/2/18	6 P.M.	Hard frost during the night with some mist during this morning – Visit of inspection by D.D.M.S. VII Corps.	JH
"	4/2/18	6 PM.	Frost has gone followed by mist & rain. Visit of Inspection by A.D.M.S. 39th Div. Orders received to draw up scheme for rapid evacuation of (1) sick & wounded from this M.D.S (2) Personnel (3) Valuable Stores & Transport – west of NURLU. Also orders to decide, in consultation with Area Commandant concerned, upon suitable accomodation for a Dressing Station, in connection with the scheme of defence of each of the villages – FINS + SOREL LE GRAND. Dental Surgeon due from 55 C.C.S. did not attend.	JH
"	5/2/18	7 PM	Dull, foggy & wet day. Daily inspection	JH

D. D. & L., London, E.C. (A8004) Wt. W1771/M2 31 750,000 5/17 Sch. 52 Forms/C2118/14

FIELD AMBULANCE 6/2/18.

Instructions regarding War Diaries and Intelligence Summaries are contained in F. S. Regs., Part II. and the Staff Manual respectively. Title pages will be prepared in manuscript.

(2)

WAR DIARY
or
~~INTELLIGENCE SUMMARY.~~

(Erase heading not required.)

Army Form C. 2118.

FINS-NURLU ROAD.
Map Reference 57c

Place	Date	Hour	Summary of Events and Information	Remarks and references to Appendices
FINS-NURLU ROAD. V.18.C.	6/2/18	7 PM.	Considerable numbers of sick admitted daily – no trench feet – a few cases of diarrhoea attributable to the recent severe cold.	JM
"	8/2/18	5 PM.	Surprise visit of Inspection by G.O.C. 39th Division at 11.45 AM. and DDMS at 2.30 PM –	JM
"	9/2/18	6 PM	Defence scheme mentioned on 4/2/18 above. Sites for Dressing stations have been fixed as follows. FINS V12.b.2.1 and SOREL LE GRAND W13.C.3.4. Has been a dull day, windy & some rain.	JM
"	10/2/18	7 PM.	Windy night. dry wind blowing today. Visit of Inspection at 11.30 AM by ADMS 39th Division. By order of D.D.M.S. VII Corps a Medical Board was held here at 11 AM constituted as follows. President Lt Col S. MILLER M.C. RAMC. (SR) Members – Capt J. MORRIS MC RAMC (TF) and Capt A.E. KNIGHT. MC RAMC (TC). to examine Lieut T.C. FARMER 6th Bn The BUFFS.	JM
"	11/2/18	7 PM.	Bright Sunshiny day. N.W wind blowing. drying up the ground well. Progress made with gardening for growing vegetables. The Nissen hut opposite the Sick officers ward has now been fitted up as a Dining Room for officer Patients – 5 Places only per Division weekly for Dental treatment and to attend at BRAY-SUR-SOMME. Dental Surgeon from 55 C.C.S. has Returned to ~~Eng~~ ENGLAND.	JM JM

D. D. & L., London, E.C.
(A8004) Wt. W1771/M2 31 750,000 5/17 Sch. 52 Forms/C2118/14

Instructions regarding War Diaries and Intelligence Summaries are contained in F. S. Regs., Part II. and the Staff Manual respectively. Title pages will be prepared in manuscript.

(3)

WAR DIARY
or
~~INTELLIGENCE SUMMARY.~~
(*Erase heading not required.*)

FINS-NURLU ROAD
Map Reference Sheet 57c

Army Form C. 2118.

Place	Date	Hour	Summary of Events and Information	Remarks and references to Appendices
FINS-NURLU ROAD (V 18, c)	12/2/18	5.PM.	Bright Sunshiny dry day. Orders received to run small Ambulance train on light Railway from AX13 Siding to C.C.S at TINCOURT calling at D.R.S. NURLU, and 16th Div. M.D.S. at VILLERS-FAUCON. Train consists of 2 covered Wagons each to take 12 stretcher cases - warmed by oil stoves. To be equipped here with stretchers, blankets, bed pans, urinals &c. The Wagons which should have been at the siding ~~has~~ at 12 noon have not yet arrived. Warned of possible visit of C in C on Friday next 15/2/18.	JHB
"	13/2/18	6 P.M.	Very heavy rain during the night, dull wet day. Ambulance Wagons arrived during the night, in a very dirty & battered condition. They were cleaned out & repaired here, & fitted up - accommodation is cramped.	JHB
"	14/2/18	6 P.M.	Dull showery day - I attended a Conference at the ADMS's office at 10.30 AM when a very instructive & interesting discussion took place with reference to front line work, sick rate, diarrhoea & scabies &c. The C in C was seen in the area during the afternoon, I have sent in a report as to total lack, at present, of Dental treatment in the Division.	JHB
	15/2/18	7.P.M.	Very cold night with hard frost. Dull grey misty day, with a little sunshine in the afternoon. Daily Inspection. Daily work - gardening, general repairs and protection against bombs pushed on.	JHB

D. D. & L., London, E.C.
(A8004) Wt. W1771/M2 31 750,000 5/17 Sch. 52 Forms/C2118/14

Army Form C. 2118.

WAR DIARY
or
INTELLIGENCE SUMMARY.
(Erase heading not required.)

Instructions regarding War Diaries and Intelligence Summaries are contained in F. S. Regs., Part II. and the Staff Manual respectively. Title pages will be prepared in manuscript.

(4)

FINS-NURLU ROAD
Map Reference Sheet 57c.

Place	Date	Hour	Summary of Events and Information	Remarks and references to Appendices
FINS-NURLU ROAD (V.18.C)	16/2/18	10 P.M.	Hard frost during the night. Bright sunshiny day. Visit by A.D.M.S. at 9.45 AM when he assisted at an operation – Amputation of forearm –. Visit of D.D.M.S. VII Corps enquiring about the Ambulance Train (DECAUVILLE RAILWAY) now running between here & TINCOURT.	JHH
			About 7 P.M. tonight the enemy made an air raid on this area, dropping many bombs one of which struck the Divisional Canteen at FINS. Killing 10. and wounding 15 men. one of whom died shortly after admission. A second bomb struck a Dugout occupied by men of the 39th D.A.C. Killing 2 outright, and wounding 8 other men. of whom one died shortly after admission. A third bomb caused four casualties at EQUACOURT – wounded. I was informed of the casualties at FINS by Telephone, & at once sent 2 M.O's with stretchers blankets &c and 20 bearers. I telephoned for 5 M.A.C cars, and was able to collect these cases dress them all, and evacuate them to C.C.S. before 9 o'clock. p.m.	JHH
"	17/2/18	5 P.M.	A beautiful sunny morning after a bright moonlight night & hard frost. The enemy continued bombing until 11 P.M. last night. He has not yet begun this evening.	
	18/2/18	6. P.M.	The enemy began dropping bombs about 7 P.M. last evening, and continued with short intervals until 1 A.M. Fortunately without causing any casualties in this neighbourhood. The night was ideal for his work.	JHH

D. D. & L., London, E.C.
(A8004) Wt. W1771/M2 31 750,000 5/17 Sch. 52 Forms/C2118/14

Army Form C. 2118.

Instructions regarding War Diaries and Intelligence Summaries are contained in F. S. Regs., Part II. and the Staff Manual respectively. Title pages will be prepared in manuscript.

(5)

WAR DIARY
or
INTELLIGENCE SUMMARY.
(Erase heading not required.)

FINS-NURLU ROAD
Map Reference Sheet 57^c

Place	Date	Hour	Summary of Events and Information	Remarks and references to Appendices
FINS-NURLU ROAD (V 18.C)	18/2/18 (Contd)		There was very hard frost again last night. Today has been very bright sunny. Conditions appear ideal for another raid tonight. The enemy has not yet commenced	[initials]
"	19/2/18	7 PM.	Frost continues. Today has been a delightful one of sunshine. Very little enemy bombing from the air last night. A.D.M.S. visited this afternoon to inspect one officer and 2 O.R.	[initials]
"	20/2/18	3 PM.	It froze hard again last night, and there was some ground mist, but although it was beautifully moonlight overhead no enemy aircraft came over.	[initials]
"	21/2/18	6 PM.	Last evening about 5 PM it commenced to rain & rained practically all night. This morning it cleared & the sun shone all afternoon.	[initials]
"	22/2/18	7 PM	Another wet night. Wet drizzling morning. At 3pm. The Corps Commander (VIIth Corps) & D.D.M.S. visited this Main Dressing Station & made a tour of inspection. They appeared satisfied with everything and all the arrangements.	[initials]
"	24/2/18	6 PM.	Fine night strong NW wind blowing. Sunshiny afternoon. Work on Dressing Stations at FINS & SOREL LE GRAND proceeding well	[initials]

D. D. & L., London, E.C. (A8004) Wt. W1771/M2 31 750,000 5/17 Sch. 52 Forms/C2118/14

Instructions regarding War Diaries and Intelligence Summaries are contained in F. S. Regs., Part II. and the Staff Manual respectively. Title pages will be prepared in manuscript.

(6)

WAR DIARY
or
~~INTELLIGENCE SUMMARY.~~
(Erase heading not required.)

Army Form C. 2118.

FINS - NURLU ROAD.
Map Reference Sheet 57C

Place	Date	Hour	Summary of Events and Information	Remarks and references to Appendices
FINS-NURLU ROAD V.18 C.	25/2/18	6 P.M.	A very wet night, & some rain during the morning. Afternoon no rain but strong North wind blowing.	[illegible]
"	26/2/18	9 A.M.	Fine morning following cold night & frost. Progress in agricultural preparations. A.D.M.S. Operation Order No: 39 received at 7 P.M.	[illegible]
"	27/2/18	9 A.M.	Weather milder but rather stormy. Arrangements completed for mutual relief between this unit and the S. AFRICAN. Field Ambulance on the 2nd inst.	[illegible]
"	28/2/18	9 A.M.	Stormy morning, some rain & snow showers. Orders received from A.D.M.S. at 1 P.M. for no further action to be taken in connection with forthcoming relief until receipt of further orders. R.A.M.C. Operation Order No: 39 Cancelled received at 2.30 P.M. Attended Conference at office of A.D.M.S. at 8 P.M. Admissions for the month were: Sick — Officers 35, O.R. 1387; Wounded — Officers 9, O.R. 259	[illegible]

A Whittingham [?] Lt Col
R.A.M.C.

D. D. & L., London, E.C. (A5004) Wt. W1771/M2 31 750,000 5/17 Sch. 52 Forms/C2118/14

Original

Secret

Instructions regarding War Diaries and Intelligence Summaries are contained in F. S. Regs., Part II. and the Staff Manual respectively. Title pages will be prepared in manuscript.

(1)

WAR DIARY
or
~~INTELLIGENCE SUMMARY.~~

(Erase heading not required.)

March 1918

Map Reference. Sheet 57c.

Army Form C. 2118.

Place	Date	Hour	Summary of Events and Information	Remarks and references to Appendices
FINS–NURLU Road – V.18.c.	1/3/18	9AM	Very bright sharp morning, following hard frost during the night – R.A.P. at FINS completed – Preparations made to deal with an emergency –	A.H.
"	2/3/18	9AM	Bitterly cold N.E. wind, blowing very hard – Good reserve of dressings etc now established – A good deal of snow fell during the day – Captain J. MORRIS. M.C. assumes the acting rank of Major as Commander of "B" Section, in accordance with G.R.O. 3448 of 20/2/18, under authority of the Divisional Commander –	A.H.
"	3/3/18	9AM	Not so cold – inclined to rain – D.A.D.M.S. VII Corps and A/A.D.M.S. 39 Division visited the site in the morning; reduction of canvas was discussed and general arrangements for an emergency – Decided that number of patients remaining should for the present be reduced to a minimum –	A.H.
"	4/3/18	9AM	Rough morning, some snow showers – D.D.M.S. 7th Corps visited the site at 12.45 PM – He expressed the opinion ~~that~~ the wagons should be loaded up as far as possible, and I have asked that our wagons may be placed at my disposal in order to have this done – Four G.S. wagons are at present earmarked for other purposes & cannot be loaded until released from these duties –	A.H.

D. D. & L., London, E.C.
(A8004) Wt. W1771/M2 31 750,000 5/17 Sch 52 Forms/C2118/14

Instructions regarding War Diaries and Intelligence Summaries are contained in F. S. Regs., Part II. and the Staff Manual respectively. Title pages will be prepared in manuscript.

(2)

March 1918 –

WAR DIARY
or
~~INTELLIGENCE SUMMARY.~~
(Erase heading not required.)

Map Reference Sheet 57c.

Army Form C. 2118.

Place	Date	Hour	Summary of Events and Information	Remarks and references to Appendices
FINS - NURLU Road - V. 18. C	5/3/18 –	9 AM.	Weather still very stormy – Orders received to strike some of the Canvas here –	A.L.L.
"	6/3/18.	9 AM.	Frost during the night – Bright cold morning – Canvas struck in accordance with orders received – "B" + "C" Section Medical Store Wagons packed –	A.L.L.
"	7/3/18	9 AM.	Fine but dull – 6 large Hpl marquees + 13 small Hpl marquees handed over for conveyance to Corps Rest Station – The Consulting Surgeon to the 5th Army revisited the site at 12.30 PM. and saw the dressing rooms (walking + lying) –	A.L.L.
"	8/3/18.	9 AM.	Fine bright morning following sharp frost –	A.L.L.
"	9/3/18	9.30 AM.	Beautiful weather continues – I attended lectures + demonstrations at the 7th Corps Gas School, returning to HQ at 5.45 PM –	A.L.L.
"	10/3/18	9 AM.	Fine weather continues – Parade Service at 11 AM – Captain C. WITTS. M.C. RAMC + two nursing orderlies left to attend the 5th Army RAMC School of Instruction at 61 CCS –	A.L.L.

D. D. & L., London, E.C.
(A8004) Wt. W1771/M2 31 750,000 5/17 Sch. 52 Forms/C2118/14

Instructions regarding War Diaries and Intelligence Summaries are contained in F. S. Regs., Part II. and the Staff Manual respectively. Title pages will be prepared in manuscript.

132nd FIELD AMBULANCE 11/3/18

(3)

March 1918.

WAR DIARY
or
~~INTELLIGENCE SUMMARY.~~
(Erase heading not required.)

Army Form C. 2118.

Map References :- Sheets 57C. 62C.

Place	Date	Hour	Summary of Events and Information	Remarks and references to Appendices
I 18. c.	11/3/18	9AM.	Fine weather continues - Advance party arrived from the South African Field Ambulance - I visited HAUT ALLAINES to which place the unit will proceed tomorrow in mutual relief of the S.African Fld Amb - Wagons were loaded -	A.H.
	12/3/18	9AM.	Brilliantly fine weather continues - The unit proceeded by march route to HAUT ALLAINES and established headquarters at I 4. a. 5.0. at 12.30 PM - Accommodation consists of a ruined house and 7 Nissen huts for the personnel - All is not being opened up - 1/Lt W. J. EGAN MORC USA and Lt [illegible] HARROLD RAMC were admitted to Hpl suffering from slight pyrexia and ~~transferred~~ to the 7th Corps Rest Station - I called on the A.D.M.S. at 5.30 PM -	A.H.
HAUT ALLAINES	13/3/18	9AM.	Fine weather continues - Captain A.W. ULOTH RAMC rejoined the unit from Fifth Army RAMC School of Instruction & course in Sanitation -	A.H.
	14/3/18	9AM.	Cold wind blowing from the North - Box respirator inspection & drill - Additional protection provided for Nissen huts of personnel -	A.H.

D. D. & L., London, E.C. (A8004) Wt. W1771/M2 31 750,000 5/17 Sch. 52 Forms/C2118/14

Instructions regarding War Diaries and Intelligence Summaries are contained in F. S. Regs., Part II. and the Staff Manual respectively. Title pages will be prepared in manuscript.

132nd FIELD AMBULANCE 15/3/18.

(4)

WAR DIARY
or
~~INTELLIGENCE SUMMARY.~~
(Erase heading not required.)

Army Form C. 2118.

March 1918 –

Map Reference Sheet 62c.

Place	Date	Hour	Summary of Events and Information	Remarks and references to Appendices
HAUT ALLAINES	15/3/18	9AM.	Fine weather continues, but still sharp cold wind from N.E. – Captain A.W. ULOTH. RAMC proceeded to take over medical charge of the 7th Corps reinforcement camp – 1/Lieut. M.G. MORALES. MORC.USA. was evacuated to CCS suffering from laryngitis – The ADMS. visited the unit during the afternoon –	AHL.
"	16/3/18	9AM.	Fine weather – some frost – Attended medical Board at the Office of the ADMS. at 11.30 AM, with Major J. MORRIS. MC –	AHL.
"	17/3/18	9AM.	Fine weather continues, less cold – Divine Service parade at 11.15 AM – 1/Lt W.V. EGAN. MORC.USA. rejoined from Hospital –	AHL.
"	18/3/18	9AM.	Weather warm + fine – Morning occupied with physical exercise, box respirator + squad drill parades – I visited the ADMS. about 6.45 PM –	AHL.
"	19/3/18	9AM.	Visited LONGAVESNES + VILLERS FAUCON + studied present evacuation from their areas with F.Amb. Commanders occupying these sites – The weather has changed to rain – 1/Lt. M.G. MORALES. MORC. USA. rejoined at 5 P.M. –	AHL.
"	20/3/18	9AM.	Inclined to rain – Captain WITTS. M.C. rejoined from 5th Army School of Instruction – 1/Lt MORALES relieved Captain ULOTH. RAMC as M.O i/c 7th Corps Reinforcement Camp –	AHL.

D. D. & L., London, E.C.
(A8004) Wt. W1771/M2 31 750,000 5/17 Sch. 52 Forms/C2118/14

Instructions regarding War Diaries and Intelligence Summaries are contained in F.S. Regs., Part II. and the Staff Manual respectively. Title pages will be prepared in manuscript.

(5)

March 1918 –

WAR DIARY
or
~~INTELLIGENCE SUMMARY.~~
(Erase heading not required.)

Map Reference: —
Sheet 62C.

Army Form C. 2118.

Place	Date	Hour	Summary of Events and Information	Remarks and references to Appendices
HAUT ALLAINES.	21/3/18.	5 AM.	Preliminary bombardment of enemy offensive – Unit moved to its battle station near NURLU, & parked about D4.C.0.0: owing to shell fire it was necessary to move the park into a quarry situated about D.3.d. central. One bearer subdivision & 3 horsed ambulances proceeded to assembly point of 117 Infantry	
		1 AM.	Brigade at W.25.a. under charge of Major W.T. BROWN. M.C. – Kept in close touch with new Brigade H.Q. at NURLU – Major BROWN. M.C. Capt. ULOTH. & bearer subdivision moved with 117 Infantry Brigade during the evening to SAULCOURT: Division is to dig a line from PAULCOURT to TINCOURT WOOD. 118 Infantry Brigade at LONGAVESNES – About midnight received orders to get in touch with 16 Division F.A., and proceeded to TINCOURT – Saw the A.D.M.S. 16 Div. who gave me	Ah
NURLU.	22/3/18.	2 AM.	instructions to move my unit to TINCOURT – Then visited 118 Brigade H.Q., and also saw Major BROWN. M.C.; arranged that his H.Q. should be at	
		4 AM.	LONGAVESNES, and his bearer reserve held here – Evacuation will be by car to TINCOURT – Visited D.H.Q. and discussed situation with D.A.D.M.S. and returned	
		8.30 AM.	to TINCOURT & found unit marching in: took over old C.C.S. site at J.23.b.5.5. At 10 AM received orders from A.D.M.S. 16 Div. to move forthwith to DOINGT: Sent this order to A.D.M.S. 29 Div. for confirmation which was given, and unit proceeded to DOINGT, arriving there at 3.30 PM – parked at I.36.b. central. A.D.M.S. visited the unit there at 5 P.M. –	Ah.
DOIGNT.	23/3/18.	5 AM.	Operation orders received from A.D.M.S.: no word from Major BROWN. M.C. as to his	

D. D. & L., London, E.C.
(A8004) Wt. W1771/M2 31 750,000 5/17 Sch. 52 Forms/C2118/14

Army Form C. 2118.

Instructions regarding War Diaries and Intelligence Summaries are contained in F. S. Regs., Part II. and the Staff Manual respectively. Title pages will be prepared in manuscript.

(6)

WAR DIARY
or
~~INTELLIGENCE SUMMARY.~~
(Erase heading not required.)

March 1918.

Map Reference — Sheet 62.C.

Place	Date	Hour	Summary of Events and Information	Remarks and references to Appendices
DOIGNT.	23/3/18.	5 AM.	new location, Major MORRIS. M.C took a bearer division to report to 117 Brigade H.Q. at DRIENCOURT — I visited BUIRE where it was reported 118 Brigade H.Q. were situated: no H.Q. found, but on my return ~~to~~ DOINGT I found a dispatch from Major BROWN M.C, who had established his H.Q. at J 10.b.6.8. I visited	
		7 AM.	him, taking two Sunbeam Cars up to him — Bearers under Major MORRIS. M.C. had arrived at DRIENCOURT & found no H.Q: he dealt with casualties he found between here & BUSSU, at BUSSU & between BUSSU & PERONNE as he fell back in accordance with the development of the situation —	
		9 AM.	In the meantime I returned to DOINGT and received orders from A.D.M.S. 16 Div. to move to H29. central at once — Unit therefore left DOIGNT being last	
H 29. Central —			unit out of the village: our infantry could be seen retiring from next crest in direction of the village — Captain ULOTH. took another car up to BUSSU, in spite of the road being badly blocked with traffic & he got nearly up to J.10, & he filled his car and got it away — Unit passed through PERONNE slowly, crossed the river & reached H 29. central	
		1.30 PM.	about 1.30 PM — and parked there — here there was intense congestion of traffic, and some casualties were dealt with following enemy aircraft Machine Gun fire — Majors MORRIS. & BROWN. rejoined with their personnel about 3 PM. having evacuated all wounded they had collected —	AL

D. D. & L., London, E.C. (A8004) Wt. W1771/M2 31 750,000 5/17 Sch. 52 Forms/C2118/14

Instructions regarding War Diaries and Intelligence Summaries are contained in F. S. Regs., Part II. and the Staff Manual respectively. Title pages will be prepared in manuscript.

(7)

March 1918.

WAR DIARY
or
~~INTELLIGENCE~~ ~~SUMMARY.~~
(Erase heading not required.)

Army Form C. 2118.

Map Reference. Sheet 62C. + AMIENS. 17

Place	Date	Hour	Summary of Events and Information	Remarks and references to Appendices
H 29. Central.	24.3.18.	6.30 PM.	We got in touch with 118 Infantry Brigade, established nearby at 6.30 PM. + found we were about a ~~thousand~~ yards from our Front line. About midnight received orders to move farther back, and moved to H 25. d. 4.0: Major Brown M.C. remained with 118 Infantry Bde. H.Q. to act as Liaison Officer + control the forward situation, with bearers + motor ambulances.	AH.
H. 25. d. 4.0.	25.3.18	6 AM.	Evacuation was satisfactory all day. My H.Q. moved to C 27. 6. 6. 2. at about 8 PM, having previously moved to C 29. a. 5.5. about 2 PM. Captain WITTS. M.C. + bearer subdivision had gone to FEUILLERES with cars to clear 117 Infantry Brigade about noon, and he had a successful evacuation here. At midnight Major BROWN. MC. + Captain WITTS. M.C. established their H.Q. at HERBECOURT.	AH.
C 27. 6. 6. 2.	26.3.18	9 AM.	A.D.M.S. visited us. Evacuation carried on all day very successfully. In the afternoon I sent most of the transport to 184 Fd Amb, as we were under observation of enemy. My H.Q. remained until midnight, when I received orders to move back to CAPPY. I visited HERBECOURT at 10 PM, and saw O.C. bearers, + we discussed the situation for the following day. He retired with Bde H.Q. during the night to ~~[illegible]~~ DOMPIERRE AH. and had to fall back to CHUIGNES later.	
CAPPY.	26.3.18	9 AM.	In accordance with orders received from D.A.D.M.S. personally at CAPPY about 9.30 AM. on the 26th inst, I left CAPPY as soon as possible clearing all wounded: unit moved to MERICOURT-SUR-SOMME: I visited Major BROWN. M.C. at CHUIGNES	AH.

D. D. & L., London, E.C. (A8004) Wt. W1771/M2131 750,000 5/17 Sch. 52 Forms/C2118/14

Instructions regarding War Diaries and Intelligence Summaries are contained in F. S. Regs., Part II. and the Staff Manual respectively. Title pages will be prepared in manuscript.

(8)

WAR DIARY
or
~~INTELLIGENCE SUMMARY.~~
(Erase heading not required.)

March 1918.

Map Reference — Sheet — AMIENS 17 —

Army Form C. 2118.

Place	Date	Hour	Summary of Events and Information	Remarks and references to Appendices
MERICOURT-SUR-SOMME.	26/3/18	11 AM.	about 11 A.M.: as the troops fell back all available cars were run up and filled + got away – on returning to MERICOURT I found orders awaiting me to hand over to 134 Fd Amb.: thereupon sent orders to my forward parties to rejoin me on handing over to Major COYLE. RAMC. of 134 Fd Amb – and moved in accordance with orders received to CERNY, where the unit concentrated again – In accordance with orders received at about 5 P.M., the unit moved to WARFUSÉE-ABANCOURT arriving there at 8 P.M., + billeting in an empty farm –	AAh
WARFUSÉE-ABANCOURT.	27/3/18	4 A.M.	Orders received to proceed to VILLERS-BRETONNEUX; unit moved there and took over nearly all the Fd Amb. transport of the Division: we remained at VILLERS BRETONNEUX all day; the A.D.M.S. visited us; about 5 P.M. we were very	
		5 P.M.	busy for about an hour and passed a large number of wounded through to C.C.S. by car + lorries commandeered – Unit then moved to GENTELLES + spent the night there –	AAh
GENTELLES.	28/3/18	10 AM.	Received orders + moved to DOMART, arriving there at noon: we left at 3 P.M. + marched via BOVES to SAINS-EN-AMIENOIS, reached at 8.55 P.M –	AAh
SAINS-EN-AMIENOIS –	29/3/18		We remained at SAINS all day –	AAh
1	30/3/18	2 P.M.	A.D.M.S. visited us and ordered me to move in the direction of DURY.	

D. D. & L., London, E.C. (A8004) Wt. W1771/M2 31 750,000 5/17 Sch. 52 Forms/C2118/14

Instructions regarding War Diaries and Intelligence Summaries are contained in F. S. Regs., Part II. and the Staff Manual respectively. Title pages will be prepared in manuscript.

(9)

WAR DIARY
or
~~INTELLIGENCE SUMMARY.~~
(Erase heading not required.)

March 1918 –

Sheet – AMIENS 17. Map Reference –

Army Form C. 2118.

Place	Date	Hour	Summary of Events and Information	Remarks and references to Appendices
SAINS-EN-AMIENOIS –	30/3/18 –	2 PM.	Unit moved to a point near the Y in DURY, and later in the evening on to SALEUX, going into billets about 2 AM. on 31/3/18 –	AH.
SALEUX –	31/3/18	2 PM.	Orders received to move to BOVELLES: unit on arrival bivouacked in a field about 400 yards S.E. of BOVELLES –	AH.

A. Whittyshire –
Lt Col.
O.C. 132 Fld Amb –

Original -

C O N F I D E N T I A L.

W A R   D I A R Y

O F

132nd. FIELD AMBULANCE.

FROM:- 1st.MARCH 1918.   TO:- 31st.MARCH 1918.

(VOLUME 3)

Vol 25

140/2849

132nd Field Ambulance

March 1918

Second - Original -

Apr. 1918.

C O N F I D E N T I A L

W A R D I A R Y

OF

132nd. FIELD AMBULANCE

FROM:- 1st. APRIL 1918. TO:- 30th. APRIL 1918.

(Volume 3) 26

140/2400

Vol 26

ORIGINAL

Secret

(1)

Instructions regarding War Diaries and Intelligence Summaries are contained in F. S. Regs., Part II. and the Staff Manual respectively. Title pages will be prepared in manuscript.

Army Form C. 2118.

WAR DIARY
or
INTELLIGENCE SUMMARY.
(Erase heading not required.)

April – 1918 –

Map Reference – Sheet AMIENS. 17 – DIEPPE 16 –

Place	Date	Hour	Summary of Events and Information	Remarks and references to Appendices
BOVELLES.	1/4/18.	9 AM.	Unit remained in its bivouac all day –	A.H.
"	2/4/18.	8 AM.	Unit moved to ARAINES & took 45 slight sick cases in –	A.H.
ARAINES.	3/4/18	Noon.	Unit moved to FOUCAUCOURT and opened up accomodation for sick: orders received to hold unit in readiness to entrain at a very early date –	A.H.
FOUCAUCOURT.	4/4/18	10 AM.	Dull showery weather –	A.H.
"	5/4/18	9 AM.	Dull weather continues – A.D.M.S. visited the unit at 3 PM, and directed that all cases be evacuated except the very slightest, as accomodation here is poor –	A.H.
"	6/4/18.	9 AM.	Fine weather – Lt MORALES. MORCUPA rejoined from 7th Corps Reinforcement Camp – Orders received re move tomorrow from 118 Infantry Brigade at 10 PM – last night –	A.H.
"	7/4/18	9 AM.	Fine bright morning – Unit packed up & marched at 11.20 AM – arriving at FRETTEMEULE at 3 PM, & going into billets – Lt. W.F. TISDALE RAMC is transferred to 134 Fd. Amb. and struck off the strength from today's date –	A.H.
FRETTEMEULE.	8/4/18	10.15 AM	Unit proceeded to OUST-MAREST & billeted for the night –	A.H.

D. D. & L., London, E.C.
(A8004) Wt. W1771/M2 31 750,000 5/17 Sch. 52 Forms/C2118/14

Instructions regarding War Diaries and Intelligence Summaries are contained in F. S. Regs., Part II. and the Staff Manual respectively. Title pages will be prepared in manuscript.

(2)

WAR DIARY
or
~~INTELLIGENCE SUMMARY.~~
(Erase heading not required.)

Army Form C. 2118.

April 1918 –

Map Reference – DIEPPE 16. HAZEBROUCK 5A – ABBEVILLE 14.

Place	Date	Hour	Summary of Events and Information	Remarks and references to Appendices
OUST-MAREST.	9/4/18 –	10 AM	Transport moved off, followed by dismounted personnel at 12.15 PM, & proceeded to entrain at EU: train left at 2.19 PM, and reached ARQUES at 11 PM, detrained & went into billets –	AM
ARQUES.	10/4/18.	10 AM.	Unit remained at ARQUES all day: visited the ADMS. at 6.30 PM – weather cold & dull –	AM
ARQUES.	11/4/18.	10 AM.	Dull morning – Unit proceeded by march route to WATTEN arriving there at 1.30 PM –	AM
WATTEN.	12/4/18.	9 AM.	Fine morning – Equipment of site and checking of Fd. Amb. Equipment –	AM
"	13/4/18.	9 AM	Dull & cold – Major W.T. BROWN. MC. left for temporary duty at the office of the ADMS – Refitting of personnel as supplies become available – General clean up of wagons, with a view to repainting of same if time is available –	AM
"	14/4/18	6 P.M.	Dull & very cold – Cleaning & painting of vehicles proceeding – Lt W.V. EGAN. M.O. R.C. U.S.A – Lt M.G. MORALES. MO. R.C. USA. & Lt W.T. SHAW RAMC departed for duty with 133 Fd Ambulance in accordance with instructions of ADMS 39th Div.	AM

D. D. & L., London, E.C. (A8004) Wt. W1771/M2 31 750,000 5/17 Sch. 52 Forms/C2118/14

Instructions regarding War Diaries and Intelligence Summaries are contained in F. S. Regs., Part II. and the Staff Manual respectively. Title pages will be prepared in manuscript.

(3)

April. 1918

WAR DIARY
or
~~INTELLIGENCE SUMMARY.~~
(*Erase heading not required.*)

Army Form C. 2118.

Map Reference. DIEPPE 16
HAZEBROUCK. 5A ABBEVILLE. 14

Place	Date	Hour	Summary of Events and Information	Remarks and references to Appendices
WATTEN	15/4/18	6.P.M.	Another very cold day, cloudy, & threatening rain. Cleaning up of vehicles, & refitting carried on. Four American Infantry soldiers just admitted. These are the first admissions from 77th Division A.E.F newly arrived for training and instruction with 39th (British) Division.	JMD
"	16/4/18	10 A.M.	Dull cold & drizzly morning, hindering the cleaning & painting of vehicles. Repairs to vehicles commenced, with material drawn from C.R.E. 39th Div yesterday.	JMD
"	17/4/18	9 A.M.	Fine & mild. Good progress has been made in the repainting of wagons.	AHL
"	18/4/18	9 A.M.	Weather cold & wet; interfering with repainting.	AHL
"	19/4/18	9 A.M.	Weather cold. Some showers of sleet. Repainting of transport is proceeding. Medical Board held during the afternoon.	AHL
"	20/4/18	9 A.M.	Weather inclined to be showery. This hampers repainting of transport & tends to spoil the work. General refit proceeding.	AHL

D. D. & L., London, E.C.
(A8004) Wt. W1771/M2 31 750,000 5/17 Sch. 52 Forms/C2118/14

Instructions regarding War Diaries and Intelligence Summaries are contained in F. S. Regs., Part II. and the Staff Manual respectively. Title pages will be prepared in manuscript.

(4)

WAR DIARY
or
~~INTELLIGENCE SUMMARY.~~
(Erase heading not required.)

April 1918. Map Reference – HAZEBROUCK 5A.

Army Form C. 2118.

Place	Date	Hour	Summary of Events and Information	Remarks and references to Appendices
WATTEN	21/4/18	9AM.	Beautiful weather – Sunday – Parade Service at 11AM –	Alh
	22/4/18	9AM	Fine weather continues – The 39 Division Tivolies visited the Fld Ambulance and gave a splendid performance – The A.D.M.S. + D.A.D.M.S. attended the performance –	Alh
	23/4/18	9AM.	Fine weather continues – The repainting of transport is now well on, and will soon be completed –	Alh
	24/4/18	9AM.	Fine weather continues – Orders received re instruction of United States personnel in Water Purification –	Alh
	25/4/18	2PM.	Instruction in Water Purification given to American personnel who attended –	Alh
	26/4/18	9AM.	Fine weather continues – Repainting of all vehicles is now complete except for a few tyres which remain to be done –	Alh

D. D. & L., London, E.C.
(A8004) Wt. W1771/M2 31 750,000 5/17 Sch. 52 Forms/C2118/14

Instructions regarding War Diaries and Intelligence Summaries are contained in F. S. Regs., Part II. and the Staff Manual respectively. Title pages will be prepared in manuscript.

Army Form C. 2118.

WAR DIARY
or
~~INTELLIGENCE SUMMARY.~~
(Erase heading not required.)

(5)

April 1918.

Map Reference:— Sheet HAZEBROUCK 5A.

Place	Date	Hour	Summary of Events and Information	Remarks and references to Appendices
WATTEN.	28/4/18.	9 AM.	Weather showery & overcast. Some readjustment has been made in the accommodation here, giving a better Medical Inspection and Dressing room. Major W.T. BROWN. M.C. left to report for duty to the D.D.M.S. TROUVILLE during the afternoon and is struck off the strength of the Field Ambulance from this date. Major J. MORRIS. M.C. left at 7 P.M. for temporary duty with the A.D.M.S.	Ath
"	29/4/18.	9 AM.	Weather dull & cold. Concert given by the Inland Water Transport in the evening.	Ath
"	30/4/18	9 AM.	Weather overcast & mild. Lt. F.C PETERS. M.R.C. 306 Ambulance Coy, and Lt. W. HARRIS. M.R.C. 306 Field Hpl, of 77 Div. A.E.F, reported their arrival and are attached to the unit for duty.	Ath

Ath[illegible] Lt Col.
R.A.M.C.
O.C. 132nd FIELD AMBULANCE

D. D. & L., London, E.C.
(A8004) Wt. W1771/M2 31 750,000 5/17 Sch. 52 Forms/C2118/14

C O N F I D E N T I A L

W A R D I A R Y

O F

132nd. FIELD AMBULANCE

FROM 1st. MAY 1918. TO 31st. MAY 1918.

(VOLUME 27)

Original – Confidential – (1)

Instructions regarding War Diaries and Intelligence Summaries are contained in F. S. Regs., Part II. and the Staff Manual respectively. Title pages will be prepared in manuscript.

May 1918 –

WAR DIARY
or
~~INTELLIGENCE SUMMARY.~~
(Erase heading not required.)

Army Form C. 2118.

Map Reference – HAZEBROUCK. 5A –

Place	Date	Hour	Summary of Events and Information	Remarks and references to Appendices
WATTEN.	1/5/18.	9AM.	Dull cold weather – This site has been improved by the addition of some equipment obtained from the B.R.C.S. – Major MORRIS. M.C. returned from temporary duty at the Office of the A.D.M.S –	A.H.
"	2/5/18.	9AM.	Beautiful Spring weather – Construction of a meat safe commenced – Captain WITTS M.C. delivered lecture to the Medical Officers of the 77 Div. A.E.F. on the "Medical equipment of a Bn: its uses and abuse" – The ~~[illegible]~~ Division Surgeon, and his Staff Officer, of the 77 Div. A.E.F. visited the site at 6.30 P.M. and looked over it –	A.H.
"	3/5/18.	9AM.	Fine weather continues – Major Morris M.C. delivered lectures on ~~Nomenclature~~ Nomenclature of Diseases etc to 77 Div. A.E.F. Medical Officers –	A.H.
"	4/5/18.	9AM.	Fine weather continues; some heavy rain fell during the night. Captains C. WITTS. M.C. & A.W. ULOTH. RAMC left at 11.15 AM to return to report to A.D.M.S. 25 Div for duty, and are struck off the strength from today's date – No: C/1030 Sgt: E.S. STINCHCOMBE A.S.C. (M.T.) and No: M2/132732 Pte. D.C. KAY. A.S.C. (M.T.) awarded the MILITARY MEDAL. Authy. 39 D.R.O. No: 32. dated 3/5/18 –	A.H.

D. D. & L., London, E.C. (A8004) Wt. W1771/M2 31 750,000 5/17 Sch. 52 Forms/C2118/14

Instructions regarding War Diaries and Intelligence Summaries are contained in F. S. Regs., Part II. and the Staff Manual respectively. Title pages will be prepared in manuscript.

(2)

May 1918 –

WAR DIARY
or
INTELLIGENCE SUMMARY.
(Erase heading not required.)

Army Form C. 2118.

Ref Refuse – Sheet HAZEBROUCK. 5A.

Place	Date	Hour	Summary of Events and Information	Remarks and references to Appendices
WATTEN.	5/5/18.	9AM	Weather dull + showery – Divine Service held at 11AM – Thunderstorm in the evening –	AH.
"	6/5/18.	2PM.	All available horsed + mechanical transport left to carry detraining Details to their billets – Weather fine + warm – Work commenced on shelves in Pack Store –	AH.
"	7/5/18	9AM	Very wet morning, following heavy rain through the night –	AH.
	8/5/18	9AM.	Beautiful weather – 1 Lts W.V. EGAN and M.G. MORALES. M.R.C. U.S.A, and Lieut: T.W. SHAW. RAMC are posted to 133 Field Ambulance from 14/4/18 and are struck off the strength of this unit from that date, under instructions received from the ADMS –	AH.
"	9/5/18	9AM.	Fine weather continues – Construction of meat safe and Pack Store almost completed –	AH.
"	10/5/18	9AM.	Dull + cooler – Preliminary Orders received re disposal of Personnel of unit –	AH.
"	11/5/18	9AM.	Warm + fine – Orders received as to entraining of personnel at 2.50AM. 12/5/18 – At 3.30 PM. the 306 Ambulance Company and 306	

D. D. & L., London, E.C.
(A8004) Wt. W1771/M2 31 750,000 5/17 Sch. 52 Forms/C2118/14

Instructions regarding War Diaries and Intelligence Summaries are contained in F. S. Regs., Part II. and the Staff Manual respectively. Title pages will be prepared in manuscript.

(3)

WAR DIARY
or
~~INTELLIGENCE SUMMARY.~~
(Erase heading not required.)

Army Form C. 2118.

May 1918.   Map Reference: Sheet HAZEBROUCK. 5A.

Place	Date	Hour	Summary of Events and Information	Remarks and references to Appendices
WATTEN.	11/5/18	3.30 P.M.	Field Hospital of 77 Div. American Exp. Force arrived and went into billets. These units are to be attached for training in Field Ambulance work on R.A.M.C. lines –	AHL
	12/5/18	9 A.M.	Cold & dull – The 306 Field Ambulance, formed of above U.S.A. units having put in staff to relieve my personnel, the latter 136 strong entrained at 4 P.M. for R.A.M.C. Base Depot ROUEN, under charge of 1/Lt BOYERS of 133 Field Ambulance – A training Cadre is now left consisting of the Officer Commanding, Q.M.r, and 22 Other Ranks R.A.M.C. – Transport, horse and mechanical, remains as before – The training Cadre remains in every department to give all the assistance in its power to the 306 Field Ambulance –	AHL
	13/5/18	9 A.M.	Wet & cold – Orders received to hand over all equipment to 306 Field Ambulance A.E.F. – this was commenced –	AHL
	14/5/18	9 A.M.	Beautiful weather – Handing over of equipment continued –	AHL

D. D. & L., London, E.C.
(A8004) Wt. W1771/M2 31 750,000 5/17 Sch. 52 Forms/C2118/14

Instructions regarding War Diaries and Intelligence Summaries are contained in F. S. Regs., Part II. and the Staff Manual respectively. Title pages will be prepared in manuscript.

(4)

WAR DIARY
or
~~INTELLIGENCE SUMMARY.~~
(Erase heading not required.)

Army Form C. 2118.

May 1918 –

Map Reference – Sheet HAZEBROUCK 5A –

Place	Date	Hour	Summary of Events and Information	Remarks and references to Appendices
WATTEN.	15/5/18.	9 A.M.	Beautiful weather continues – Handing over of equipment continued – Considerable enemy activity (aircraft) at nightfall –	AHu
〃	16/5/18	9 AM	Fine weather continues – Handing over & training of new unit continued –	AHu
〃	17/5/18	9 AM.	Weather very hot & fine – Major J. MORRIS. M.C. accompanied 1/6 Cheshire Rgt on manoeuvres arranged for American Division – 306 Field Ambulance is taking part in these, establishing an Advanced Dressing Stn. at 3D.10.70, an A.D.S. at WATTEN (present site) and Main Dressing Stn at LE QUILLEVAL –	AHu
〃	18/5/18	9 AM.	Weather continues very hot & fine – All sites in connection with manoeuvres visited during the day – Handing over of all equipment Stores and Transport completed during the day –	AHu
〃	19/5/18	9 AM.	Fine weather continues – Accompanied Division Surgeon on tour of inspection during the morning – & visited M.D.S. at QUILLEVAL – In the afternoon went to 133 Fld Ambulance, who held a Sports meeting –	AHu

D. D. & L., London, E.C.
(A8004) Wt. W1771/M2 31 750,000 5/17 Sch. 52 Forms/C2118/14

Instructions regarding War Diaries and Intelligence Summaries are contained in F. S. Regs., Part II. and the Staff Manual respectively. Title pages will be prepared in manuscript.

(5)

May 1918.

WAR DIARY
or
INTELLIGENCE SUMMARY.
(Erase heading not required.)

Army Form C. 2118.

Ref Reference – Sheet HAZEBROUCK 5A –

Place	Date	Hour	Summary of Events and Information	Remarks and references to Appendices
WATTEN.	20/5/18	9AM.	Beautiful weather continues – Training of unit continued – M.D.S. at QUILLEYAL + other posts closed on conclusion of tactical exercise –	Alh.
"	21/5/18	9AM.	Fine weather + very hot – Training of unit continued: pitching of tents and examination of panniers: at 4PM. held a Conference of Officers and went into the subject of Medical Organisations at the Front and system of evacuation –	Alh.
"	22/5/18	9AM.	Very fine hot weather continues – Training continued in contents of panniers + equipment of operating room in an A.D.S.: Personnel + equipment of the various medical Organisations in the Forward Area formed subject of the Officers' Conference at 12 noon – Very good progress is being made in all departments –	Alh.
"	23/5/18	9AM	Cooler – high wind and much dust – Gas was dealt with at an Officers' Conference at 12 noon –	Alh.

D. D. & L., London, E.C.
(A8004) Wt. W1771/M2 31 750,000 5/17 Sch. 52 Forms/C2118/14

Instructions regarding War Diaries and Intelligence Summaries are contained in F. S. Regs., Part II. and the Staff Manual respectively. Title pages will be prepared in manuscript.

(6)

May 1918.

WAR DIARY
or
INTELLIGENCE SUMMARY.
(Erase heading not required.)

Army Form C. 2118.

Map Reference – Sheet HAZEBROUCK 5A.

Place	Date	Hour	Summary of Events and Information	Remarks and references to Appendices
WATTEN.	24/5/18	9AM	Rain has fallen during the night and is falling steadily this morning; Major General W. G. MACPHERSON. CB. CMG. visited the site at 4.30 PM in the afternoon.	Alh
	25/5/18	9AM.	Fine weather, bright sunshine. Gas shells and protection against gas formed subject of a Conference of Officers at 11.45 AM.	Alh
	26/5/18	9AM.	Fine weather continues. Lt + QM A.E HARROLD RAMC left for England in accordance with instructions received and is struck off the strength from today's date.	Alh
	27/5/18	9AM	Fine weather continues. I visited ~~the~~ A.D.M.S. at 11.45 AM. Major J. MORRIS. M.C. left to proceed on leave.	Alh
	28/5/18	9AM.	Fine weather. Cool. No C/1030 Sgt. E.S. STINCHCOMBE MM ASC (M.T.) receives a mention in Despatches (London Gazette 25/5/18).	Alh

D. D. & L., London, E.C.
(A8004) Wt. W1771/M2 31 750,000 5/17 Sch. 52 Forms/C2118/14

132nd FIELD AMBULANCE 29/5/18.

Instructions regarding War Diaries and Intelligence Summaries are contained in F. S. Regs., Part II. and the Staff Manual respectively. Title pages will be prepared in manuscript.

(7)

May. 1918.

WAR DIARY
or
~~INTELLIGENCE SUMMARY.~~

(Erase heading not required.)

Army Form C. 2118.

Map Reference – Sheet HAZEBROUCK 5A –

Place	Date	Hour	Summary of Events and Information	Remarks and references to Appendices
WATTEN.	29/5/18	9AM.	Weather dull + cool – Officers' Conference at 11.30 AM when the subject dealt with was Marching and March Discipline –	AL
"	30/5/18	9AM	Weather fine + hot –	AL
"	31/5/18	9AM	Fine weather continues – Officers' Conference held at 11.30 AM when the duties of a Regimental Medical Officer were dealt with – The unit attached to this training Cadre has made good progress in every department of Field Ambulance work, and in running the site here since it arrived on 11/5/18 has become familiar with the reception + disposal of all kinds of sick, and the treatment + selection of cases suitable for retention in this Field Ambulance site – also with the methods of obtaining all kinds of supplies for them –	AL

132nd FIELD AMBULANCE 1/6/18.

A Littlejohns – Lt Col –
R.A.M.C
O.C. 132nd FIELD AMBULANCE.

ORIGINAL

Vol 28

140/3076.

CONFIDENTIAL

WAR DIARY

OF

132nd. FIELD AMBULANCE

FROM 1st. JUNE 1918. TO 30th. JUNE 1918.

(VOLUME 28)

1

June 1918.

Instructions regarding War Diaries and Intelligence Summaries are contained in F. S. Regs., Part II. and the Staff Manual respectively. Title pages will be prepared in manuscript.

WAR DIARY
or
~~INTELLIGENCE SUMMARY.~~
(Erase heading not required.)

Army Form C. 2118.

Map Reference: — HAZEBROUCK 5A —

Place	Date	Hour	Summary of Events and Information	Remarks and references to Appendices
WATTEN	1/6/18	9AM	Fine weather, very hot — At 11.30 AM Officers' Conference held when the duties of a Regimental M.O. were dealt with —	Alh
	2/6/18	9AM	Fine weather continues — Sunday; training during past week has made good progress —	Alh
	3/6/18	9AM	Cooler + rather windy, with a great deal of dust — Officers Conference at 11·30 AM on 'Sanitation' in The Field —	Alh
	4/6/18	9AM	Weather dull + cool — At a conference with the Officers the remainder of the ground was covered as regards Sanitation in the Field — All sides of this subject have been dealt with both for temporary and more permanent camps —	Alh
	5/6/18	9AM	Weather hot + much dust. The 306 Field Ambulance, American E.F. received orders to be prepared to move out tomorrow —	Alh

D. D. & L., London, E.C. (A8004) Wt. W1771/M2 31 750,000 5/17 Sch. 52 Forms/C2118/14

Instructions regarding War Diaries and Intelligence Summaries are contained in F. S. Regs., Part II. and the Staff Manual respectively. Title pages will be prepared in manuscript.

WAR DIARY
or
~~INTELLIGENCE SUMMARY.~~
(Erase heading not required.)

Army Form C. 2118.

Map Reference – Sheet HAZEBROUCK 5A –

Place	Date	Hour	Summary of Events and Information	Remarks and references to Appendices
WATTEN	6/6/18.	9 AM.	Very hot day – The 306 Field Ambulance received orders to move at 11.30 AM, and having completed all its arrangements moved off at 3 PM, in good order, thus completing its training so far as this training cadre is concerned – Visited the A.D.M.S. in the evening, and later called upon the Division Surgeon 80th Division, American E.F. and arranged to collect sick from some of his units tomorrow –	A.H.
	7/6/18	9 AM.	Very fine & hot weather – Site got ready for reception of patients with what remains in the way of equipment – Indents for B.R.C.S. stores passed to A.D.M.S. for approval – These stores were approved & delivered by B.R.C.S. at 6.30 PM –	
		7 PM.	Captain R. McBRAYER M.C. U.S.A. reported for duty with 2 O.R.	A.H.
	8/6/18.	10 AM	Fine weather continues – attended Conference at Office of the A.D.M.S. at 10 AM – 1/Lt E. W. REEVES. M.R.C. U.S.A. and 8 O.R. reported for duty –	A.H.

D. D. & L., London, E.C.
(A8004) Wt. W1771/M2 31 750,000 5/17 Sch. 52 Forms/C2118/14

Instructions regarding War Diaries and Intelligence Summaries are contained in F. S. Regs., Part II. and the Staff Manual respectively. Title pages will be prepared in manuscript.

(3) June. 1918 –

WAR DIARY
or
~~INTELLIGENCE SUMMARY.~~
(*Erase heading not required.*)

Army Form C. 2118.

Map Reference: —
Sheet HAZEBROUCK. 5A –

Place	Date	Hour	Summary of Events and Information	Remarks and references to Appendices
WATTEN	9/6/18	9 AM.	Fine weather continues – Case of diphtheria discovered amongst Civilian population and reported to A.D.M.S. –	AH.
"	10/6/18	9 AM.	Cooler – Some showers – Visited NORTKERQUE to look for a Field Ambulance site, but did not see anything suitable –	AH.
"	12/6/18	9 AM.	Spent the whole day in search for a site, but the area is already full – Selected village of LA WATTINE for approval of A.D.M.S. –	AH.
"	13/6/18	9 AM.	Weather very hot + stuffy – Held a conference for Officers at 2 PM + took them over the Medical Organisation + evacuation from the Front – Orders received to stand fast at WATTEN —	AH.
"	14/6/18	9 AM.	Dull + cool – Officers Conference at noon subject – "Duties of a RMO" – Lt + Qm. M.D. COWTAN. RAMC. reported his arrival and is taken on the strength from todays date –	AH.
"	15/6/18	9 AM.	Some rain during the night – weather cool – Officers' Conference Duties of a RMO. concluded –	AH.

D. D. & L., London, E.C.
(A8004) Wt. W1771/M2 31 750,000 5/17 Sch. 52 Forms/C2118/14

Instructions regarding War Diaries and Intelligence Summaries are contained in F. S. Regs., Part II. and the Staff Manual respectively. Title pages will be prepared in manuscript.

WAR DIARY
or
~~INTELLIGENCE SUMMARY~~.
(Erase heading not required.)

Army Form C. 2118.

(4) June 1918

Map Reference:- Sheets — HAZEBROUCK 5A + CALAIS 13 —

Place	Date	Hour	Summary of Events and Information	Remarks and references to Appendices
WATTEN.	16/6/18.	8.30 A.M.	Fine weather continues, but still cool — I proceeded to BOURNONVILLE to inspect accommodation there for a Field Ambulance, in accordance with orders received from the ADMS, and submitted a report on the subject on return — Captain R. McBRAYER + Lt E.W. REEVES and the 10 Other Ranks M.C. U.S.A, attached here for duty, left at 5.30 P.M. to report to O.C. 112 Field Ambulance at LICQUES for duty —	AM
"	17/6/18	9 A.M	Fine weather, warmer — Remaining cases here transferred to 112 Field Ambulance at LICQUES — Warning notice received to be ready to move to VIEIL MOULIER at an early date —	AM
"	18/6/18	9 A.M.	Dry weather continues, with a good deal of dust — Site cleaned up and everything prepared for moving — Orders received	
		11 P.M.	at 11 P.M. to move to BOURNONVILLE tomorrow —	AM

D. D. & L., London, E.C. (A8004) Wt. W1771/M2 31 750,000 5/17 Sch. 52 Forms/C2118/14

Instructions regarding War Diaries and Intelligence Summaries are contained in F. S. Regs., Part II. and the Staff Manual respectively. Title pages will be prepared in manuscript.

WAR DIARY
or
~~INTELLIGENCE~~ SUMMARY.
(Erase heading not required.)

Army Form C. 2118.

(5) June 1918 –

Map Reference:– Sheets HAZEBROUCK 5A. CALAIS 13 –

Place	Date	Hour	Summary of Events and Information	Remarks and references to Appendices
WATTEN.	19/6/18	9AM	Unit moved during the day to BOURNONVILLE –	[illegible]
BOURNONVILLE	20/6/18	9AM.	Weather inclined to be wet – All stores and equipment on charge have now been got down to new site, at present occupied by 44 Field Ambulance –	[illegible]
"	21/6/18	9AM.	Notification received that the 311 Ambulance Coy & Field Hpl. of 78 Div. Am. Ex. F., will arrive here tomorrow – No. 65795 Sgt. A.C. PIPER. RAMC is awarded the Meritorious Service Medal in the London Gazette dated June 17th 1918 –	[illegible]
"	22/6/18	9AM.	Fine weather, cool & windy – Orders received that 44 Field Ambulance will remain here and take on the training of the part of the 78 Am. Div. Sanitary Train which is arriving today –	[illegible]
"	23/6/18	9AM.	Fine weather, cool –	
"	25/6/18	9AM	Orders received warning to be ready to move to ABBEVILLE at short notice to reequip –	[illegible]

D. D. & L., London, E.C. (A8004) Wt. W1771/M2 31 750,000 5/17 Sch. 52 Forms/C2118/14

Instructions regarding War Diaries and Intelligence Summaries are contained in F. S. Regs., Par. II. and the Staff Manual respectively. Title pages will be prepared in manuscript.

(6)

132nd FIELD AMBULANCE
June 1918

WAR DIARY
or
~~INTELLIGENCE SUMMARY.~~
(Erase heading not required.)

Army Form C. 2118.

Map Ref
Calais 13. Hazebrouck 5A
Abbeville 14.

Place	Date	Hour	Summary of Events and Information	Remarks and references to Appendices
Bournonville	26/6/8	5pm	Lt Col A. Littlejohns R.A.M.C. admitted No 44 Fld Amb & evacuated to No 14 St. Hosp.	M.L.
ABBEVILLE	27/VI/18	10.PM.	On instructions from A.D.M.S. 39th Div. I joined the Training Cadre of the (132) Field Ambulance at BOULOGNE on its way to ABBEVILLE to re-equip, and assumed command. Arrived at ABBEVILLE 8.45 PM. I reported to A.D.M.S. ABBEVILLE at 9.15 PM. who instructed me to proceed to the Chinese Camp at MOUTORT, and also as to drawing Transport, Ordnance Stores and Medical & Surgical Equipment.	JH
	28/VI/18	5.PM.	The camp is shared with 112 Field Ambulance. Horse Transport as per Army Form G. 1098-120 of January 1918 was drawn at 10 AM today. Ordnance equipment to be drawn at 6 PM today and Medical & Surgical Equipment to be drawn from No 13 A.D Med Stores at 9 AM tomorrow. 121 RAMC other ranks have rejoined the unit today from the Base.	JH
	29/VI/18	8.PM.	Glorious Summer weather. At 5.30 PM yesterday I received orders for A.D.M.S. ABBEVILLE to be ready to move today. I therefore proceeded to draw Ordnance & Medical Equipment forthwith. Medical Equipment was drawn from No 13 A.D. Med Stores complete with the exception of Water Testing Cases – "Horrocks" & "Poison" none being available. Ordnance Equipment was not drawn complete – a considerable number of items not having been supplied	

A6945 Wt. W11422/M1160 350,000 12/16 D. D. & L. Forms/C./2118/14.

Instructions regarding War Diaries and Intelligence Summaries are contained in F. S. Regs., Pur. II. and the Staff Manual respectively. Title pages will be prepared in manuscript.

WAR DIARY
or
~~INTELLIGENCE SUMMARY.~~
(Erase heading not required.)

Army Form C. 2118.

Map Ref
Calais 13. Hazebrouck 5A
Abbeville 14

132nd FIELD AMBULANCE June 1918

Place	Date	Hour	Summary of Events and Information	Remarks and references to Appendices
ABBEVILLE	Cont'd 29/VI/18	8PM	from the base. I reported personally to A.D.M.S ABBEVILLE at 10 AM that I would be prepared to move off at 2PM., the Deficiencies not being of vital importance. Later I forwarded him a list of these, and forwarded indent for same to DADOS 39th Div.	[initials]
"	30/VI/18	9PM	Horse transport moved off en route for Divisional HQ (39) at WOLPHUS. last night at 9.30 PM. under charge of Lt + QM M.D. COWTAN D.C.M. RAMC. Orders received to report with personnel at The TRIAGE for entraining at 8AM. tomorrow, with 3 days Rations.	[initials]

132nd FIELD AMBULANCE 2/VII/18

J Morris Major R.A.M.C. T.F.
O.C. 132nd FIELD AMBULANCE.

A6945 Wt. W11422/M1160 350,000 12/16 D. D. & L. Forms/C./2118/14.

ORIGINAL.

SECRET.

CONFIDENTIAL.

WAR DIARY

OF

132nd FIELD AMBULANCE.

From JULY 1st to JULY 31st 1918.

(Volume 29)

Instructions regarding War Diaries and Intelligence Summaries are contained in F. S. Regs., Part II, and the Staff Manual respectively. Title pages will be prepared in manuscript.

(1)

July 1918

WAR DIARY
or
INTELLIGENCE ~~SUMMARY.~~
(Erase heading not required.)

Army Form C. 2118.

Map Reference
CALAIS 13. HAZEBROUCK 5A
ABBEVILLE 14.

Place	Date	Hour	Summary of Events and Information	Remarks and references to Appendices
ETAPLES.	1/VII/18	8 P.M.	Reported to R.T.O. TRIAGE, ABBEVILLE at 7.45 AM, entraining strength 1 officer 125 O.R. Train left at 10.50 AM Destination AUDRUICQ. Arrived ETAPLES 2.30 P.M. had to detrain & spent the night at No 9 Rest Camp having to Report to R.T.O. New Siding at 6.30 A.M. tomorrow. Enemy Air Raid during the night. No casualties amongst personnel at No 9 Rest Camp.	JMM
AUTINGUES	2/VII/18	7 P.M.	Train left ETAPLES at 7.25 arriving at AUDRUICQ 1 P.M. Received orders to proceed to AUTINGUES, where I arrived at 3.50 P.M. and established my H.Q. Horse Transport under Lt QM M.D. COWTAN D.C.M. RAMC arrived at 4.45 pm having proceeded by Road from ABBEVILLE staging as follows:- Night of 29/30-6-18 RUE. Night 30/VI/18 - 1/VII/18 CUCQ Night 1/2nd - VII - 18 DESVRES. no incident of special note having occurred.	JMM
"	3/VII/18	7 P.M.	Weather keeps gloriously fine. Billets are good, but some of the men prefer to bivouac. Work of sorting out equipment &c into Sections commenced & good progress made. As only 19 G.S. Panniers and no Medical Comfort Panniers (– all available –) were drawn the remainder of the equipment is temporarily stored in sacks. Painting of Transport, Red Crosses &c commenced.	JMM
"	4/VII/18	2 P.M.	All indents for equipment not available for issue at Ordnance & Medical Depot Stores at ABBEVILLE have been sent in this morning. ~~Painting~~ & Cleaning & painting of	

A6945 Wt. W11422/M1160 350,000 12/16 D. D. & L. Forms/C./2118/14.

Army Form C. 2118.

WAR DIARY
or
~~INTELLIGENCE SUMMARY.~~
(Erase heading not required.)

Instructions regarding War Diaries and Intelligence Summaries are contained in F. S. Regs., Part II, and the Staff Manual respectively. Title pages will be prepared in manuscript.

(2)

July 1918

Map Reference
CALAIS 13 HAZEBROUCK 5A
ABBEVILLE 14.

Place	Date	Hour	Summary of Events and Information	Remarks and references to Appendices
AUTINGUES	Contd 4/VII/18	2 PM	Transport is proceeding well	[initials]
"	5/VII/18	5 PM	Weather remains good. Rain threatens. Good progress with cleaning & painting of Transport. Lt Col G.A.D. HARVEY. CMG. RAMC arrived and took command of the unit this afternoon.	[initials]
"	5/7/18	5 P.M.	Took over command of 138th Field Ambulance this day (authority D.M.S 2nd Army No P2/264, 1/7/18.) Received orders from ADMS to be in readiness to move by road to 2nd Corps area on 6/7/18, at 9.30 pm, necessary steps taken. At 11-30 pm ADMS notified that move would not take place till 7th inst.	[initials]
"	6/7/18		Captain J. MAC RAE RAMC & 1st Lieut J.G. RILEY M.O.R.C. reported for duty. Received orders from ADMS to proceed on 7th & 8th inst by road in two ~~days~~ stages to LISTER CAMP (Sheet 19 W.23 A.4.8), marching the first day to VOLKERINCKHOVE & reporting there for billets to the Commandant 22nd Corps School	
"	~~7/7/18~~	8 pm	~~[struck out]~~ Captain D.B.I. HALLETT RAMC & Lieut T. McLAREN RAMC reported for duty.	[initials]
VOLKERINGK-HOVE	7/7/18	5-30 am	The whole unit with the exception of one N.C.O & two men left as a rear party marched to VOLKERINGKHOVE, arriving there at 3-30 p.m. A halt of two & a half hours	

A6945 Wt. W11422/M1160 350,000 12/16 D. D. & L. Forms/C./2118/14.

Instructions regarding War Diaries and Intelligence Summaries are contained in F. S. Regs., Part II. and the Staff Manual respectively. Title pages will be prepared in manuscript.

3 July 1918

WAR DIARY
or
~~INTELLIGENCE SUMMARY.~~
(Erase heading not required.)

Map References HAZEBROUCK 5A. BELGIUM & part of FRANCE 1/100,000

Army Form C. 2118.

Place	Date	Hour	Summary of Events and Information	Remarks and references to Appendices
VOLKERINGKHOVE	7/7/18	10 p.m.	hours at EST MONT for the mid day meal. No men fell out on the march. The distance covered was 17 miles, weather fine & warm	J.A.D.W.
LISTER CAMP ROUSEBRUGGE	8/8/17	6. p.m.	Marched from ~~[illegible]~~ Camp at VOLKERINGKHOVE to LISTER CAMP, ROUSEBRUGGE, starting at 5-30 AM and arriving at destination at 3 p.m. A long halt of 2½ hours was made in the middle of the day for dinner. Very hot day & distinctly oppressive at times, nevertheless only one man fell out. The total distance covered was approximately 18 miles. The horses stood the march well. The Division Surgeon 30th Division AmEF under whose jurisdiction the unit now comes visited the camp. He was accompanied by the D.D.M.S 2nd Corps	J.A.D.W.
"	9/8/17		The Division Surgeon 30th Divn Am EF & the O.C. 134th Fd Ambulance visited the Camp & a discussion was held on the allocation of duties to the Fd Ambulances of the division. The personnel were employed in cleaning up the Camp, which was in an untidy condition, & arranging for the reception of cases.	J.A.D.W.

A6945 Wt. W11422/M1160 350,000 12/16 D. D. & L. Forms/C./2118/14.

Instructions regarding War Diaries and Intelligence Summaries are contained in F. S. Regs., Part II. and the Staff Manual respectively. Title pages will be prepared in manuscript.

4

July 1918

WAR DIARY

or

~~INTELLIGENCE SUMMARY.~~

(Erase heading not required.)

Army Form C. 2118.

Map References BELGIUM & part of FRANCE 19 & 28

Place	Date	Hour	Summary of Events and Information	Remarks and references to Appendices
LISTER CAMP ROUSEBRUGGE	10/7/18		Routine duties carried out, & one ward opened for the reception of cases	[illegible]
"	11/7/18		Commenced receiving patients. The holding party left at AUTINGUES returned	[illegible]
"	12/7/18		Nothing special to report. Heavy rain fell during the morning & came through a number of the huts	[illegible]
"	13/7/18		The Division Surgeon 30th American Divn visited the hospital at 8-30 am. The D.D.M.S. & D.A.D.M.S. 2nd Corps inspected the hospital in the afternoon. I attended a conference of Field Ambulance Commanders at the office of the Division Surgeon 30th American Divn at 6 p.m.	[illegible]
"	14/7/18		Captain H. L. MORRIS Dental Corps National Guard U.S. Army & an enlisted assistant reported for temporary duty with the ambulance. Captain J. MacCrae Rame left for temporary duty in the office of the Division Surgeon 30th American Divn. I visited the R.A.P.s & Bearer posts which would function in the event of the Blue line (EAST POPERINGHE) being occupied by the 30th American Divn.	[illegible]
"	15/7/18		Received verbal orders from D.D.M.S. 2nd Corps to move ambulance to TUBBY CAMP Ref 19/W.17.d.8.6. & take over the running of the	

Instructions regarding War Diaries and Intelligence Summaries are contained in F. S. Regs., Par. II, and the Staff Manual respectively. Title pages will be prepared in manuscript.

5
July 1918

WAR DIARY
or
~~INTELLIGENCE SUMMARY.~~
(Erase heading not required.)

Army Form C. 2118.

Map references
BELGIUM & part of FRANCE
Sheets 19, 27 & 28

Place	Date	Hour	Summary of Events and Information	Remarks and references to Appendices
ROUSBRUGGE, LISTER CAMP	15/7/18		Corps skin centre as well as a Divisional Rest Station for the 30th American Divn from the 102nd Field Ambulance 34th Divn as soon as the 102nd Fd Ambulance moves to another area. Visited TOBBY CAMP with Major MORRIS my 2nd in Command & the Quarter Master & arranged details of taking over with The O.C. 102 Fd Ambulance	S.D.H.
TOBBY CAMP	16/7/18		Took over Corps skin centre & Divl Rest station from 102 Fd ambulance at 2 pm. The latter ambulance did not however move out till 4 am on 17/7/18. 170 patients in hospital	S.D.H.
"	17/7/18		Camp inspected by the Divn Surgeon 30th American Divn & the D.D.M.S. 2nd Corps.	S.D.H.
"	18/7/18		Took Captain HALLETT & Lieut McLAREN and their bearer NCOs round R.A.P.S, bearer relay posts & A.D.S. to be used in the event of the BLUE line being manned.	S.D.H.
"	19/7/18		Camp inspected by Divl Surgeon 30th American Divn. Work proceeding on new bath house for patients in the Corps skin centre also recovering of the huts with tarred paper which is badly needed – the rain coming thro' most of the huts in many places during the heavy thunderstorms experienced lately.	S.D.H.

A6945 Wt. W11422/M1160 350,000 12/16 D. D. & L. Forms/C./2118/14.

Army Form C. 2118.

WAR DIARY
or
~~INTELLIGENCE~~ SUMMARY.
(*Erase heading not required.*)

Instructions regarding War Diaries and Intelligence Summaries are contained in F. S. Regs., Part II. and the Staff Manual respectively. Title pages will be prepared in manuscript.

6
July 1918

MAP REFERENCES
BELGIUM & part of FRANCE
Sheets 19, 27 NE & 28 N.W.

Place	Date	Hour	Summary of Events and Information	Remarks and references to Appendices
TUBBY CAMP	20/7/18		Very heavy thunderstorms today & the ground became very wet & muddy. Captain ULOTH reported arrival from temporary duty in the office of the A.D.M.S. 39th Div^n.	[signature]
"	22/7/18		Division Surgeon 30th American Div^n visited the ambulance	[signature]
"	23/7/18		Captain HALLETT, Lieut. McLAREN & self attended a lecture on gas warfare by Colonel GILCHRIST M.C., USA at NINE ELMS. Very heavy rain all morning.	[signature]
"	24/7/18		Division Surgeon 30th American Division inspected the D.R.S. & Corps Skin Centre	[signature]
"	26/7/18		Work progressing on the new bath house in the Corps Skin centre, also resetting of huts & repairing roofs generally throughout the whole camp	[signature]
"	27/7/18		Very heavy rain, camp in a very muddy state notwithstanding various improvements in the surface drainage system.	[signature]
"	28/7/18		A British aeroplane returning from a bombing raid landed close to the camp owing to engine trouble; the observer had a flesh wound of the left forearm. I placed a guard over the machine. D.D.M.S. visited camp.	[signature]

A6945 Wt. W11422/M1160 350,000 12/16 D. D. & L. Forms/C./2118/14.

Instructions regarding War Diaries and Intelligence Summaries are contained in F. S. Regs., Par. II. and the Staff Manual respectively. Title pages will be prepared in manuscript.

7 July 1918

WAR DIARY
or
~~INTELLIGENCE SUMMARY.~~
(Erase heading not required.)

Army Form C. 2118.

MAP REFERENCES
BELGIUM & part of FRANCE
Sheets 19, 27 NE & 28 NW.

Place	Date	Hour	Summary of Events and Information	Remarks and references to Appendices
TUBBY CAMP ROOSEBRUGGE	30/7/18		The aeroplane was removed by a party from Aerodrome. Major DALE RAMC sanitary expert at army headquarters inspected sanitary arrangements of the camp.	[signature]
"	31/7/18		The D.M.S. 2nd Army inspected the Corps Skin Centre & Divisional Rest Station. He was accompanied by the D.D.M.S. 2nd Corps and Division Surgeon 30th American Division.	[signature]

[signature] Harvey
Lt Col RAMC
OC 132 Field Ambulance

TUBBY CAMP
31/7/18.

A6945 Wt. W11422/M1160 350,000 12/16 D. D. & L. Forms/C./2118/14.

Original
Secret

37

98 L 30

140/3200.

CONFIDENTIAL

WAR DIARY

OF

132nd FIELD AMBULANCE.

From 1st AUGUST to 31st AUGUST 1918.

(VOLUME 30)

6 Aug. 1918.

Instructions regarding War Diaries and Intelligence Summaries are contained in F. S. Regs., Part II. and the Staff Manual respectively. Title pages will be prepared in manuscript.

(1) August 1918

WAR DIARY
or
~~INTELLIGENCE SUMMARY~~.
(Erase heading not required.)

Army Form C. 2118.

MAP REFERENCES
BELGIUM & Part of
FRANCE SHEETS 19, 27 & 28

Place	Date	Hour	Summary of Events and Information	Remarks and references to Appendices
TUBBY CAMP ROOSEBRUGGE	2/8/18		Division Surgeon informed me personally that a party consisting of 10 Officers & 107 other ranks 105 Sanitary Train Amer force would report to me at about 9 am on 3/8/18 for instruction in Field Ambulance duties	[illegible]
"	3/8/18		The party of 105 Sanitary train reported here for instruction at 9-45 am four Officers & 24 O.R. proceeded in accordance with instructions to LEISHMAN CAMP, ROUSEBRUGGE for instruction there, the remainder remaining here. In the afternoon instructions were received that one Veterinary Officer & 3 O.R. of the 105 Sanitary train were to proceed to 108 Mobile Vet. Section Amer Force – the move was carried out at once. I visited the H.Q. 1/3 West Riding Field Ambulance at L'EBBE FARM & arranged to remove to this site the majority of wooden bedsteads in his charge to be utilized in the Corps Skin Centre, in accordance with instructions received from D.D.M.S. 2nd Corps. I gave a lecture to the Officers & Other ranks of 105 Sanitary Train on the general duties of a Field Ambulance. A Schedule of training for the 105 Sanitary train was drawn up & is attached marked appendix 1.	[illegible] appendix attached

A6945 Wt. W11422/M1160 350,000 12/16 D. D. & L. Forms/C./2118/14.

Instructions regarding War Diaries and Intelligence Summaries are contained in F. S. Regs., Par. II. and the Staff Manual respectively. Title pages will be prepared in manuscript.

(2)
August 1918

WAR DIARY
or
INTELLIGENCE SUMMARY.
(*Erase heading not required.*)

Army Form C. 2118.

MAP REFERENCES
BELGIUM & Part of FRANCE
Sheets 19. 27 & 28

Place	Date	Hour	Summary of Events and Information	Remarks and references to Appendices
TUBBY CAMP ROUSBRUGGE	4/8/18		Instruction of personnel of 105 Sanitary Train continued, double banking of personnel with personnel of this unit being carried out & a lecture & demonstration on the medical equipment being given to all ranks	JSDW
"	5/8/18		Lectures given to Officers of 105 Sanitary Train on the duties of a Regimental Medical Officer & to the whole unit on the evacuation of the forward area. Division Surgeon visited the Corps Skin Centre.	JSDW
"	6/8/18		Lectured to personnel of 105 Sanitary Train on classification of casualties & disposal, procedure when patients admitted to D.R.S. & duties of orderlies in charge of wards. 4 Officers & 2nd OR 105 San. Train proceeded to ½ W. Riding F.A.	JSDW
"	7/8/18		Captain W.O.K. lectured on water duties & demonstrated the water cart to the Sanitary Train. DDMS 2nd Corps & 19th Corps visited D.R.S. Division Surgeon 30th American Div. visited ambulance.	JSDW
"	8/8/18		Captain McCrae lectured to attached personnel on sanitary duties in camps & billets. Division Surgeon visited ambulance & instructed Lt & Qr Mr COWTAN to proceed to ABBEVILLE by car to assist Qr Master COLLINS U.S.A. to take over equipment & transport of 2 field ambulances for use of the 30th American Division	JSDW
"	9/8/18		Four Officers & 2nd O.R. of 105 Sanitary Train who proceeded on 3/8/18 to ½ West Riding Field	

A6945 Wt. W11422/M1160 350,000 12/16 D. D. & L. Forms/C./2118/14.

Instructions regarding War Diaries and Intelligence Summaries are contained in F. S. Regs., Par. II. and the Staff Manual respectively. Title pages will be prepared in manuscript.

3
August 1918

WAR DIARY
or
~~INTELLIGENCE~~ SUMMARY.
(Erase heading not required.)

MAP REFERENCES
BELGIUM & part of FRANCE
Sheets 19. 27 & 28

Army Form C. 2118.

Place	Date	Hour	Summary of Events and Information	Remarks and references to Appendices
TUBBY CAMP ROUSEBRUGGE	9/8/18		Field Ambulance returned. 1 Officer & 24 O.R. proceeded to 1/3 West Riding Field Ambulance in accordance with instructions. The Motor personnel & drivers complete of two Field Ambulances arrived from the base & remain here & train drivers of 105 Sanitary Train & eventually be handed over to that unit	JCDW
"	10/8/18		I lectured to the party of 105 San^y Train which returned yesterday – the men & officers have been posted to various duties in the Ambulance.	JCDW
"	12/8/18		Party of 105 Sanitary Train returned from instruction at M.D.S & A.D.S. 1 Officer & 21 O.R. proceeded to M.D.S for instruction. D.D.M.S. visited Corps Skin depot.	JCDW
"	13/8/18		Division Surgeon visited ambulance. Received orders that move of the personnel of 105 Sanitary Train from here to BALLANCE CAMP, 27 E.6.d.6.4. is postponed for the present. I lectured to the personnel of the train.	JCDW
"	14/8/18		Division Surgeon visited Ambulance.	JCDW
"	15/8/18		The party of 105 Sanitary Train in accordance with orders received from the Division Surgeon 30th American Division proceeded to BALLANCE CAMP Sheet 27. E.6.d.6.4. The personnel & cars of the two Field Ambulances who arrived here on 9/8/18 proceeded one half to BALLANCE CAMP the other to AMBULANCE CAMP Sheet 27 F.25 b.6.9. in accordance with orders received from Div^l Surgeon 30th American Div^n.	JCDW
"	17/8/18		I visited the advanced Army Dysentery Centre at HILLHOEK Sheet 27. L.20.b.8.8. also the	

[illegible]

Instructions regarding War Diaries and Intelligence Summaries are contained in F. S. Regs., Par. II. and the Staff Manual respectively. Title pages will be prepared in manuscript.

(4) August 1918

WAR DIARY
or
INTELLIGENCE ~~SUMMARY~~.
(Erase heading not required.)

Map References. BELGIUM & part of FRANCE SHEETS 19, 27 & 28

Army Form C. 2118.

Place	Date	Hour	Summary of Events and Information	Remarks and references to Appendices
TUBBY CAMP ROUSEBRUGGE	17/8/18		Laterie POPERINGHE, Ref 27/F.5.d.5.9. which is being prepared as a reserve advanced dressing station; In accordance with orders received from Division Surgeon I detailed a party consisting of one Sergeant & 12 men to hold this post & continue the work of protecting & making the post suitable for an A.D.S.	[illegible]
"	19/8/18		Visited the Laterie POPERINGHE and instructed the NCO as to the continuation of the work on this post.	[illegible]
"	21/8/18		Visited the Laterie POPERINGHE & H.Q. 134 Field Ambulance at MOORE PARK Sheet 28 G.4.D.5.7.	[illegible]
"	23/8/18		Paid the personnel of the ambulance. Division Surgeon visited the ambulance	[illegible]
"	25/8/18		Annual sports held today; DDMS & Division Surgeon were present.	[illegible]
"	26/8/18		Very heavy rain during the night & camp in consequence very muddy & wet.	[illegible]
"	28/8/18		D.D.M.S. 2nd Corps inspected Corps Skin centre	[illegible]
"	29/8/18		Div. Surgeon 30th American Div. inspected D.R.S. & Corps Skin Centre	[illegible]
"	30/8/18		Visited R E dump at PESELHOEK 28/A 21.a.6.5 and arranged for supply of wood for stand on which to place tank for bath in Corps Skin Centre. From 6 p.m. today this unit ceases to be under 2nd Corps British & comes under 2nd Corps Amer.	[illegible]

A6945 Wt. W11422/M1160 350,000 12/16 D. D. & L. Forms/C./2118/14.

Instructions regarding War Diaries and Intelligence Summaries are contained in F. S. Regs., Par. II, and the Staff Manual respectively. Title pages will be prepared in manuscript.

(5) August 1918

WAR DIARY
or
~~INTELLIGENCE SUMMARY.~~
(*Erase heading not required.*)

Map References BELGIUM & Part of FRANCE SHEETS 19, 27 & 28.

Army Form C. 2118.

Place	Date	Hour	Summary of Events and Information	Remarks and references to Appendices
TUBBY CAMP ROOSEBRUGGE	31/8/18		Received orders from Divl Surgeon 30th American Divn that their Medical officers are being sent here on the 1st – 3rd & every succeeding 3rd day for instruction in the Corps Main Centre with particular reference to diagnosis of cases. This will continue till all Medical Officers with the 105th Sanitary Train & 119 & 120th Regiments have been trained.	[illegible]

[illegible] Lt Col RAMC
OC 132 Field Ambulance
31/8/18.

ORIGINAL
SECRET

WO 31

140/3259

C O N F I D E N T I A L

WAR DIARY

OF

132nd FIELD AMBULANCE

From 1st SEPTEMBER 1918 TO 30th SEPTEMBER 1918.

4

Sept. 1918

(VOLUME 31.)

Instructions regarding War Diaries and Intelligence Summaries are contained in F. S. Regs., Par. II. and the Staff Manual respectively. Title pages will be prepared in manuscript.

(1) September 1918

WAR DIARY
or
INTELLIGENCE ~~SUMMARY~~.
(Erase heading not required.)

Map References
BELGIUM & part of FRANCE
Sheets 19, 27

Army Form C. 2118.

Place	Date	Hour	Summary of Events and Information	Remarks and references to Appendices
TUBBY CAMP ROUSBRUGGE	1/9/18		Received a secret warning order that this unit will be relieved on 5th Sept by a unit of the 35th British Division. The Major General Commanding 30th American Division inspected the hospital & Corps skin centre this evening at 6-30 pm.	[illegible]
"	2/9/18		Received instructions from D.S. to return to duty all patients possible by noon 3/9/18. Received orders from D.S. to hand over the D.R.S. & Corps skin centre to 107 British Field Ambulance & move to BALLANCE CAMP 27/F.7.a.5.6 handing over & move to be completed by 4 pm. 3/9/18	[illegible]
"	3/9/18		Handed over D.R.S. & Corps skin centre at TUBBY CAMP to 107 British Field Ambulance & marched to BALLANCE CAMP 27/F.7.a.5.6 arriving there at 3 p.m.	[illegible]
BALLANCE CAMP	4/9/18		Received notification of date & time when this unit is to entrain for another area. In accordance with DG/129/1 forwarded by Divl. Surgeon returned to No 2 Canadian advanced depot of medical stores the following:- Field medical panniers prs 1, Field surgical panniers prs 1, Surgical haversacks 12, Medical companions 2, Field fracture boxes 3.	[illegible]
"	5/9/18		D.D.M.S. & Divl. Surgeon visited camp	[illegible]
"	7/9/18		Unit moved by train from PROVEN 27/A.7.6. at 7 am to WAVRANS	

A6945 Wt. W11422/M1160 350,000 12/16 D. D. & L. Forms/C./2118/14.

Instructions regarding War Diaries and Intelligence Summaries are contained in F. S. Regs., Par. II. and the Staff Manual respectively. Title pages will be prepared in manuscript.

(2)

Sepr 1918

WAR DIARY
or
~~INTELLIGENCE~~ SUMMARY.
(Erase heading not required.)

Map References
LENS 11.

Army Form C. 2118.

Place	Date	Hour	Summary of Events and Information	Remarks and references to Appendices
HERNICOURT LENS 11.2 D.61.83	7/9/18		detraining at 5 pm. orders were received on detraining to march to HERNICOURT	[initials]
			LENS 11 2.D. 61,83 and billet there. Troops & transport were all settled in billets by 7-30 pm. &	
"	~~[illegible]~~		arrival report sent to Div^l Surgeon 30th American Div^n	
"	8/9/18		Reported personally to the Div^l Surgeon. Was informed that the unit is in the I Corps & I Army	[initials]
			(British). Very heavy rain last night & today & the transport lines are in a very wet &	
			muddy condition. Received copy of I Corps medical arrangements & also Divisional	
			arrangements while in this area.	
"	10/9/18		Paid the Men. Visited Corps H.Q. I Corps. can ... ascertained that	[initials]
			the nearest Field Cashier is at LABUSSIERE. Made up new horse lines.	
"	11/9/18		Very wet during night	
"	13/9/18		Division Surgeon visited Ambulance. Moved horses under cover in farm buildings as owing to the heavy	[initials]
"	~~[illegible]~~		rain of the last few days the lines are under water. The unit was paraded for Squad drill	
"	14/9/18		Paper chase for the unit - distance about 4 miles.	[initials]
"	15/9/18		Received warning order to be ready to move unit within the next 48 hours	[initials]
"	16/9/18		Received orders for the ambulance to move to PUCHVILLERS area LENS 11 6.E.9.7. on 17th & 18th	
			instant. The transport to go by road leaving on 17th & the personnel by tactical train leaving on	

Instructions regarding War Diaries and Intelligence Summaries are contained in F. S. Regs., Part. II. and the Staff Manual respectively. Title pages will be prepared in manuscript.

(3) Sept 1918

WAR DIARY
or
~~INTELLIGENCE SUMMARY.~~
(Erase heading not required.)

LENS II.

Army Form C. 2118.

Place	Date	Hour	Summary of Events and Information	Remarks and references to Appendices
HERNICOURT	16/9/18		18th unit at 8 am entraining at WARRANS D.3.4.9 (LENS II) & detraining at BELLE EGLISE F.6.7.8.	[illegible]
″	17/9/18		Transport left at 7-30 am on march to new area joining the 60th American Brigade en route & staging at BOUQUEMAISON E4.1.6 (LENS II). Billeting party of one Officer & 2 O.R. sent on to new area. Received orders that the unit will be billeted at VAUCHELLES F.5.6.3 in the new area	[illegible] [illegible]
″	18/9/18		Unit entrained at 8 am & reached BELLE EGLISE F.6.7.8 at 1.15 p.m. where it was met by guide who led it to LOUVENCOURT F5.9.2. where billets had been obtained as the billeting party had found that there were no billets available in VAUCHELLES. Arrival report despatched to Div Surgeon 30th American Div.	[illegible]
LOUVENCOURT F5.9.2 (LENS II)	19/9/18		Division Surgeon visited Ambulance	[illegible]
″	20/9/18	9-45 pm	Received warning order that unit will move by bus on nights of 22-23 & 23-24 and transport to move on nights 21-22 & 22-23	[illegible]
″	21/9/18	8-40 am	Received order from D.S. for a billeting party to report at HERISSART to Captain FAIR at 9 am this morning. Sent Capt MACRAE in charge of party by car. Attended a conference at Division Surgeons Office at 8.30 pm.	[illegible]

A6945 Wt. W11422/M1160 350,000 12/16 D. D. & L. Forms/C./2118/14.

Instructions regarding War Diaries and Intelligence Summaries are contained in F. S. Regs., Par. II, and the Staff Manual respectively. Title pages will be prepared in manuscript.

(4)
Sept 1918

WAR DIARY
or
~~INTELLIGENCE SUMMARY.~~
(Erase heading not required.)

Army Form C. 2118.

LENS 11, FRANCE 62.C

Place	Date	Hour	Summary of Events and Information	Remarks and references to Appendices
BUIRE 62.C.J.28 A.4.4			The unit less horse transport & motor transport proceeded by bus from LOUVENCOURT to TINCOURT area Sheet 62C.J. & took over a site at BUIRE Sheet 62 C.J.28 A.4.4 embussing at 10 pm & arriving at destination at 6-15 am.	[initials]
"	23/9/18		Received orders to take over the Divisional Gas Centre at BUIRE from the 1st Australian Field Ambulance & also to take over the Advanced Dressing Station at HERVILLY & evacuation of casualties from the line, relief to be complete by midnight 23-24/9/18. Reconnoitred the line & arranged for reliefs. Received orders to hand over Advanced Dressing Station & evacuation from the line to 119th American Field Ambulance relief to be completed by midnight 25-26/9/18	[initials]
"	24/9/18		Arranged system of relief with OC 119th (Am) Field Ambulance. Visited ADS.	[initials]
"	25/9/18		Visited the RAPs of right sector & ADS. Relief completed by 11-30 pm	[initials]
"	26/9/18		Received orders to establish a Divisional Walking Wounded Post at TEMPLEUX Sheet 62C.L.2b. Reconnoitred suggested site & found no place suitable to catch the [illegible] of the Division (? from 31st Div (Am)) decided to establish post in open field at Sheet 62C L.1.D.5.2. in tents & huts. Also ordered to open a Divisional Gas Center at MARQUAIX Sheet 62 C. K.14.D.8.8, three NISSEN huts to be erected there for the purpose by Australian	[initials]

Instructions regarding War Diaries and Intelligence Summaries are contained in F. S. Regs., Par. II. and the Staff Manual respectively. Title pages will be prepared in manuscript.

(5)
Sepr 1918

WAR DIARY
or
INTELLIGENCE ~~SUMMARY~~.
(Erase heading not required.)

Army Form C. 2118.

FRANCE 62.C

Place	Date	Hour	Summary of Events and Information	Remarks and references to Appendices
BUIRE	26/9/18		Pioneers & tentage will be used in addition.	[initials]
MARQUAIX 62.C.L.1d.52	27/9/18		Moved here today, three small Nissen huts in process of erection, & one large Nissen hut salved from another site will also be erected. MAJOR MORRIS, Lt McLAREN & two tent subdivisions proceeded to TEMPLEUX & started to erect walking wounded post there. Visited TEMPLEUX in the evening. Huts which are to be erected have not yet arrived.	[initials]
"	28/9/18		Visited TEMPLEUX & found three NISSEN huts in process of erection - they should be completed by this evening. Three huts completed at MARQUAIX & work proceeding on the fourth. Received orders from D.S. to place my bearer personnel & 2 officers at the disposal of 13th Field Ambulance, also the three horse ambulances. Motor ambulances already placed at the disposal of Major MORGAN 119 (Amer) Field Ambulance	[initials]
"	29/9/18		30th Div. attacked this morning at 6 am. Walking wounded Post at TEMPLEUX & gas centre at MARQUAIX opened to receive patients. Visited the W.P. at 2-30pm & found everything going smoothly except that Decauville trains were not running frequently enough to clear patients, reported this to Division Surgeon personally.	[initials]

A6945 Wt. W11422/M1160 350,000 12/16 D. D. & L. Forms/C./2118/14.

Instructions regarding War Diaries and Intelligence Summaries are contained in F. S. Regs., Par. II. and the Staff Manual respectively. Title pages will be prepared in manuscript.

(6)
Sept 1918

WAR DIARY
or
INTELLIGENCE ~~SUMMARY~~.
(Erase heading not required.)

Army Form C. 2118.

Map references
FRANCE 62 C

Place	Date	Hour	Summary of Events and Information	Remarks and references to Appendices
MARQUAIX	29/9/18		Number of cases treated in Walking Wounded Post & Divisional Gas Centre respectively between 6am & 6pm was 8 officers 589 OR, 3 officers 150 OR	JWH
"	30/9/18		Visited W.W.P. all going smoothly - no of cases treated in 24 hours ending 6pm today 18 officers 408 OR. Cases treated in Gas Centre for same period numbered 7 officers 276 O.R. Had difficulty in clearing gas cases from Gas Centre & reported fact to Assistant Division Surgeon who arranged for extra cars & so enabled me to clear the centre.	JWH
	"	9.30pm	Received warning order that unit is to move to another area & arranged for billeting party to report to HQ 68th Bde at 9am 1/10/18.	JWH

J W Harvey
Lt Col RAMC
OC 132 Fd Amb.

A6945 Wt. W11422/M1160 350,000 12/16 D. D. & L. Forms/C./2118/14.

Original.
SECRET.

982 32

145/13321

C O N F I D E N T I A L

W A R   D I A R Y

OF

132nd FIELD AMBULANCE

FROM 1st OCTOBER 1918 to 31st OCTOBER 1918.

(Volume 32)

6

Oct 1918

Appendicitis I

Schedule of training for personnel of 108 Sanitary Train, 30th American Divn.

Lectures & demonstrations under the following headings.

1 General outline of the work of a Field Ambulance
2 Medical equipment of a Field Ambulance
3 Duties of a Regimental Medical Officer
4 General system of evacuation of casualties
5 Methods of dealing with casualties & their classification.
6 Sanitation in camps & billets & sanitary appliances etc
7 Water duties & the water cart
8 Infectious diseases, isolation, disinfection & disinfestation.
9 Special campaign affections – Trench foot, shell shock – Trench fever & conditions due to vermin

In addition officers & other ranks will be attached to the various offices wards & duties in camp for instruction under the following headings.

(1) Head quarters Office
(2) Quartermasters Store

(3) Reception room
(4) Cook house
(5) Sanitation
(6) Water cart
(7) Horse transport
(8) Motor transport
(9) Nursing duties
(10) Dispensary
(11) Pack store
(12) Baths
(13) Fumigator, disinfector & disinfestor.

J. D. Harvey
Lt Col
O.C. 132 Fd Amb

3/8/18.

Instructions regarding War Diaries and Intelligence Summaries are contained in F. S. Regs., Par. II, and the Staff Manual respectively. Title pages will be prepared in manuscript.

(1)

October 1918

WAR DIARY
or
~~INTELLIGENCE~~ SUMMARY.
(*Erase heading not required.*)

Army Form C. 2118.

FRANCE 62.C.

Place	Date	Hour	Summary of Events and Information	Remarks and references to Appendices
MARQUAIX	1/10/18		At 6-45 p.m last night received a warning order that the Division will shortly move to a new area. In accordance with instruction received in the order sent off a billeting party of one NCO & 1 man as I had no Officer available to report to 59th Brigade H.Q at 9 am this morning. Very few gas cases received during the night 30 Sep - 1st Oct. Visited the Walking Wounded Collecting post this afternoon and arranged for handing over of post to an ambulance of the 2nd Australian Divn in accordance with orders received from Division Surgeon dated 1/10/18. Also made the necessary preparatory arrangements to hand over the gas Centre at MARQUAIX to an ambulance of the 5th Australian Divn. Received orders from Divn Surgeon that on notification that the forward area is cleared the gas Centre will close.	[signature]
MARQUAIX	2/10/18		Received notification from O.C. 134 Fd Ambulance at 2-30 am that the forward area was cleared – Closed gas Centre.	[signature]
		1200	Unit marched off to BIACHES I.25 d central in accordance with orders received from Divn Surgeon No 17-A dated 1/10/18. As no relieving unit had arrived to take over the site & excess stores a holding party was left.	
BIACHES	3/10/18		In accordance with orders arranged for a camp hospital to treat slight cases from	[signature]

A6945 Wt. W11422/M1160 350,000 12/16 D. D. & L. Forms/C./2118/14.

Instructions regarding War Diaries and Intelligence Summaries are contained in F. S. Regs., Par. II. and the Staff Manual respectively. Title pages will be prepared in manuscript.

(2)
October 1918

WAR DIARY
or
~~INTELLIGENCE~~ SUMMARY.
(*Erase heading not required.*)

Army Form C. 2118.

FRANCE 62.C
62.b

Place	Date	Hour	Summary of Events and Information	Remarks and references to Appendices
BIACHES	3/10/18		from the 119th Infantry billeted in this village, also arranged with regimental surgeon for removal of serious cases to C.C.S.	[initials]
"	4/10/18		Received warning order for a move of the Division & verbal orders from D.S. that this ambulance would run the forward area & A.D.S. taking over from the 2nd AUSTRALIAN Divn. Visited A.D.S. of 2nd AUSTRALIAN Divn situated at G.16.d.8.2 Sheet 62b, and ascertained forward arrangements & returned at 9-30 pm & reported to the Divl Surgeon. While out orders arrived for transport to move tonight to the TINCOURT area & for the personnel to move by bus tomorrow morning at 9-30 to TEMPLEUX-LA-GUERARD L.1.d.7.2. Sheet 62.c & to be joined there by the transport & await further orders.	[initials]
TEMPLEUX L.1.d.7.2 Sheet 62c	5/10/18		Personnel arrived here by bus at 1315 & transport half an hour later. Informed verbally by D.S. that we should probably take over A.D.S. & forward area from 8th Australian Field Ambulance before 1000 tomorrow. Sent up advance party with Major MORRIS & Capt JOHNSTON with necessary equipment & personnel for A.D.S. & relief of forward posts.	[initials]
A.D.S. G.16.d.8.2. Sheet 62b	6/10/18		During the night received definite written orders to take over A.D.S. & running of forward area	[initials]

A6945 Wt. W11422/M1160 350,000 12/16 D. D. & L. Forms/C./2118/14.

Instructions regarding War Diaries and Intelligence Summaries are contained in F. S. Regs., Part II, and the Staff Manual respectively. Title pages will be prepared in manuscript.

(3)
October 1918

WAR DIARY
or
~~INTELLIGENCE~~ SUMMARY.
(Erase heading not required.)

FRANCE
Sheets 62 b & C.

Army Form C. 2118.

Place	Date	Hour	Summary of Events and Information	Remarks and references to Appendices
A.D.S. G.16.d.7.2 Sheet 62 b QUARRIES	6/10/18		area by 0900 ~~[illegible]~~ today. Detailed Major MORRIS MC AAMC to be in charge of area forward of A.D.S. Took over A.D.S. & forward area from 8th Australian Field Ambulance & reported to Div. Surgeon that I had done so.	JADS
"	7/10/18	am	Visited forward car loading posts & RAPs of right sector with Major MORRIS & reconnoitred for site of A.D.S. in the event of an advance.	JADS
		1800	Reported to me by an NCO that Major MORRIS was killed while visiting an R.A.P. despatched Lt McLAREN to bring in body. Asked Div. Surgeon for experienced officer to assist me & reported Major MORRIS death to him & also to DDMS Army by wire. Instructed Lt FERRAN M.C. U.S.A to carry on at DAIMLER POST pending arrival of another officer.	
		2315	Major WALL MC AAMC reported for duty & detailed him to take over charge of forward area in lieu of Major MORRIS. Notified by Major MORROW that attack by our troops will take place at 05.10 8/10/18	
"	8/10/18		117th & 118 Infantry attacked at 0510 & gained objectives. Casualties were evacuated promptly to A.D.S. Some delay there owing to blocking of road to M.D.S. & the 25 MAC cars were at my disposal. The rush of wounded was not cleared off till 1200. In all	JADS

(4) Oct 1918

Instructions regarding War Diaries and Intelligence Summaries are contained in F. S. Regs., Part II. and the Staff Manual respectively. Title pages will be prepared in manuscript.

WAR DIARY
or
INTELLIGENCE SUMMARY.
(Erase heading not required.)

Army Form C. 2118.

FRANCE
62 b & c & 57 B.

Place	Date	Hour	Summary of Events and Information	Remarks and references to Appendices
QUARRIES	8/10/18		All 531 casualties were evacuated in the 24 hours 0800 8/10/18 – 0800 9/10/18. All stretcher cases	[illegible]
MONTBREHAIN I.1.d.2.5. Sheet 62 C	9/10/18	0500	Received orders from D.D. to advance A.D.S. to the MONTBREHAIN area. Reconnoitred & found a school lately used as a GERMAN hospital which I decided upon.	[illegible]
		0730	Sent one tent subdivision forward to open in the meanwhile one tent subdivision operated at QUARRIES till forward A.D.S. ready to receive. Forward A.D.S. opened at 1030 & rear A.D.S. moved at once to join up. Dressers attached at once. Casualties not heavy & evacuated expeditiously notwithstanding the change of location.	
BUSIGNY V.10.d.0.2 Sheet 57 B	10/10/18		On account of advance of troops reconnoitred site in this village at 07-30 and moved one tent subdivision here at 1130 today & opened an advanced dressing station. 119 Field Ambulance taking over site at MONTBREHAIN at 1730 & opening M.D.S. & gas centre there. Casualties not heavy & evacuation carried out satisfactorily notwithstanding the fact that the roads were in a very bad condition due to rain, many lorries being bogged & thus causing great delay in traffic. The car loading point for right sector which had been at PRÉMONT U.28.d.8.4 sheet 62b was moved to BECQUIGNY V.25.a.6.2 sheet 57.b & cars were sent up to RAPs when this was found possible.	[illegible]

A6945 Wt. W11422/M1160 350,000 12/16 D. D. & L. Forms/C./2118/14.

Instructions regarding War Diaries and Intelligence Summaries are contained in F. S. Regs., Part II. and the Staff Manual respectively. Title pages will be prepared in manuscript.

(5)

Oct 1918

WAR DIARY
or
~~INTELLIGENCE~~ SUMMARY.
(*Erase heading not required.*)

Sheets 62.B & 57.B.

Army Form C. 2118.

Place	Date	Hour	Summary of Events and Information	Remarks and references to Appendices
BUSIGNY	11/10/18	1645	Received orders to hand over A.D.S. & evacuation of forward area to 108 Sanitary Train. Arranged for this with officers of 108 Sanitary Train detailed i.e. Major CRAUS taking over A.D.S. & Major CRANSTON evacuation of forward area, relief to be completed by 0800 12/10/18. Headquarters of this ambulance remaining at MONTBREHAIN.	[illegible]
MONTBREHAIN	12/10/18		Relief completed by 0800 & all personnel & equipment returned here by car. Ordered to get in touch with HQ 119th Infantry & arrange for evacuation of sick to the sick collecting station at MONT BREHAIN – sent a motor ambulance to the Regimental Surgeon of 119 Infantry to be at his disposal for carrying out this duty. As there are no billets in area allotted to this unit for billeting obtained permission of D.S. to remain in present billets here.	[illegible]
"	13/10/18		Field ambulance in rest at MONT BREHAIN.	[illegible]
"	14/10/18		MAJOR J.A. BENNETT reported his arrival for duty.	[illegible]
"	15/10/18		Weather fine & dry with light [illegible]. Attended conference HdQrs 30th Divn received warning orders at 21.45, all necessary instructions given. Sent Capt HALLETT RAMC to reconnoitre BOHAIN in view of possibility of establishing a MDS there, or ADS. Reported to Div'l Surgeon 30th Divn. Proceeded in afternoon to IX Corps HQ Qrs to draw cash [illegible] – [illegible]	[illegible signature] Major
	16.10.18		Received verbal orders from Div'l Surgeon 30 Divn to send party to or near to BOHAIN.	

A6945 Wt. W11422/M1160 350,000 12/16 D. D. & L. Forms/C./2118/14.

Instructions regarding War Diaries and Intelligence Summaries are contained in F. S. Regs., Part II, and the Staff Manual respectively. Title pages will be prepared in manuscript.

(6)
October 1918

WAR DIARY
or
~~INTELLIGENCE SUMMARY~~. Sheets 62B & 57B/

(Erase heading not required.)

Army Form C. 2118.

Place	Date	Hour	Summary of Events and Information	Remarks and references to Appendices
MONTBREHAIN 16·10·18	16·10·18	4 pm	despatched CAPT HALLETT & 90 Stretcher bearers together with Lt McLAREN & 25 NCOs & men of Bearer Section to bivouac W of BOHAIN. established at Sheet 62B/D14 b33. Ordered remainder of unit & personnel 14 vehicles (H.T.) to be in readiness to march at 0830 tomorrow. 4 Cars M. Amb cars despatched to OC 118 Fd Amb at BUSIGNY 57B/V9c66.	JMB
BOHAIN	17·10·18		Established M.D.S. at BOHAIN Sheet 62B/D21b37. notified ADS. Sent CAPT HALLETT & 88 SBs to BUSIGNY to report at LE ROND POINT Sheet 57B/V24a18 to O.C. 118 F.A. Capt ACUFF, Lts MYLL, KAMINISKI, LIGON, JOHNSON reported to me for duty also two bandsmen [musical] for whom I have no employment. Evacuation of cases delayed greatly owing to scarcity of MAC cars, took action on this & asked OC MAC for more, asked the Div Surgeon to divert lorries returning empty. Many passed cases.	JMB
— do —	18·10·18		10 further MAC cars reported this morning. MAC cars now evacuating to BIHECOURT IX Corps CCS. evacuation satisfactory. Divisional surgeon visited MDS here today. Accompanied him to ADS at MOLAIN & W.W. Collecting post at VAUX-ANDIGNY. Yesterday evacuated until ~~[illegible]~~ 0600 today 268 lying & 95 sitting. From 0600 to 1800 evacuated 224 lying & 99 sitting. Weather fine & dry. Town shelled about 2200 hours. Casualties nil from same.	JMB

A6945 Wt. W11422/M1160 350,000 12/16 D. D. & L. Forms/C./2118/14.

Instructions regarding War Diaries and Intelligence Summaries are contained in F. S. Regs., Part II, and the Staff Manual respectively. Title pages will be prepared in manuscript.

Army Form C. 2118.

WAR DIARY
or
~~INTELLIGENCE SUMMARY.~~
(Erase heading not required.)

October 1918 Sheets 57B & 62B

Place	Date	Hour	Summary of Events and Information	Remarks and references to Appendices
BOHAIN	19/10/18	1600	Inspected all stables, returned 2 bands to MONTBREHAIN. Received verbal warning from D.S. that we should probably entrain tomorrow & that I was to return all American personnel to their respective units, carried out 1900. D.S. instructed me verbally to close MDS at 23.59. & also similar instructions that all equipment above mob. scale would be taken over by MAC, instructed R.Ms accordingly. 13 men admitted & 2 died from 213 Bde RFA 46th Br Divn result of shelling [Bosch] of this town, in addition 2 deaths from same shell. Packed as far as possible. 1 NCO & 1 man of this unit wounded near MOLAIN – returned to duty.	JMB
– do –	20/10/18		At 22.10 hrs last night received warning order from DS that 30th Divn was to be relieved by the 1st Divn. Continued packing. Have received no orders respecting the return of my Motor Ambulances & personnel of Bearers (1 O & 88 OR). As the unit is presumably about to move I asked officially (~~memo~~ Memo to O.C. 118 Fd Amb.) that same might be returned to me. 803 cases evacuated since opening MDS. Received order #30 from DS respecting movement of unit; MAC (37th) to take over all stores above mob. scale. Red X equipment to be kept. Weather wet roads heavy, march discipline on road lamentable. JMB	JMB

A6945 Wt. W11422/M1160 350,000 12/16 D. D. & L. Forms/C./2118/14.

Instructions regarding War Diaries and Intelligence Summaries are contained in F. S. Regs., Part II. and the Staff Manual respectively. Title pages will be prepared in manuscript.

8

October

WAR DIARY
or
INTELLIGENCE SUMMARY.
(Erase heading not required.)

Army Form C. 2118.

Sheet 62 B
Lens 11

Place	Date	Hour	Summary of Events and Information	Remarks and references to Appendices
QUARRY near BELLICOURT	21/10/18		Marched 0900. Handed over all stores received from 118, 119 FA yesterday; & some received from 134 FA. Notified DS Army location – Sheet 62B/G 16 c 7 4. Major Wroth & Capt Macrae reported back from leave.	
MARQUAIX	22/10/18		Marched to MARQUAIX, detailed Major Wroth as entraining officer. Proceeded to HEILLY then after finding no area allotted there went on to BAIZIEUX & eventually by getting information by means of telephone at a POW camp found BONNAY is allotted for billeting this unit, I carry out accordingly.	WWB
			Yesterday I sent on CAPT HALLETT as billeting officer to find a representative officer of A. Army, the rendezvous being given me as POINT NOYALE, not finding this on map I conclude	WWB
BONNAY		1200	PONT NOYELLE to place, cross roads there 1900 – 2000. Capt HALLETT informs me that no officer was there from 1830 – 2030. At 2000 hours today after completing billeting some American officer handed me "a chit" signed by someone undesignated that 132 FA was now to be billeted in BAIZIEUX	WWB
BAIZIEUX	23/10/18		Arranged billeting in BAIZIEUX. Representative officer of DS came here at 1320 hours & instructed me to arrange billeting for unit now in CONTAY. I obtain this in writing. Area Comdt at CONTAY knows nothing of this as 119 A. FA are there in chateau	WWB
VADENCOURT		2100	at VADENCOURT. At this time after having arranged accommodation in two towns within 24 hours we are left standing in the cold. I sent in Capt Hallett to QUERRIEU to D.S. to obtain written instructions for the guidance of the Area Comdt at CONTAY	WWB

A6945 Wt. W11422/M1160 350,000 12/16 D. D. & L. Forms/C./2118/14.

Army Form C. 2118.

WAR DIARY
or
~~INTELLIGENCE SUMMARY~~.
(Erase heading not required.)

Instructions regarding War Diaries and Intelligence Summaries are contained in F. S. Regs., Part II. and the Staff Manual respectively. Title pages will be prepared in manuscript.

9
October 1918

Lens 11

Place	Date	Hour	Summary of Events and Information	Remarks and references to Appendices
VADENCOURT	23/10/18		VADENCOURT About 22.30 hours came into Chateau at Vadencourt found party of 119 American FA. there without instructions. At 23.90 retired & instructed all others to go there having carried out billeting arrangements in 3 places i.e. BONNAY, BAIZIEUX & CONTAY within 36 hours. Have maintained communication with my unit at MARROAIX, HEILLY & SUZANNE throughout these changes & have kept them au fait with the situation throughout its many vicissitudes	MB
do	20/10/18		Personnel arrived here this morning after detraining at ALBERT at 04.00 hours & marched here 8½ miles. Sick commenced coming in. Visit from MAJOR NORRIS [avert to D.S.] who promised to expedite all my demands for drugs, blankets, stretchers etc which have been sent in officially. Made all arrangements for establishment of a "Camp Infirmary".	MB
do	25/10/18		Weather fine. Influenza comprises most cases of sickness in FA. Apart from this other cases are unsuitable for treatment here in the existing situation – i.e. equipment & stretchers beyond Mob. scale. Evacuation to 41 Sty AP ASYLUM. Fine adm issued.	MB
do	26/10/18		As equipment asked for from HdQrs 30th American Div has not yet arrived & the inflow of sick continues to increase visited HdQrs at OVERBIED with my QM. Evacuation of serious cases continued i.e. anyone who is really ill, Temp 103° & upwards	MB
do	27/10/18		Weather fine nothing of moment to report	MB

2353 Wt. W2544/1454 700,000 5/15 D. D. & L. A.D.S.S./Forms/C. 2118.

Instructions regarding War Diaries and Intelligence Summaries are contained in F. S. Regs., Part II. and the Staff Manual respectively. Title pages will be prepared in manuscript.

10 October 1918

WAR DIARY
or
~~INTELLIGENCE SUMMARY~~. Map Lens 11

(Erase heading not required.)

Army Form C. 2118.

Place	Date	Hour	Summary of Events and Information	Remarks and references to Appendices
VADENCOURT	28/10/18		Difficulty in obtaining drugs. Asst. D.S. called & told me that Drugs & dressings were now to be drawn from 41 Sty H ASYLUM (near AMIENS). Gave instructions for motor Ambulance to call there accordingly – find they cannot supply without authority from LofC. All H.T. overhauled also saddlery & harness. Inflow of Influenza cases continues. Weather is dry & fine which should have beneficial effect on this epidemic	[initials]
– do –	29/10/18		Am informed by message (telephone) that Indents for Med & Surgical Stores to be obtained from DOIGNT, action taken accordingly. Influenza still continues to be much "in evidence", 42 cases evacuated to 41 Sty H. Weather fine & dry. 2 Soyer stoves arrive from Store. Obtain 2 cars from 134 FA to help evacuation	[initials]
– do –	30/10/18		Weather fine & dry, camp satisfactory. Admissions less today, Influenza seems to be decreasing.	
– do –	31/10/18		Returned from leave & reported to D.S. in writing. Number of cases in hospital 68 practically all Influenza. Admissions to 1200 today 27. Division Surgeon visited the ambulance this morning prior to my return.	[signature] Lt Col RAMC

[signature]
Lt Col RAMC
OC 132 Fd Ambulance
31/10/18

D. D. & L., London, E.C.
(A8004) Wt. W1771/M2 31 750,000 5/17 Sch. 52 Forms/C2118/14

SECRET
ORIGINAL.

Vol 33

140/3401

C O N F I D E N T I A L

W A R D I A R Y

O F

132nd F I E L D A M B U L A N C E.

Nov 1918

(Volume 33)

Instructions regarding War Diaries and Intelligence Summaries are contained in F. S. Regs., Part II. and the Staff Manual respectively. Title pages will be prepared in manuscript.

WAR DIARY
or
~~INTELLIGENCE SUMMARY.~~
(Erase heading not required.)

(1) November 1918

LENS II.

Army Form C. 2118.

Place	Date	Hour	Summary of Events and Information	Remarks and references to Appendices
VADENCOURT	1/11/18		Division Surgeon visited the ambulance but did not make an inspection. Cases of influenza still occurring among division but on the whole the numbers appear to be decreasing. Beautiful sunny day.	JADH
— do —	2/11/18		Damp muggy day, nothing of interest to report.	JADH
— do —	4/11/18		All those Officers NCOs & men of the unit not on duty marched to to attend Corps field day II American Corps leaving camp at 0800 & returning at 1800, beautiful sunny day. Influenza seems to be decreasing among the troops of the Division.	JADH
— do —	5/11/18		Troops again attended II American Corps field day but as it was a pouring wet day they were sent back to camp early arriving here at 1230 very wet. Arranged to have clothes dried in Russian pit. Orders received from Division Surgeon for Captain McRAE to return to England & report to War Office on expiration of contract, which happens today.	JADH

D. D. & L., London, E.C. (A8004) Wt. W1771/M2 31 750,000 5/17 Sch. 52 Forms/C2118/14

Instructions regarding War Diaries and Intelligence Summaries are contained in F. S. Regs., Part II. and the Staff Manual respectively. Title pages will be prepared in manuscript.

2.

November 1918

WAR DIARY
or
INTELLIGENCE ~~SUMMARY~~.
(*Erase heading not required.*)

FRANCE
57.D.

Army Form C. 2118.

Place	Date	Hour	Summary of Events and Information	Remarks and references to Appendices
VADENCOURT U.28.A.1.9	6/11/18		Captain J McRAE RAMC departed for ENGLAND on expiration of his contract, to report to the War Office. Very wet day.	JADH
– do –	7/11/18		Nothing of interest to report.	
– do –	8/11/18		Division Surgeon visited Ambulance. The number of cases of Influenza shows slight signs of diminution in number & the cases are less severe	JADH
– do –	9/11/18		Beautiful fine day – nothing special to note.	JADH
– do –	11/11/18		Armistice signed between allies & United States of America & Germany, hostilities to cease at 1100 today. Influenza decreasing markedly.	JADH
– do –	13/11/18		Fine weather still continues. Influenza epidemic seems to be ended	JADH
– do –	14/11/18		Inspection of whole Division & march past, by Divisional General at 1000	JADH
– do –	15/11/18		Very cold night but beautiful fine day	JADH
– do –	16/11/18		Received orders to proceed by road to ABBEVILLE on 17th inst staying night of 17/18 at PICQUINY; on arrival at ABBEVILLE equipment & transport is to be handed in & RAMC Officers & OR are to proceed to RAMC depot ETAPLES. Patients in hospital to be evacuated to 2/1 Stationary hospital.	JADH

D. D. & L., London, E.C.
(A6004) Wt. W1771/M2 31 750,000 5/17 Sch. 52 Forms/C2118/14

Instructions regarding War Diaries and Intelligence Summaries are contained in F. S. Regs., Part II. and the Staff Manual respectively. Title pages will be prepared in manuscript.

(3)

WAR DIARY
or
~~INTELLIGENCE SUMMARY.~~
(*Erase heading not required.*)

Army Form C. 2118.

November 1918

France 57 D. &
ABBEVILLE.

Place	Date	Hour	Summary of Events and Information	Remarks and references to Appendices
PICQUIGNY	17/11/18		Unit marched here today, leaving YADENCOURT at 0715 & arriving at 1530 & was accommodated in billets.	[signature]
ABBEVILLE	18/11/18		Marched here today arriving at 1515, accommodated at night in A.H.T.D. Arranged to hand in equipment, horses, transport etc tomorrow 20/11/18.	[signature]
-do-	19/11/18		Handed in all equipment, horses, transport except motor ambulances by B.O.O. & obtained receipts. At 1400 received verbal orders to stand by for further orders & not to hand in equipment. These orders were confirmed on the phone by D.G.A.M.S.	[signature]
-do-	20/11/18		Nothing special to report	[signature]
-do-	22/11/18		MAJOR J. A. BENNETT RAMC admitted to No 2 Stationary Hospital suffering from eczema & debility	[signature]
-do-	23/11/18 - 30/11/18		Unit standing by for further orders in accordance with instructions received on 19/11/18 & confirmed by D.G.M.S. Troops exercised daily by route marches	[signature]

[signature]
Lt Col RAMC
OC 132 Field Ambulance

D. D. & L., London, E.C.
(A8004) Wt. W1771/M2 31 750,000 5/17 Sch. 52 Forms/C2118/14

SECRET. (ORIGINAL)

34

140/3401

CONFIDENTIAL WAR DIARY

of the

132nd FIELD AMBULANCE.

For the month of DECEMBER. 1918.

14 Dec. 1918

Army Form C. 2118.

WAR DIARY
or
~~INTELLIGENCE SUMMARY.~~
(Erase heading not required.)

Instructions regarding War Diaries and Intelligence Summaries are contained in F. S. Regs., Part II. and the Staff Manual respectively. Title pages will be prepared in manuscript.

(1) Dec 1918

ABBEVILLE 14.

Place	Date	Hour	Summary of Events and Information	Remarks and references to Appendices
ABBEVILLE	1/12/18		Standing by for further instructions at A.H.T.D.	[illegible]
— do —	2/12/18		In accordance with orders received Lt T. McLAREN proceeded to England to report at Adastral House, London.	[illegible]
— do —	3/12/18 – 7/12/18		Standing by for further instructions	[illegible]
— do —	7/12/18		Received orders to proceed on 9/12/18 to Ramc depot ETAPLES with unit which is to be disbanded there	[illegible]
— do —	9/12/18		Unit proceeded by train to ETAPLES to Ramc depot.	[illegible]
— do —	11/12/18		Unit disbanded, Officers & Other Ranks being taken on the strength of Ramc depot ETAPLES.	[illegible]

J. S. Harvey
Lt. Col. RAMC

D. D. & L., London, E.C.
(A8004) Wt. W1771/M2 31 750,000 5/17 Sch. 52 Forms/C2118/14

www.ingramcontent.com/pod-product-compliance
Lightning Source LLC
Chambersburg PA
CBHW080537020526
44117CB00034B/2253